PARENTS AND EDUCATORS PRAISE
THE CORE KNOWLEDGE SERIES

"Though I have twenty-five years' teaching experience, this is my first year as a Core Knowledge teacher. Now, for the first time in a long time, I am excited about teaching again. As for my students, I seriously believe that many of them would eliminate summer vacation to get on with the business of learning!"

—*Joan Falbey, teacher, Three Oaks Elementary School, Fort Myers, Florida*

"Thank you for writing such wonderful books! My children and I have thoroughly enjoyed them. Your books have been a great source and a guide to us. I have a degree in elementary education and I think this is the best curriculum I have encountered."

—*Barbara de la Aguilera, parent, Miami, Florida*

"For three years, we have been using elements of the Core Knowledge program, and I have watched as it invigorated our students. These books should be in every classroom in America."

—*Richard E. Smith, principal,*
Northside Elementary School, Palestine, Texas

"Hirsch made it quite clear [in *Cultural Literacy*] that respect for cultural diversity is important but is best achieved when young people have adequate background knowledge of mainstream culture. In order for a truly democratic and economically sound society to be maintained, young people must have access to the best knowledge available so that they can understand the issues, express their viewpoints, and act accordingly."

—*James P. Comer, M.D., professor, Child Study Center,*
Yale University (in Parents *magazine)*

The
CORE KNOWLEDGE
Series

Resource Books for
Kindergarten Through Grade Six

Bantam Books

New York

Core Knowledge®

What Your Third Grader Needs to Know

Fundamentals of a Good Third-Grade Education

(Revised Edition)

Edited by E. D. Hirsch, Jr.

Published in the United States by Bantam Books, an imprint of Random House, a division of Penguin Random House LLC, New York.

BANTAM BOOKS and the HOUSE colophon are registered trademarks of Penguin Random House LLC.

CORE KNOWLEDGE is a trademark of the Core Knowledge Foundation.

Originally published in hardcover in the United States in 1992. A revised hardcover edition was published in 2001 by Doubleday, an imprint of the Knopf Doubleday Publishing Group, a division of Penguin Random House LLC, and subsequently in trade paperback in 2002 by Delta Books, an imprint of Random House, a division of Penguin Random House LLC.

Library of Congress Cataloging-in-Publication Data
Hirsch, E.D. Jr.
What your third grader needs to know (revised and updated) : fundamentals of a good third-grade education / edited by E.D. Hirsch, Jr. — Revised and updated
pages cm
Includes bibliographical references and index.
ISBN 978-0-553-39466-5 (paperback) — ISBN 978-0-553-39468-9 (ebook)
1. Third grade (Education)—Curricula—United States.   2. Curriculum planning—United States.   I. Hirsch, E. D. (Eric Donald).   II. Title.
LB1571.W55 2015
372.24'1—dc23
2015007746

Printed in the United States of America on acid-free paper

randomhousebooks.com

2 4 6 8 9 7 5 3 1

Book design by Diane Hobbing

Editor in Chief of the Core Knowledge Series: E. D. Hirsch, Jr.

Editors, Revised Edition: John Holdren, Susan Tyler Hitchcock

Project Managers and Art Editors: Alice Wiggins, Emma Earnst

Writers: John Hirsch (Math), Michele Josselyn (Visual Arts),
Mary Beth Klee (American History), Barbara Lachman (Music),
Deborah Mazzotta (World History), Christiana Whittington (Music),
Words & Numbers (All)

Artists and Photographers: Steve Henry, Sara Holdren, Bob Kirchman,
Gail McIntosh, Jane Sickon

Art and Photo Research, Art and Text Permissions: Emma Earnst,
Alice Wiggins, Words & Numbers

Acknowledgments

This series has depended on the help, advice, and encouragement of some two thousand people. Some of those singled out here already know the depth of our gratitude; others may be surprised to find themselves thanked publicly for help they gave quietly and freely for the sake of the enterprise alone. To helpers named and unnamed we are deeply grateful.

Advisers on multiculturalism: Minerva Allen, Barbara Carey, Frank de Varona, Mick Fedullo, Dorothy Fields, Elizabeth Fox-Genovese, Marcia Galli, Dan Garner, Henry Louis Gates, Jr., Cheryl Kulas, Joseph C. Miller, Gerry Raining Bird, Connie Rocha, Dorothy Small, Sharon Stewart-Peregoy, Sterling Stuckey, Marlene Walking Bear, Lucille Watahomigie, Ramona Wilson

Advisers on elementary education: Joseph Adelson, Isobel Beck, Paul Bell, Carl Bereiter, David Bjorklund, Constance Jones, Elizabeth LaFuze, J. P. Lutz, Sandra Scarr, Nancy Stein, Phyllis Wilkin

Advisers on technical subject matter: Marilyn Jager Adams, Karima-Diane Alavi, Richard Anderson, Judith Birsh, Cheryl Cannard, Barbara Foorman, Paul Gagnon, David Geary, Andrew Gleason, Ted Hirsch, Henry Holt, Blair Jones, Connie Juel, Eric Karell, Morton Keller, Joseph Kett, Charles Kimball, Mary Beth Klee, Barbara Lachman, Karen Lang, Michael Lynch, Diane McGuinness, Sheelagh McGurn, Joseph C. Miller, Jean Osborn, Vikas Pershad, Margaret Reed, Donna Rehorn, Gilbert Roy, Nancy Royal, Mark Rush, Janet Smith, Ralph Smith, Keith Stanovich, Paula Stanovich, Nancy Strother, Nancy Summers, Marlene Thompson, James Trefil, Patricia Wattenmaker, Nancy Wayne, Christiana Whittington, Linda Williams, Lois Williams

Conferees, March 1990: Nola Bacci, Joan Baratz-Snowden, Thomasyne Beverley, Thomas Blackton, Angela Burkhalter, Monty Caldwell, Thomas M. Carroll, Laura Chapman, Carol Anne Collins, Lou Corsaro, Henry Cotton, Anne Coughlin, Arletta Dimberg, Debra P. Douglas, Patricia Edwards, Janet Elenbogen, Mick Fedullo, Michele Fomalont, Mamon Gibson, Jean Haines, Barbara Hayes, Stephen Herzog, Helen Kelley, Brenda King, John King, Elizabeth

La-Fuze, Diana Lam, Nancy Lambert, Doris Langaster, Richard LaPointe, Lloyd Leverton, Madeline Long, Allen Luster, Joseph McGeehan, Janet McLin, Gloria McPhee, Marcia Mallard, William J. Maloney, Judith Matz, John Morabito, Robert Morrill, Roberta Morse, Karen Nathan, Dawn Nichols, Valeta Paige, Mary Perrin, Joseph Piazza, Jeanne Price, Marilyn Rauth, Judith Raybern, Mary Reese, Richard Rice, Wallace Saval, John Saxon, Jan Schwab, Ted Sharp, Diana Smith, Richard Smith, Trevanian Smith, Carol Stevens, Nancy Summers, Michael Terry, Robert Todd, Elois Veltman, Sharon Walker, Mary Ann Ward, Charles Whitten, Penny Williams, Clarke Worthington, Jane York

Schools: Special thanks to Three Oaks Elementary for piloting the original Core Knowledge Sequence in 1990. And thanks to the schools that have offered their advice and suggestions for improving the Core Knowledge Sequence, including (in alphabetical order): Academy Charter School (CO); Coleman Elementary (TX); Coral Reef Elementary (FL); Coronado Village Elementary (TX); Crooksville Elementary (OH); Crossroads Academy (NH); Gesher Jewish Day School (VA); Hawthorne Elementary (TX); Highland Heights Elementary (IN); Joella Good Elementary (FL); Mohegan School–CS 67 (NY); The Morse School (MA); Nichols Hills Elementary (OK); North East Elementary (MD); Ridge View Elementary (WA); R. N. Harris Elementary (NC); Southside Elementary (FL); Thomas Johnson Elementary (MD); Three Oaks Elementary (FL); Vienna Elementary (MD); Washington Core Knowledge School (CO). And to the many other schools teaching Core Knowledge—too many to name here, and some of which we have yet to discover—our heartfelt thanks for "sharing the knowledge"!

Benefactors: The Brown Foundation, The Challenge Foundation, Mrs. E. D. Hirsch, Sr., The Walton Family Foundation

Our grateful acknowledgment to these persons does not imply that we have taken their (sometimes conflicting) advice in every case, or that each of them endorses all aspects of this project. Responsibility for final decisions must rest with the editors alone. Suggestions for improvements are very welcome, and we wish to thank in advance those who send advice for revising and improving this series.

This book is dedicated to
Lucy Alexander Hirsch,
born March 20, 2000

A Note to Teachers

We hope you will find this book useful, especially those of you who are teaching in the growing network of Core Knowledge schools. Throughout the book, we have addressed the suggested activities and explanations to "parents," since you, as teachers, know your students and will have ideas about how to use the content of this book in relation to the lessons and activities you plan. If you are interested in the ideas of teachers in Core Knowledge schools, please write or call the Core Knowledge Foundation (801 East High Street, Charlottesville, VA 22902; 434-977-7550) for information on ordering collections of lessons created and shared by teachers in Core Knowledge schools. Many of these teacher-created lessons are available through the Core Knowledge website at the following address: www.coreknowledge.org.

Author's earnings from sales of the Core Knowledge Series go to the nonprofit Core Knowledge Foundation. E. D. Hirsch, Jr., receives no remuneration for editing the series nor any other remuneration from the Core Knowledge Foundation.

Contents

I. Language and Literature

II. History and Geography

III. Visual Arts

IV. Music

V. Mathematics

VI. Science

General Introduction to the Series

Schools and Your Child

If Charles Dickens were alive today, observing the state of American schools, he might be tempted to observe anew that it is the best of times and the worst of times. Seldom has there been more attention and energy aimed at our nation's education system. Unacceptable inequities in achievement between income and ethnic groups, long viewed with alarm, are being addressed with unprecedented urgency and resources. Years of dismay over lackluster performance have created a sense of crisis, even fear, that if we do not set our educational house in order, American competitiveness, our economy, and even our way of life are at risk. The response has been an unprecedented era of educational dynamism and innovation. Seen through this lens, it might seem to be the best of times for American education.

Yet for all our admirable focus, urgency, and investment, we have surprisingly little to show for it. Reading test scores for American 17-year-olds, the ultimate report card for our schools, have hardly budged in 40 years. That's two generations with no discernible progress. How can this be? We have tried testing every child and holding teachers accountable. We have built charter schools and filled classrooms with computers. We have even made it the law of the land that every child read at grade level, but to no avail. Surely it is the worst of times.

Do not blame teachers. They are among our most committed and generous-spirited citizens. We have not lacked urgency, idealism, or even resources. What we have lacked is a coherent plan for educating all children to proficiency.

The book you hold in your hands exemplifies an essential building block of that coherent plan.

Why Knowledge Matters in the Era of Google

American public education sprang from the 19th-century idea of the common school. We sent our children to learn reading and writing, but also a common curriculum of history, geography, math, and other subjects. Such schools also strived to create virtuous, civic-minded citizens for the new nation. As the United States matured and became more diverse, the idea of a common curriculum gradually melted away. Today we have all but abandoned the idea that there is a body of knowledge that every child should learn in school, and that the broad mission of education is to maximize each individual's potential. However, there is good reason to believe that the idea of common schooling is even more relevant and effective today than ever before.

Ask yourself: *"Would I rather have my child go to school to gain knowledge of history, science, art, or music? Or should schools emphasize skills such as critical thinking and problem solving?"* The answer should ideally be both. Knowledge and skills are not two different things; they are two sides of the same coin. Thinking skills are what psychologists call "domain specific." In plain English, this means that you cannot think critically about a subject you know little about. If we want our children to be broadly competent readers, thinkers, and problem solvers, they must have a rich, broad store of background knowledge to call upon, enabling them to flex those mental muscles.

Unfortunately, too many of our schools have lost touch with this critical insight. It is commonly believed to be a fool's errand to think we can teach children all they need to know—far better simply to spark in children a lifelong love of learning. Indeed, many well-intentioned educators believe the in-depth study of a few topics, practice with a variety of "thinking skills," and access to the Internet are all anyone needs today. Why clutter our minds with facts and trivia when you can just Google them? Today's classroom and curriculum, it is commonly argued, should be built around "21st-century skills" such as media literacy and working cooperatively to solve "authentic" problems. These are the skills that will ensure them a lifetime of learning, productivity, and engaged citizenship. The rest is mere trivia. Right?

On its surface, the idea that skills are more important than knowledge has a basic, commonsense appeal. Why should your child learn about the thirteen colonies, the solar system, or who painted *The Scream*? What child hasn't asked, "Why do we need to know this?" Unfortunately, this benign, even obvious-sounding idea contains a great paradox: it takes knowledge to gain knowledge. Those who repudiate a coherent, knowledge-rich curriculum on the grounds that you can always look things up have failed to learn an important lesson from cognitive science: deemphasizing factual knowledge prevents children from looking things up effectively. When you have just a little bit of information about a subject, you cannot evaluate the importance of new knowledge. When you know nothing, you're flying blind, like reading a book whose words you don't know. Thus, emphasizing procedural skill at the expense of factual knowledge hinders children from learning to learn. Yes, the Internet has placed a wealth of information at our fingertips. But to be able to use that information—to absorb it, to add to our knowledge—we must already possess a storehouse of knowledge. That is the paradox disclosed by cognitive research.

Common Knowledge, Not "One Size Fits All"

All children are different. Like the idea that skills are more important than knowledge, there is a warm, intuitive appeal to the idea that we should tailor schooling to allow every child to find what most excites and engages him and let those interests drive his "child-centered" education. But again, this ignores some fundamental facts about how we learn.

Language and vocabulary—like critical thinking and problem solving—also depend a great deal on a broad base of shared knowledge. When a sportscaster describes a surprising performance by an underdog basketball team as "a Cinderella story," or when a writer compares an ill-fated couple to Romeo and Juliet, they are making an assumption that their audience will know and understand the reference. So much of our language depends on a shared body of knowledge. Yes, you must know the words. But you must also understand the context in order to understand and be understood. The word "shot," for example, means something different in a doctor's office, on a basketball court, or when a technician says your dishwasher is beyond fixing. Fluency depends on context, and context is largely a function of shared background knowledge.

Yet it remains all too easy to deride a knowledge-rich curriculum as "mere facts" and "rote learning." The idea that there is a common body of knowledge that all children should know to enable them to read, communicate, and work cooperatively with others does sound old-fashioned. But the overwhelming evidence argues that this is precisely the case. Learning builds on learning: children (and adults) gain new knowledge only by building on what they already know. It is essential to begin building solid foundations of knowledge in the early grades, when children are most receptive, because for the vast majority of children, academic deficiencies from the first six grades can permanently impair the success of later learning. Poor performance of American students in middle and high school can be traced to shortcomings inherited from elementary schools that have not imparted to children the knowledge and skills they need for further learning.

All of the highest-achieving and most egalitarian elementary school systems in the world (such as those in Sweden, France, and Japan) teach their children a specific core of knowledge in each of the first six grades, thus enabling all children to enter each new grade with a secure foundation for further learning. U.S. schools, with their high student mobility rates, would especially benefit from a carefully sequenced core curriculum in the elementary and middle school years.

Commonly Shared Knowledge Makes Schooling More Effective

We know that the one-on-one tutorial is the most effective form of schooling, in part because a parent or teacher can provide tailor-made instruction for the individual child. But in a non-tutorial situation—in, for example, a typical classroom with 25 or more students—the instructor cannot effectively impart new knowledge to all the students unless each one shares the background knowledge upon which the instructor is building the lesson.

Consider this scenario. In third grade, Ms. Franklin is about to begin a unit on early explorers—Columbus, Magellan, and others. In her class, she has some students who were in Mr. Washington's second-grade class last year and some students who were in Ms. Johnson's second-grade class. She also has a few students who have moved in from other towns. As Ms. Franklin begins the unit on explorers, she asks the children to look at a globe and use their fingers to trace a route across the Atlantic Ocean from Europe to North America. The students who had Mr. Washington look blankly at her: they didn't learn that last year. The students who had Ms. Johnson, however, eagerly point to the proper places on the globe, while two of the students who came from other towns pipe up and say, "Columbus and Magellan again? We did that last year."

When all the students in a class share the relevant background knowledge, a classroom can begin to approach the effectiveness of a tutorial. Even when some children in a class do not have elements of the knowledge they were supposed to acquire in previous grades, the existence of a specifically defined core makes it possible for the teacher or parent to identify and fill the gaps, giving all students a chance to fulfill their potentials in later grades.

Commonly Shared Knowledge Makes Schooling Fairer and More Democratic

When all the children who enter a grade can be assumed to share some of the same building blocks of knowledge, and when the teacher knows exactly what those building blocks are, then all the students are empowered to learn. In our current system, children from disadvantaged backgrounds too often suffer from unmerited low expectations that translate into watered-down curricula. But if we specify the core of knowledge that all children should share, then we can guarantee equal access to that knowledge and compensate for the academic advantages some students are offered at home. In a Core Knowledge school, all children enjoy the benefits of important, challenging knowledge that will provide the foundation for successful later learning.

Commonly Shared Knowledge Helps Create Cooperation and Solidarity in Our Schools and Nation

Diversity is a hallmark and strength of our nation. American classrooms are usually made up of students from a variety of cultural backgrounds, and those different cultures should be honored by all students. At the same time, education should create a school-based culture that is common and welcoming to all because it includes knowledge of many cultures and gives all students, no matter what their background, a common foundation for understanding our cultural diversity.

Commonly Shared Knowledge Creates the Conditions That Make Higher-Order Thinking Possible

"We don't just read about science. We do science," a teacher in New York City recently wrote. One of the greatest misconceptions in contemporary education is the idea that in order to best prepare students for college and careers, we should train them to "think like an expert." In other words, we should help them understand and practice what scientists, historians, and other highly skilled professionals do. But it is clear from cognitive science that to think like an expert, you must know what the expert knows. Unfortunately, there are no shortcuts to expertise. Deep knowledge and practice are essential. Yet our schools, under the mistaken idea that knowledge is less important than skills, try to teach children to engage learning by doing, under the assumption that skills trump knowledge. They do not. You cannot have one without the other.

All of our most cherished goals for education—reading with understanding, critical thinking, and problem solving—are what psychologists call "domain-specific" skills. Simply put, there is no such thing as an all-purpose critical thinker or problem solver. Such skills are a function of your background knowledge.

What Knowledge Needs to Be Taught?

One of the primary objections to a content-rich vision of education is that it offends our democratic sensibilities. The title of this book—*What Your Third Grader Needs to Know*—can easily be viewed as presumptuous: "Who are you to say what knowledge matters? Why do you get to decide what goes in my child's curriculum and what gets left out?" Deciding what we want our children to know can be a politically and emotionally charged minefield. No grade-by-grade sequence of knowledge or course of study will satisfy everyone. But it is educationally reckless to ignore what we know about the importance of a broad knowledge base. The effort may be difficult, but we are duty-bound to try.

The content in this and other volumes in the Core Knowledge Series is based on a document called the *Core Knowledge Sequence*, a grade-by-grade sequence of specific content guidelines in history, geography, mathematics, science, language arts, and fine arts. As the core of a school's curriculum, it offers a solid, coherent foundation of learning while allowing flexibility to meet local needs. The entire sequence, from preschool to eighth grade, can be downloaded for free at the Core Knowledge Foundation's website (www.coreknowledge.org/download-the -sequence).

The Core Knowledge Foundation invested a considerable amount of time, energy, and resources in an attempt to find a consensus on the most enabling knowledge—the content that would most enable all children to read, write, listen, and speak with understanding.

Shortly after the establishment of the Core Knowledge Foundation in 1987, we analyzed the many reports issued by state departments of education and by professional organizations—such as the National Council of Teachers of Mathematics and the American Association for the Advancement of Science—that recommend general outcomes for elementary and secondary education. We also tabulated the knowledge and skills, through grade 6, specified in the successful educational systems of several other countries, including France, Japan, Sweden, and Germany.

In addition, we formed an advisory board on multiculturalism that proposed a specific knowledge of diverse cultural traditions that American children should all share as part of their school-based common culture. We sent the resulting materials to three independent groups of teachers, scholars, and scientists across the country, asking them to create a master list of the knowledge children should have by the end of grade 6. About 150 education professionals (including college professors, scientists, and administrators) were involved in this initial step.

These items were amalgamated into a master plan, and further groups of teachers and specialists were asked to agree on a grade-by-grade sequence of the items. That sequence was then sent to some 100 educators and specialists who participated in a national conference to hammer out a working agreement on an appropriate core of knowledge for the first six grades; kindergarten, grades 7 and 8, and preschool were subsequently added to the sequence.

This important meeting took place in March 1990. The conferees were elementary school teachers, curriculum specialists, scientists, science writers, officers of national organizations, representatives of ethnic groups, district superintendents, and school principals from across the country. A total of 24 working groups decided on revisions in the *Core Knowledge Sequence*. The resulting provisional sequence was further fine-tuned during a year of implementation at a pioneering school, Three Oaks Elementary, in Lee County, Florida.

In only a few years, many more schools—urban and rural, rich and poor, public and private—joined in the effort to teach Core Knowledge. Based largely on suggestions from these schools, the *Core Knowledge Sequence* was revised in 1995; separate guidelines were added for kindergarten and a few topics in other grades were added, omitted, or moved from one grade to another to create an even more coherent sequence for learning. Because the sequence is intended to be a living document that provides a foundation of knowledge that speakers and writers assume their audiences know, it has been—and will continue to be—periodically updated and revised. In general, however, there is more stability than change in the sequence.

The purpose of the *Core Knowledge Sequence* is not to impose a canon. It is an attempt to *report* on a canon—to identify the most valuable, empowering knowledge across subject areas, and to create a plan for imparting it from the first days of school.

Knowledge Still Matters

· ·

This book, as well as the work of the Core Knowledge Foundation and the efforts of Core Knowledge teachers in hundreds of schools nationwide, swims strongly against the anti-knowledge tide of mediocrity that threatens to drag down our schools, our children, and ultimately our nation.

A broad, rich store of background knowledge is not merely nice to have. Knowledge is the essential raw material of thinking. Cognitive scientist Daniel Willingham observes, "Knowledge is not only cumulative, it grows exponentially. Those with a rich base of factual knowledge find it easier to learn more—the rich get richer. In addition, factual knowledge enhances cognitive processes such as problem solving and reasoning. The richer the knowledge base, the more smoothly and effectively these cognitive processes—the very ones that teachers target—operate. So, the more knowledge students accumulate, the smarter they become."

If all of our children are to be fully educated and participate equally in civic life, then we must provide each of them with the shared body of knowledge that makes literacy and communication possible. This concept, so central to the new Common Core State Standards adopted by more than 40 states, and to the Core Knowledge Foundation's goal of equity and excellence in education, manifests itself in the *Core Knowledge Sequence*—and in these popular grade-by-grade books. It is a pleasure to introduce this latest refinement of them to a new generation of readers.

E. D. Hirsch, Jr.
Charlottesville, Virginia

I
Language and Literature

Reading, Writing, and Your Third Grader: A Note to Parents

The best way to nurture your child's reading and writing abilities is to provide rich literary experiences and find frequent and varied opportunities to work and play with language.

By the end of second grade, children have developed a reading vocabulary of familiar words and can decode the letter sound patterns of many unfamiliar one- and two-syllable words. During third grade, as they increase their knowledge about words (including the concepts of syllables, prefixes, and suffixes), they put that knowledge to work, decoding unfamiliar multisyllabic words. If a child has not mastered the skill of decoding simple words, that practice should continue.

By third grade, the mental process of turning letters into sounds should be nearly automatic. This year, children focus more on meaning as they read. Their reading vocabulary expands tremendously, as does their ability to read longer and more complex literature. They read for information and begin to use nonfiction reference books like children's dictionaries and encyclopedias. They learn the distinction between fiction and nonfiction, and they read and enjoy longer and more complicated "chapter books."

In third grade, children continue to learn about language as they write it: identifying parts of speech, properly using punctuation, and recognizing sentence types. They begin to shape their own writing, understanding how paragraphs relate in a larger whole and exerting more control over vocabulary and structure.

Parents can do many things to help their children reach these new levels of understanding language:

- **Read aloud to your child.** While third graders are beginning to read on their own, they also still enjoy listening.

Continue reading aloud, both fiction and nonfiction, even as your child becomes an independent reader.

• **Have your child read aloud to you.** Build your child's ability to read independently by encouraging her to read poems and stories aloud. Encourage your child to change the inflection in her voice to mimic natural speaking patterns in dialogue or to emphasize a character's emotions.

• **Visit the library with your child.** Not only will visiting the library open up your child to a variety of books about different cultures and subjects, but it will also teach your child responsibility. Your child will learn to treat books with care and return them on time.

• **Encourage your child to write letters or keep a journal.** Get your child excited about writing by challenging him to write letters to characters he has read about. After reading about Alice's adventures, he might write a letter to Caterpillar about Caterpillar's first impressions of Alice. Encourage your child to sound out words as he writes.

• **Play word games with your child.** Scrabble, Hangman, Boggle, and other popular games that involve spelling, word recognition, and vocabulary development combine fun with language facility.

• **Find language wherever you go.** Use road signs, advertising, magazines—the written word all around you—to keep your child thinking and talking about language.

• **Support your child's interests through reading.** When your child shows an interest in something special—insects or baseball, Davy Crockett or ballet—go together to the library to find more to read on that subject or download e-books about those topics with your child and read the stories together.

The more a child reads and writes, the more fluent in language that child becomes. By using these strategies, you communicate the enjoyment of reading and writing and help build the foundation for learning that will last a lifetime.

Suggested Resources

The American Heritage First Dictionary (Houghton Mifflin). Simple words, clear definitions, and ample visuals provide a helpful introduction to how a dictionary works.

E. D. Hirsch, Jr., *A First Dictionary of Cultural Literacy* (Houghton Mifflin). Some entries may be difficult for a third grader, but this book can serve as a single-volume encyclopedia of American culture.

Macmillan Dictionary for Children (Simon & Schuster). This dictionary offers 35,000 expanded entries with easy-to-read pronunciations, synonym lists, and color illustrations.

The World Book Student Discovery Encyclopedia (World Book Inc.). This multivolume reference is structured like a standard encyclopedia but designed and written so third graders can look things up and read entries easily.

Amplify Education is the source for purchase of the Core Knowledge Language Arts program. The Core Knowledge Language Arts program for grade 3 is available for free download from www .coreknowledge.org/ckla-files. These materials are designed to teach basic phonics, spelling, vocabulary development, reading comprehension, grammar, and composition skills.

Literature

Introduction

This selection of poetry, stories, and myths can be read aloud or, in many cases, read independently by third graders. We hope you'll take it as a starting point in your search for more literature for your child to read and enjoy.

We have included both traditional and modern poetry. Poems can be silly, written for the sheer enjoyment of rhythm and rhyme, or they can be serious. Rhythm and rhyme make poetry the perfect literature for a third grader to memorize.

The stories selected here include classic folktales from many cultures and excerpts from great works of children's literature. Some of them have been chosen as literary links to topics elsewhere in the book. In the case of book-length works, we can provide only short excerpts, hoping that you and your child will read the rest on your own.

This book continues the effort, begun in previous books, to share the wealth of classical mythology. Because third graders learn about ancient Rome, several myths were chosen to convey a sense of Roman history. Likewise, we offer some Norse mythology. Parents can coordinate readings about literature and history. Age-old myths also give parents the opportunity to discuss traditional virtues such as friendship, courage, and honesty.

Poetry

. . . .

By Myself

by Eloise Greenfield

When I'm by myself
And I close my eyes
I'm a twin
I'm a dimple in a chin
I'm a room full of toys
I'm a squeaky noise
I'm a gospel song
I'm a gong
I'm a leaf turning red
I'm a loaf of brown bread
I'm a whatever I want to be
An anything I care to be
And when I open my eyes
What I care to be
Is me

Catch a Little Rhyme
by Eve Merriam

Once upon a time
I caught a little rhyme

I set it on the floor
but it ran right out the door

I chased it on my bicycle
but it melted to an icicle

I scooped it up in my hat
but it turned into a cat

I caught it by the tail
but it stretched into a whale

I followed it in a boat
but it changed into a goat

When I fed it tin and paper
it became a tall skyscraper

Then it grew into a kite
and flew far out of sight . . .

Do It Yourself

What happens after the rhyme turns into a kite and flies out of sight? Write your own couplets to extend the poem.

Dream Variations

by Langston Hughes

To fling my arms wide
In some place of the sun,
To whirl and dance
Till the white day is done.
Then rest at cool evening
Beneath a tall tree
While night comes on gently,
    Dark like me—
That is my dream!

To fling my arms wide
In the face of the sun,
Dance! Whirl! Whirl!
Till the quick day is done.
Rest at pale evening . . .
A tall, slim tree . . .
Night coming tenderly
    Black like me.

Knoxville, Tennessee
by Nikki Giovanni

I always like summer
best
you can eat fresh corn
from daddy's garden
and okra
and greens
and cabbage
and lots of
barbecue
and buttermilk
and homemade ice-cream
at the church picnic
and listen to
gospel music
outside
at the church
homecoming
and go to the mountains with
your grandmother
and go barefooted
and be warm
all the time
not only when you go to bed
and sleep

What About You?

Ask your child what his favorite season is. Help him to make a list of what he likes so he can write a poem in the style of "Knoxville, Tennessee."

The Crocodile
by Lewis Carroll

How doth the little crocodile
    Improve his shining tail,
And pour the waters of the Nile
    On every golden scale!

How cheerfully he seems to grin!
    How neatly spreads his claws,
And welcomes little fishes in
    With gently smiling jaws!

Lewis Carroll's Inspiration

Lewis Carroll borrowed the rhythm and rhyme for "The Crocodile" from a serious poem by Isaac Watts called "Against Idleness and Mischief," which began like this:

How doth the little busy bee
    Improve each shining hour,
And gather honey all the day,
    From every opening flower!

How skilfully she builds her cell!
    How neatly she spreads her wax!
And labours hard to store it well
    With the sweet food she makes.

When you compare the two poems, you see that Carroll was up to some mischief himself!

Trees

by Sergeant Joyce Kilmer

I think that I shall never see
A poem lovely as a tree.

A tree whose hungry mouth is pressed
Against the earth's sweet flowing breast;

A tree that looks at God all day,
And lifts her leafy arms to pray;

A tree that may in summer wear
A nest of robins in her hair;

Upon whose bosom snow has lain,
Who intimately lives with rain.

Poems are made by fools like me,
But only God can make a tree.

For Want of a Nail

(traditional Mother Goose rhyme)

For want of a nail, the shoe was lost,
For want of the shoe, the horse was lost,
For want of a horse, the rider was lost,
For want of a rider, the battle was lost,
For want of the battle, the kingdom was lost,
And all for the want of a horseshoe nail.

Jimmy Jet and His TV Set

by Shel Silverstein

I'll tell you the story of Jimmy Jet—
And you know what I tell you is true.
He loved to watch his TV set
Almost as much as you.

He watched all day, he watched all night
Till he grew pale and lean,
From "The Early Show" to "The Late Late Show"
And all the shows between.

He watched till his eyes were frozen wide,
And his bottom grew into his chair.
And his chin turned into a tuning dial,
And antennae grew out of his hair.

And his brains turned into TV tubes,
And his face to a TV screen.
And two knobs saying "VERT." and "HORIZ."
Grew where his ears had been.

And he grew a plug that looked like a tail
So we plugged in little Jim.
And now instead of watching TV
We all sit around and watch him.

Talk and Think
Did that really happen?
Ask your child to explain
why Jimmy Jet turns into a
television.

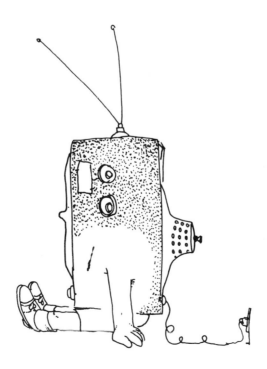

First Thanksgiving of All

by Nancy Byrd Turner

Peace and Mercy and Jonathan,
And Patience (very small),
Stood by the table giving thanks
The first Thanksgiving of all.
There was very little for them to eat,
Nothing special and nothing sweet;
Only bread and a little broth,
And a bit of fruit (and no tablecloth);
But Peace and Mercy and Jonathan
And Patience, in a row,
Stood up and asked a blessing on
Thanksgiving, long ago.
Thankful they were their ship had come
Safely across the sea;
Thankful they were for hearth and home,
And kin and company;
They were glad of broth to go with their bread,
Glad their apples were round and red,
Glad of mayflowers they would bring
   Out of the woods again next spring.
So Peace and Mercy and Jonathan,
And Patience (very small),
Stood up gratefully giving thanks
The first Thanksgiving of them all.

Make a Connection

After reading "First Thanksgiving of All," go to page 215 in the geography and history chapter and read the Thanksgiving passage with your child. Ask your child to describe how the poem captures the feeling of the first Thanksgiving.

Eletelephony

by Laura Richards

Once there was an elephant,
Who tried to use the telephant—
No! No! I mean an elephone
Who tried to use the telephone—
(Dear me! I am not certain quite
That even now I've got it right.)

Howe'er it was, he got his trunk
Entangled in the telephunk;
The more he tried to get it free,
The louder buzzed the telephee—
(I fear I'd better drop the song
Of elephop and telephong!)

All Together

This poem can be a real puzzler! Recite it aloud with your child as fast as you can and see if the mixed-up words get you tongue-tied!

Father William

by Lewis Carroll

"You are old, Father William," the young man said,
    "And your hair has become very white;
And yet you incessantly stand on your head—
    Do you think, at your age, it is right?"

"In my youth," Father William replied to his son,
    "I feared it might injure the brain;
But now that I'm perfectly sure I have none,
    Why, I do it again and again."

"You are old," said the youth, "as I mentioned before,
    And have grown most uncommonly fat;
Yet you turned a back somersault in at the door—
    Pray what is the reason of that?"

"In my youth," said the sage, as he shook his gray locks,
    "I kept my limbs very supple
By the use of this ointment—one shilling the box—
    Allow me to sell you a couple?"

"You are old," said the youth, "and your jaws are too weak
    For anything tougher than suet;
Yet you finished the goose, with the bones and the beak—
    Pray how did you manage to do it?"

"In my youth," said his father, "I took to the law,
    And argued each case with my wife;
And the muscular strength which it gave to my jaw
    Has lasted the rest of my life."

"You are old," said the youth, "one would hardly suppose
   That your eye was as steady as ever;
Yet you balanced an eel on the end of your nose—
   What made you so awfully clever?"

"I have answered three questions, and that is enough,"
   Said his father. "Don't give yourself airs!
Do you think I can listen all day to such stuff?
   Be off, or I'll kick you downstairs!"

Talk and Think
Read "Father William" and tell your child to put herself in the father's shoes. Ask your child, "How does the father feel about his son's questions at the beginning of the poem? The end?" Then ask your child to answer the same questions from the son's perspective.

Stories

. . . .

Alice's Adventures in Wonderland

(adapted from Lewis Carroll's original)

In 1865, the English author Lewis Carroll—whose real name was Charles Dodgson— introduced the world to a girl named Alice and the strange and funny world of Wonderland. Alice's Adventures in Wonderland *was so popular that Carroll wrote another book, called* Through the Looking-Glass and What Alice Found There.

Alice was beginning to get very tired of sitting by her sister on the bank and of having nothing to do: once or twice she had peeped into the book her sister was reading, but it had no pictures or conversations in it, "and what is the use of a book," thought Alice, "without pictures or conversations?"

So she was considering, in her own mind (as well as she could, for the hot day made her feel very sleepy and stupid), whether the pleasure of making a daisy-chain would be worth the trouble of getting up and picking the daisies, when suddenly a White Rabbit with pink eyes ran close by her.

There was nothing so *very* remarkable in that; nor did Alice think it so *very* much out of the way to hear the Rabbit say to itself, "Oh dear! Oh dear! I shall be too late!" But when the Rabbit actually *took a watch out of its waistcoat-pocket*, and looked at it, and then hurried on, Alice started to her feet, and burning with curiosity, she ran across the field after it, and was just in time to see it pop down a large rabbit-hole under the hedge.

The White Rabbit.

In another moment down went Alice after it, never once considering how in the world she was to get out again.

The rabbit-hole dipped suddenly down, so suddenly that Alice found herself falling down what seemed to be a very deep well.

Either the well was very deep, or she fell very slowly, for she had plenty of time as she went down to look about her, and to wonder what was going to happen next. She looked at the sides of the well, and noticed that they were filled with cupboards and bookshelves.

"Well!" thought Alice to herself. "After such a fall as this, I shall think nothing of tumbling down stairs!"

Down, down, down. Would the fall *never* come to an end? "I wonder how many miles I've fallen by this time?" she said aloud. "I must be getting somewhere near the center of the earth. Let me see: that would be four thousand miles down, I think. I wonder if I shall fall right *through* the earth! How funny it'll seem to come out among the people that walk with their heads downwards! I shall have to ask them what the name of the country is. Please Ma'am, is this New Zealand? Or Australia?"

She felt that she was dozing off when suddenly, thump! thump! down she came upon a heap of sticks and dry leaves.

Alice was not a bit hurt. She looked up: before her was another long passage, and the White Rabbit was hurrying down it. Away Alice went like the wind, and was just in time to hear the Rabbit say, as it turned a corner, "Oh my ears and whiskers, how late it's getting!" She was close behind it when she turned the corner, but the Rabbit was no longer to be seen. She found herself in a long, low hall.

There were doors all around the hall, but they were all locked. Alice sadly wondered how she was ever to get out again. Suddenly she came upon a little three-legged table, all made of solid glass; there was nothing on it but a tiny golden key. But alas! It would not open any of the doors. However, Alice then came upon a low curtain she had not noticed before, and behind it was a little door about fifteen inches high. She tried the little golden key in the lock, and it fitted!

The door led into a small passage, not much larger than a rat-hole. Alice knelt down and looked along the passage into the loveliest garden you ever saw. How she longed to get out of that dark hall, and wander about among those beds of bright flowers and those cool fountains, but she could not even get her head through the doorway.

There seemed to be no use in waiting by the little door, so she went back to the table. This time she found a little bottle on it ("which certainly was not here before," said Alice), and tied round the neck of the bottle was a paper label with the words "DRINK ME" printed in large letters.

It was all very well to say "Drink me," but the wise little Alice was not going to do *that* in a hurry: "No, I'll look first," she said, "and see whether it's marked '*poison*,' or not." However, this bottle was *not* marked "poison," so Alice ventured to taste it, and finding it very nice (it had, in fact, a sort of mixed flavor of cherry-tart, custard, pineapple, roast turkey, and hot buttered toast), she very soon finished it off.

"What a curious feeling!" said Alice, who was shutting up like a telescope. She was now only ten inches high, the right size for going through the little door into that lovely garden. But alas for poor Alice! When she got to the door, she found she had forgotten the little golden key, and when she went back to the table for it, she found she could not possibly reach it. The poor little thing sat down and cried, but soon her eye fell on a little glass box that was under the table: she opened it, and found in it a very small cake, on which the words "EAT ME" were beautifully marked in currants. "Well, I'll eat it," said Alice, and very soon finished off the cake.

"Curiouser and curiouser!" cried Alice (for she was so much surprised that she quite forgot how to speak good English). "Now I'm opening out like the largest telescope that ever was! Good-bye feet!" Her head struck against the roof of the hall: in fact she was not rather more than nine feet high, and she at once took up the little golden key and hurried to the garden door.

Poor Alice! It was as much as she could do, lying down on one side, to look through into the garden with one eye; but to get through was more hopeless than ever: she sat down and began to cry again. She went on, shedding gallons of tears, until there was a large pool around her, about four inches deep and reaching half down the hall.

After a time she heard a pattering of feet in the distance, and she hastily dried her eyes to see what was coming. It was the White Rabbit returning, splendidly dressed, with a pair of white kid gloves in one hand and a large fan in the other. He was muttering to himself, "Oh! The Duchess! Oh! *Won't* she be a savage if I've kept her waiting!"

Alice felt so desperate that she was ready to ask help of any one; so when the Rabbit came near her, she began, in a low, timid voice, "If you please, sir—" The Rabbit started violently, dropped the white kid gloves and the fan, and scurried away into the darkness as fast as he could go.

"Dear, dear!" said Alice. "How queer everything is today!" As she said this, she looked down at her hands, and was surprised to see that she had put on one of the Rabbit's little white kid gloves. "How *can* I have done that?" she thought. "I must be growing small again." She was shrinking rapidly, and in another moment, splash! She was up to her chin in salt water. She was in the pool of tears which she had wept when she was nine feet high.

Alice soon makes her way to dry ground and once again encounters the White Rabbit. But the Rabbit eludes her, leaving Alice—who has shrunk again—to wander until she comes upon a caterpillar, sitting upon a mushroom and smoking a kind of pipe called a hookah.

Alice stretched herself up on tiptoe and peeped over the edge of the mushroom, and her eyes immediately met those of a large blue caterpillar. The Caterpillar and Alice looked at each other for some time in silence. At last the Caterpillar took the hookah out of its mouth, and addressed her in a **languid**, sleepy voice.

"Who are *you?*" said the Caterpillar.

Alice replied, rather shyly, "I—I hardly know, sir, just at present—at least I know who I *was* when I got up this morning, but I think I must have changed several times since then."

"What do you mean by that?" said the Caterpillar sternly. "Explain yourself!"

"I can't explain *myself*, I'm afraid, sir," said Alice, "because I'm not myself, you see."

> ### New Word
> Does your child know the word **languid**? Have your child use context clues to guess the definition. The word "sleepy" should be a big hint! The word "languid" means "lacking strength or energy."

"I don't see," said the Caterpillar.

"I'm afraid I can't put it more clearly," Alice replied, "for being so many different sizes in one day is very confusing."

"It isn't," said the Caterpillar.

Alice felt a little irritated at the Caterpillar's making such *very* short remarks. As the Caterpillar seemed to be in a *very* unpleasant state of mind, she turned away.

"Come back!" the Caterpillar called after her. "I've something important to say!"

This sounded promising, so Alice turned and came back again.

"Keep your temper," said the Caterpillar.

"Well, I should like to be a *little* larger, sir, if you wouldn't mind," said Alice: "three inches is such a wretched height to be."

The Caterpillar and Alice.

"It is a very good height indeed!" said the Caterpillar, rearing itself up angrily as it spoke (it was exactly three inches high). "You'll get used to it in time," he said, and began smoking again.

In a minute or two the Caterpillar took the hookah out of its mouth, and yawned once or twice, and shook itself. Then it got down off the mushroom and crawled away into the grass, remarking as it went, "One side will make you grow taller, and the other side will make you grow shorter."

"One side of *what*? The other side of *what*?" thought Alice to herself.

"Of the mushroom," said the Caterpillar, just as if she had asked it aloud; and in another moment it was out of sight.

Alice stretched her arms around the mushroom and broke off a bit of the edge with each hand. Very carefully, she nibbled first at one and then at the other, and after some violent rising and shrinking, managed to bring herself back to her usual height.

Alice wandered until she came upon a cat—the Cheshire Cat—sitting on a bough of a tree and grinning from ear to ear.

"Cheshire Puss," she began, rather timidly, "would you tell me, please, which way I ought to walk from here?"

"That depends a good deal on where you want to get to," said the Cat.

"I don't care much where—" said Alice.

"Then it doesn't matter which way you go," said the Cat.

"—so long as I get *somewhere*," Alice added.

"Oh, you're sure to do that," said the Cat, "if you only walk long enough."

Alice tried another question. "What sort of people live about here?"

"In *that* direction," said the Cat, waving its right paw round, "lives a Hatter, and in *that* direction," waving the other paw, "lives a March Hare. Visit either you like: they're both **mad**."

"But I don't want to go among mad people," Alice remarked.

"Oh, you can't help that," said the Cat. "We're all mad here." Then it vanished slowly, beginning with the end of the tail, and ending with the grin, which remained some time after the rest of it had gone.

"Well! A grin without a cat! It's the most curious thing!" thought Alice.

She had not gone far before she came upon a house, with a table set out under a tree in front of the house. The March Hare and the Mad Hatter were having tea at it; a Dormouse was sitting between them, fast asleep. The table was a large one, but the three were all crowded together at one corner of it. "No room! No room!" they cried out when they saw Alice coming.

"There's *plenty* of room!" said Alice indignantly, and she sat down in a large arm chair at one end of the table.

"Have some wine," said the March Hare.

Alice looked all round the table. "I don't see any wine," she remarked.

"There isn't any," said the March Hare.

New Word

Point out to your child that the word **mad** has multiple meanings. Ask him what the word "mad" usually means. Then read the passages in which Alice and the Cheshire Cat discuss the people living in the area. Help him use context clues to discover that here "mad" means "crazy" or "insane."

What a tea party!

"Then it wasn't very civil of you to offer it," said Alice angrily.

"It wasn't very civil of you to sit down without being invited," said the March Hare.

The Hatter had been looking at Alice for some time and said, "Why is a raven like a writing desk?"

"Riddles! We shall have some fun now!" thought Alice. "I believe I can guess that," she added aloud.

"Do you mean that you think you can find out the answer to it?" said the March Hare.

"Exactly so," said Alice.

"Then you should say what you mean," the March Hare went on.

"I do," Alice repeated. "At least—at least I mean what I say—that's the same thing, you know."

"Not the same thing a bit!" said the Hatter. "Why, you might just as well say that 'I see what I eat' is the same thing as 'I eat what I see'!"

"You might just as well say," added the Dormouse, which seemed to be talking in its sleep, "that 'I breathe when I sleep' is the same thing as 'I sleep when I breathe'!"

"It *is* the same thing with you," said the Hatter. Then he turned to Alice again and asked, "Have you guessed the riddle yet?"

"No, I give it up," Alice replied. "What's the answer?"

"I haven't the slightest idea," said the Hatter.

"Nor I," said the March Hare.

"This," thought Alice, "is the stupidest tea-party I ever was at in all my life!"

Alice wanders into many more adventures in Wonderland. She meets a walking, talking deck of cards, ruled by a furious Queen of Hearts, who responds to everyone by shouting, "Off with your head!"—including Alice! You'll enjoy reading about the Queen and Alice in the full book of Alice's Adventures in Wonderland.

Aladdin and the Wonderful Lamp

This story and the next one, "Ali Baba and the Forty Thieves," come from a book called A Thousand and One Nights. *It begins with the story of a cruel sultan in Persia who chose a new wife every day and discarded her before the next morning. A clever young woman, Scheherazade [shuh-hair-uh-ZAHD], outwitted him. When it came her turn to be the wife of the sultan, she began telling him stories so fascinating that he could not wait to hear the next. By the time she had told him 1,001 stories, he had fallen in love with her, and so he spared her life. The Russian composer Rimsky-Korsakov wrote musical pieces about Scheherazade and her stories. You can learn more about them in the music section of this book, on page 277.*

There was once an idle, good-for-nothing boy called Aladdin. When his father, the tailor, died, Aladdin's mother took up spinning to earn their living.

One day a stranger approached Aladdin.

"Tell me, my son," said the stranger. "Are you not the son of the tailor?"

Aladdin answered yes, and the stranger threw his arms around him. "My dear nephew!" he cried. "Your father was my brother! And now I learn he is dead!"

Aladdin introduced the man to his mother, who had never in her life heard that her husband had a brother. She received him kindly, though, and when the man promised to set Aladdin up in business as a merchant, she believed him.

But the stranger was really a magician from faraway Africa. He had come to China in search of a magic lamp, known to give all the riches anyone could imagine. To find the lamp, the magician needed someone who would help without asking any questions. He thought Aladdin was just the right person.

The next day, the magician came to fetch Aladdin. "Come with me," he said. "I will introduce you to the other merchants." Then he led the boy out into the country.

They climbed a steep mountain to a spot where no flowers grew. "Fetch me a pile of sticks to make a fire, and I will show you a wonderful thing," the magician ordered. Aladdin did as he was told. The magician lit the fire, threw perfumes into it, and uttered magical words. The sky darkened and the earth opened at their feet. There before them was a large stone with a brass ring attached.

"Under this stone is a treasure to make you richer than a king," said the magician. "Lift the stone by the ring. Go down the stairs. You will pass many riches, but you must touch nothing. You will go into a garden, where you will see a lamp hanging from a fruit tree. Bring that lamp to me. Once you have it, you may gather any of the fruits that you see."

Aladdin could not believe what he was being asked to do, but he agreed. "Take this ring," said the magician, removing it from his finger. "It will keep you safe from harm."

Aladdin lifted the stone, stepped down the stairs, and found his way through a hallway of glittering objects, which he took care not to touch. When he found the lamp, he tucked it inside his shirt. Then he couldn't resist filling his pockets with all the glittering things he saw. He didn't know they were precious jewels. He just kept thinking, "I will gather these glass fruits to play with at home."

All those jewels weighed Aladdin down, so when he came to the top of the staircase, he could not climb out. "Give me a hand, Uncle," he cried.

"First give me the lamp," the magician answered.

But the lamp was buried deep beneath all the jewels that Aladdin was carrying. "I cannot reach it now," he said.

"Hand it up to me," said the magician.

"But I can't," Aladdin said.

The magician's anger was growing. "The lamp!" he cried, for that was all he cared about.

But Aladdin did not want to drop any jewels. "I will give it to you when I get out," he said.

The impatient magician uttered a magic chant. The stone rolled back, trapping Aladdin in the cave's black darkness. He called a thousand times for his uncle to help him, but the magician had whisked himself back to Africa. All he wanted was the lamp, and if Aladdin would not help him get that, he cared nothing for Aladdin.

For three days, Aladdin stayed in the pitch-black cave. He wept and shouted. Finally, he put his hands together to pray. As he did so, he happened to rub the ring that the magician had placed on his finger. Instantly, a genie rose before him and said, "I am the slave of him who wears the ring. What do you wish?"

Aladdin found the genie frightening, but he said, "Bring me out of this cave!" Hardly had he finished speaking when he found himself outside again. He ran home to tell his mother all that had happened. He showed her the jewels, which she thought were colored fruit as well. Then he showed her the lamp.

"It is so dirty," said Aladdin's mother. "If I clean it, perhaps I could sell it and bring home some food." She took a cloth and started rubbing it. Suddenly, there appeared a monstrous genie, far bigger than the one who had appeared when Aladdin rubbed the ring.

"I am the slave of her who holds the lamp," thundered the genie. "What do you wish?"

The poor woman almost fainted with fear. Aladdin commanded, "We are hungry! Fetch us something to eat!"

In the twinkling of an eye, the genie returned with twelve silver platters piled high with food. Aladdin and his mother ate their fill. Then they sold the silver platters and bought more food.

One day at the market, Aladdin caught a glimpse of the sultan's daughter. She was so beautiful that he fell in love at once. He told his mother that he wanted the princess for his wife.

"Have you lost your senses?" his mother said. "Your father was a poor tailor!"

"Take the beautiful glass fruit as a gift to the sultan," Aladdin answered.

His mother agreed. "O lord sultan," she said, "my son, named Aladdin, wishes to marry your daughter."

The sultan burst out laughing. "Your son and my daughter?" he boomed.

Aladdin's mother opened her handkerchief and displayed the jewels, which lit up the room. "Never have I seen jewels of such size and radiance," the sultan thought to himself.

"Your son may marry my daughter," he said to the woman, "but only after he sends forty slaves, each carrying a golden basin full of jewels like these."

Hearing the sultan's request, Aladdin rubbed his lamp. The genie reappeared. Aladdin repeated the sultan's wish. Almost instantly the genie returned with forty slaves, each carrying on his head a large golden basin filled with pearls and diamonds, rubies and emeralds.

At that, the sultan agreed to let Aladdin marry his daughter.

Aladdin was delighted. He rubbed the lamp and commanded the genie to prepare a wedding in princely style. Slaves brought him rich clothes, sweet perfumes, and a splendid horse, which he rode to the wedding. Slaves threw gold pieces into the hands of all the people who lined the streets to see him. He commanded the genie to build a palace right next to the home of the sultan, with kitchens full of golden dishes and stables full of handsome horses. Finally, at Aladdin's request, the genie spread a thick carpet from the sultan's home to Aladdin's palace so his bride's feet would not have to touch the earth.

When the sultan saw such magnificence, he was sure that Aladdin was the right husband for his daughter. They celebrated their wedding with a feast and music that lasted all day and all night. Aladdin thought that his life could not be more perfect.

But danger lurked afar. The magician caught wind of Aladdin's good fortune. "That lazy boy? Surely this must be the magic of the lamp," he said, and he whisked himself back to China. He dressed himself as a poor peddler and carried a few shiny lamps in a basket. As he walked by Aladdin's palace, he shouted, "New lamps for old!"

It just so happened that on that morning, Aladdin had gone out hunting. His wife, the princess, heard the voice from the street. "We have that ugly old lamp," she thought. "I would gladly trade it for a shiny new one." With that, she handed over Aladdin's lamp to the disguised magician.

Immediately, the magician rubbed the lamp and the genie appeared.

"Take Aladdin's palace and all that it contains," commanded the magician. "Set it down in my country of Africa."

"I hear and I obey," said the genie.

The next morning, when the sultan looked out the window, both the palace and his daughter had disappeared. He sent his soldiers out, and they dragged Aladdin before the sultan. "Find my daughter!" he stormed. "If you fail, you die!"

Poor Aladdin wandered far from the city. He walked beside a river and rubbed his hands, wondering what to do. The genie of the ring appeared once more, asking, "What do you wish?"

"Bring my palace and my beloved wife home to me," asked Aladdin.

"Alas," said the genie, "that duty belongs only to the genie of the lamp."

"Then take me to be with my wife."

Instantly, Aladdin found himself in Africa. His wife greeted him joyfully. When Aladdin heard her story, he knew that the magician had used the lamp to work his evil deed. They hit on a plan to get back the lamp.

While Aladdin kept out of sight, the princess treated the magician to a fine supper. Into his cup of wine, she slipped a poison powder. No sooner had the magician swallowed one gulp of wine than he fell on the floor, dead.

Aladdin ran in and discovered the lamp, hidden inside the magician's sleeve. He rubbed it and the monstrous genie appeared. "What do you wish?" the genie thundered.

"Take this building with all it contains," commanded Aladdin, pointing to the palace. "Carry it to China and set it down beside the sultan's home."

"I hear and I obey," replied the genie, and the palace was lifted up into the air.

The next morning when the sultan arose and looked out the window, he was overjoyed to see his daughter and her palace once again. He ordered a month of celebrations. From then on, Aladdin lived with the princess in peace and pleasure and safety. When the old sultan died, Aladdin took his throne and ruled justly over all people, rich and poor.

Ali Baba and the Forty Thieves

Here is another story told by Scheherazade to the Persian sultan to save her life and collected in A Thousand and One Nights.

Many years ago there lived two brothers in Persia, Cassim and Ali Baba. The elder brother had married the daughter of a rich merchant and lived very well. But Ali Baba had married a poor woman and barely had enough to get by.

One day, as Ali Baba was coming home from cutting wood, a troop of horsemen came riding full speed toward him. Hiding in the bushes, he watched as the horsemen, who numbered forty, climbed off their horses. Each heaved onto the ground a heavy saddlebag, and Ali Baba began to understand that these were thieves hiding their treasure.

One stood in front of a steep rock. "Open, sesame!" he cried, and a doorway appeared in the rock. The robbers entered and the door shut behind them. Ali Baba waited quietly. Then the door opened again. The leader of the thieves counted all the men as they passed by him, then cried, "Shut, sesame!" The door in the rock closed.

When the robbers were out of sight, Ali Baba tried the magic trick for himself. "Open, sesame!" he called, and the door opened.

Inside was a huge room, filled with bags of treasure and heaps of coins. Ali Baba picked up a few bags of coins—just a few—then he said the magic words that opened the door again: "Open, sesame!" Once out of the cave, he said, "Shut, sesame!" The door in the rock closed.

Ali Baba hurried home. To his poor wife, a few bags of coins were a treasure. "Let me weigh the money, to know how much we have," she said.

"Just be sure to keep our secret," Ali Baba said.

His wife ran to Cassim's house to borrow a scale with which to weigh the coins.

"What would my poor sister-in-law need to weigh?" wondered Cassim's wife. She secretly rubbed some wax on the bottom of the scale. When Ali Baba's wife returned it, a shiny gold coin stayed stuck to the wax. "Do they have so much gold that they must weigh it?" Cassim exclaimed when he heard what had happened.

Now, Cassim was rich, but he was also jealous. Early the next morning he went to his brother and demanded to know where the gold coin came from. Ali Baba told him of the cave and the special command. "I will go and fetch some treasure for myself," said Cassim.

Cassim remembered to say, "Open, sesame!" To his joy, the door opened wide, showing bags of treasure and heaps of coins. He filled ten bags as full as he could. He was so excited he forgot the magic words. "Open, barley!" he cried. "Open, oats!" But nothing he said opened the door. He was locked inside the cave of treasure.

At noon, the robbers returned to their cave. They spoke the magic words and the door in the rock opened. Cassim tried to hide, but he could not escape from forty thieves. They cut Cassim's body into four quarters and hung them inside the cave.

By nighttime, Cassim's wife was worried. Ali Baba knew where to find his brother. He went to the rock and spoke the magic words: "Open, sesame!" Then he found his worst fears to be true. He wrapped what was left of his brother's body in cloth, laid the bundle on the back of his mule, covered them with branches, and carried them back to his brother's house.

A smart young slave girl named Morgiana worked for Cassim and his wife. When she heard what Ali Baba had brought home, she agreed to help him keep it secret. She ran to the druggist's, asking for strong medicine. "My master is sick unto death," she said. "He cannot eat or speak." Having heard that, no one was surprised to hear the next day that Cassim had died and that his brother, Ali Baba, had moved into his house to console the widow and take care of unfinished business.

Now Morgiana considered Ali Baba her master, and she willingly helped him carry out his plan. She ran to the cobbler's and put two gold pieces into his hand. "I have a task for you, but it must be kept a secret," she said. She led him blindfolded to Cassim's house. She asked him to sew Cassim's body back together, so that he might be buried without anyone knowing what had happened to him. She gave the cobbler a third piece of gold for his trouble and led him blindfolded back home again.

When the forty thieves found Cassim's body missing, they realized that someone still knew the secret of how to get into their cave. They went from person to person throughout the town, trying to discover who it was. One thief happened on the cobbler, who was working at the crack of dawn.

"How can you see your work?" asked the thief. "It is scarcely light."

"I have very good eyes," said the cobbler. "Yesterday I sewed together a dead body in a room much darker than this."

"Aha!" thought the thief. To the cobbler he said, "You must be joking. Show me the house where you did such a strange job."

"I was blindfolded," said the cobbler, "but I think I can remember the way." He walked down the street, counting his steps as he went, and stopped at Cassim's doorstep.

The thief gave the cobbler a gold piece, thanked him, and sent him on his way. When he asked the neighbors, the thief learned that Ali Baba had recently lost his brother yet come into great riches. The thief was sure that Ali Baba was the man who had discovered the way into the cave. He marked Ali Baba's door with chalk.

But smart Morgiana noticed the chalk marks on the door. "Either an enemy plans to do my master wrong or a boy has been playing tricks," she thought. "Either way, it is best to guard against all possible evil." She fetched a piece of chalk and marked three other doors near her master's.

When the thief returned, he was confused by all the chalk marks. In a rage, his leader killed him on the spot. He sent another thief to find the cobbler, who pointed out Ali Baba's house, which this thief marked with red chalk.

But Morgiana was watching. She marked all the doors up and down the street with red chalk, too. Again the leader, infuriated, killed this man on the spot.

The leader decided to follow the cobbler by himself. He made no marks on Ali Baba's door. He just looked at it very carefully, so he would remember it. He went back to his fellow thieves and told them his new plan.

"Bring nineteen mules," he said. "To each mule, attach two earthen jars, big enough for a man to fit in. Put oil in only one of those jars." And do you know what he did with the other thirty-seven jars? He made the thieves crawl into them!

The leader of the thieves led the nineteen mules carrying thirty-eight jars right up to Ali Baba's door. "Sir, I have some oil to sell at market tomorrow," he told Ali Baba. "Might I stay the night with you?" Ali Baba told Morgiana to show the man to a room and feed him. As the man left the mules behind, he whispered to the thieves in hiding, "I'll be back at midnight. Come out when you hear my voice."

As Morgiana was making soup for the stranger, her lamp went out. "All I need is a little oil for the lamp, just enough to finish cooking," she said to herself. "I can borrow a bit from those jars belonging to the stranger."

So she went outside and cautiously opened the first jar. As she did so, a voice whispered, "Is it time?"

"No, not yet, be patient," she answered, wondering. She went from jar to jar, hearing a voice from each and always answering the same way, until she finally came to the jar of oil. The smart girl went back to her kitchen, lit the lamp, then built a great fire of wood, upon which she set a huge black kettle and filled it with oil from the jar outside. She heated that oil until was boiling, then poured some into each of the jars, killing the thieves inside the jars, one by one. When the leader found out, he ran away into the night, afraid for his own life.

When Morgiana told Ali Baba what had happened, he was so grateful he offered her her freedom. She thanked him, asking that she be allowed to continue living with him and his family.

But that is still not the end of the story! The leader of the forty thieves came back to town many weeks later, hoping for revenge. He learned that the son of Cassim owned a shop. He brought treasures from his secret cave and pretended to be a merchant, too. In that way he became friends with the nephew of Ali Baba.

One night, not knowing who this new merchant really was, Ali Baba invited him to dinner. "Thank you, no," the man answered. "My doctor says I must eat no salt."

"Who is this difficult man who eats no salt?" asked Morgiana.

"He is our new friend," Ali Baba answered.

But Morgiana looked closely and recognized him. Looking even more closely, she saw a dagger hidden in his robe.

Knowing that danger might befall her master, Morgiana dressed like a dancing girl and offered to entertain the visitor after dinner. She danced with grace and spirit. She swept a jeweled dagger through the air as part of the art of her dance. As the leader of the thieves reached to give the dancer a coin of gold, Morgiana plunged the dagger into his heart.

"What have you done?" cried Ali Baba. "You have murdered my new friend!"

"Nay, master, I have saved your life," answered Morgiana. She drew back the guest's robe and revealed his hidden dagger.

Again Morgiana had saved the life of Ali Baba. Since she already had her freedom, he found something even more wonderful to give her in thanks. He said that she could marry his nephew, who truly loved her. So Morgiana joined the family of Ali Baba and shared the fortunes of his house.

The Hunting of the Great Bear

This story comes from the Iroquois people, Native Americans who lived in the eastern part of today's United States, on land that we now call New York, Pennsylvania, and Ohio.

There were four hunters who were brothers. No hunters were as good as they were at following a trail. Once they began tracking their quarry, they never gave up.

One day, in the time when the cold nights return, an urgent message came to the four hunters. A great bear had appeared at a village nearby, so large and powerful that many of the villagers thought it must be some kind of monster. The people of the village were afraid.

Picking up their spears and calling to their small dog, the four hunters set forth for that village. As they came closer, they noticed how quiet the woods were. There were no signs of rabbits or deer. Even the birds were silent. They found where the great bear had reared up on hind legs and made deep scratches on a pine tree to mark its territory. The tallest of the brothers tried to touch the highest scratch mark with the tip of his spear.

"It is as the people feared," the first brother said. "This one we are to hunt is Nyah-gwaheh, a monster bear."

"The Nyah-gwaheh has special magic, but that magic will do the bear no good if we find its track," said the second brother.

"I have always heard that from the old people," said the third brother. "The Nyah-gwaheh can only chase a hunter who has not yet found its trail. When you find its trail and begin to chase it, then it must run from you."

"Brothers," said the fourth, the fattest and laziest, "did we bring along enough food to eat? It may take a long time to catch this big bear. I'm feeling hungry."

Before long, the four hunters and their small dog reached the village. It was a sad sight to see. There was no fire burning in the center of the village, and the doors of all the longhouses were closed. No game hung from the racks; no skins were stretched for tanning. All the people looked hungry.

The elder of the village appeared.

"Uncle," said the tallest brother, "we have come to help you get rid of the monster."

Then the fattest and laziest brother spoke. "Uncle, is there some food we can eat? Can we find a place to rest before we start chasing this big bear?"

The second hunter shook his head and smiled. "My brother is only joking, Uncle," he said. "We are going now to pick up the monster bear's trail."

"I am not sure you can do that, nephews," the elder said. "Though we find tracks closer and closer to the door of our lodges each morning, whenever we try to follow those tracks they disappear."

The third hunter knelt down and patted the head of their small dog. "Uncle," he said, "that is because they do not have a dog such as ours." He pointed to the two black spots above the eyes of the small dog. "Four-Eyes can see any tracks, even those many days old."

"May Creator's protection be with you," said the elder.

"I think we should have something to eat first," said the fourth hunter, but his brother did not listen.

The four hunters walked, following their little dog, who kept lifting up its head, as if to look around with its four eyes.

"Brothers," the fattest and laziest hunter complained, "don't you think we should rest? We've been walking a long time." But his brothers paid no attention to him. Though they could see no tracks, they could feel the presence of the Nyah-gwaheh. They knew that if they did not soon find its trail, the monster bear would circle around them, and then they would be the hunted ones.

The fattest and laziest brother decided to eat while they walked. He opened his pemmican pouch and shook out the strips of meat and berries he had pounded with maple sugar and dried in the sun. Pale squirming things fell out instead. The magic of the Nyah-gwaheh had changed the food into worms.

"Look what that bear did to my pemmican!" the fattest and laziest brother shouted. "Now I'm getting angry."

Meanwhile, like a giant shadow, the Nyah-gwaheh was moving through the trees. Its huge teeth shone; its eyes flashed red. Soon it would be behind them, on their trail.

Just then, though, the little dog lifted its head and yelped.

"Eh-heh!" the first brother called.

"Four-Eyes has found the trail," shouted the second brother.

"We have the track of the Nyah-gwaheh," said the third brother.

"Big Bear," the fattest and laziest one yelled, "we are after you now!"

Fear filled the heart of the great bear for the first time, and it began to run. As it broke from the cover of the pines, the four hunters saw it, a gigantic shape, so white as to appear almost naked. The great bear's strides were long and swifter than a deer's. The four hunters and their little dog were swift as well. The trail led through swamps and thickets. It was easy for the hunters to follow, for the bear pushed everything aside as it ran, even knocking down big trees. They came to a mountain and followed the trail higher and higher, every now and then catching a glimpse of their quarry over the next rise.

But the lazy hunter was getting tired of running. He pretended to fall and twist his ankle. "Brothers," he called, "I have sprained my ankle. You must carry me."

His brothers did as he asked, two of them carrying him while the third carried his spear. They ran more slowly now, but they were not falling any further behind. The day turned into night, yet they could still see the white shape ahead of them. They were at the top of the mountain now. The bear was tiring, but so were they. Four-Eyes, the little dog, was close behind the great bear, nipping at its tail as it ran.

The fattest and laziest brother asked to be put down. "I think my leg has gotten better," he said. Fresh and rested, he dashed ahead of the others. Just as the great bear turned to bite at the little dog, the fattest and laziest brother thrust his spear into the heart of the Nyah-gwaheh. The monster bear fell dead.

By the time the other brothers caught up, the fattest and laziest one had built a fire and was cutting up the bear.

"Come on, brothers," he said. "Let's eat. All this running has made me hungry!"

So they cooked the meat of the great bear, and its fat sizzled as it dripped from their fire. They ate until even the fattest and laziest brother leaned back in contentment. Just then, though, the first brother looked down.

"Brothers," the second brother exclaimed, "look below us!"

"We aren't on a mountaintop at all," said the third brother. "We are up in the sky."

Below them, thousands of lights sparkled in the darkness. The great bear had indeed been magical, and they had followed it up into the heavens.

Just then their little dog yipped twice. There, where they had piled the bones of their feast, the bear was coming back to life. It rose to its feet and began to run again, the dog close on its heels. Grabbing up their spears, the four hunters again began to chase the great bear across the skies.

So it was, as the old people say, and so still is. Each autumn the hunters chase the Great Bear across the skies and kill it. As they cut it up for meat, the blood of the bear falls from the sky and colors the leaves of the maple trees scarlet. As they cook the meat, the dripping fat bleaches the grass white.

If you look in the nighttime skies as the seasons change, you can read this story. The Great Bear is the shape some call the Big Dipper, which rotates around the North Star. During the summer, you can see the hunters and their small dog (just barely) in the Dipper's handle, running close behind the Great Bear. When autumn comes, the constellation seems to turn upside down. Then, the old people say, the lazy hunter has killed the bear. As more moons pass (which is how the old people talk about months going by), the constellations revolve. The bear slowly rises back on its feet, and the chase begins again.

> **Make a Connection**
> After reading this story with your child, turn to page 177 and read the "Eastern Woodland Peoples" passage to learn about the real Iroquois people.

Gone Is Gone

This story comes from Bohemia, which was in the Czech Republic, part of Eastern Europe. It is sometimes called "The Story of a Man Who Wanted to Do Housework."

Once there was a man named Fritzl. He had a wife named Liesi. They had a little baby, Kinndli by name, and Spitz, their dog. They had one cow, two goats, three pigs, and a dozen geese. They lived on a patch of land, and that's where they worked.

Fritzl had to plow the ground, sow the seeds, and hoe the weeds. He had to cut the hay and rake it, too, and stack it up in bunches in the sun.

Liesi had the house to clean, the soup to cook, the butter to churn, the barnyard and the baby to care for. They both worked hard, but Fritzl always thought that he worked harder. Evenings when he came home from the field, he sat down and said, "Hu! Little do you know, Liesi, what a man's work is like."

"Mine is none too easy," said Liesi.

"None too easy!" cried Fritzl. "All you do is putter and potter around the house a bit."

"Nay, if you think so," said Liesi, "we'll take it turn and turn about tomorrow. I will do your work, and you can do mine."

So the next morning, there was Liesi at peep of day, striding out across the fields. And Fritzl, where was he? He was in the kitchen, frying a string of juicy sausages, lost in pleasant thoughts.

"A mug of apple cider with my sausage," he was thinking. "That would be just the thing." Fritzl went down into the cellar where there was a big barrel full of cider.

But hulla! What was that noise up in the kitchen! When Fritzl reached the top of the stairs, there was that Spitz-dog dashing out of the kitchen door with the string of juicy sausages.

"What's gone is gone," said Fritzl, shrugging his shoulders.

But the cider, now! Had he put the cork back in the barrel? With big fast steps Fritzl went to look, but it was too late, for the cider had run all over the cellar.

"What's gone is gone," said Fritzl, scratching his head.

Now it was time to churn the butter. Fritzl filled the churn with good rich cream, took it under a tree, and began to churn with all his might. His little Kinndli was out there, playing Moo-cow among the daisies. "This is pleasant, now," thought Fritzl. "But what about the cow? I've forgotten all about her this morning."

With big fast steps Fritzl ran to the barn, carrying a bucket of cool water for the cow. The poor creature's tongue was hanging out of her mouth for thirst. She was hungry, too, so Fritzl took her from the barn to the green, grassy meadow.

But then Fritzl thought about Kinndli. She would surely get into trouble if he went all the way out to the meadow. Better keep the cow on the roof. Fritzl's house was not covered with shingles or tin or tile—it was covered with moss and sod, and a fine crop of grass and flowers grew there. The house was built into the side of a hill, so Fritzl took the cow up the little hill and onto the roof. The cow was soon munching away, so Fritzl went back to his churning.

But hulla! Kinndli was climbing up on the churn, and the churn was tipping! And now there on the grass lay Kinndli, all covered with half-churned cream and butter.

"What's gone is gone," said Fritzl, blinking his blue eyes.

The sun had climbed high up into the heavens. Noontime it was, no dinner made. Fritzl hurried off to the garden. He gathered potatoes and onions, carrots and cabbages, beets and beans, turnips, parsley, and celery. "That will make a good soup," he said, his arms so full of vegetables he could not close the garden gate behind him. He sat down in the kitchen and began cutting and paring away. How the man did work!

But now there was a great noise above him. Fritzl jumped to his feet. "That cow," he said. "She's sliding around on the roof. She might slip off and break her neck."

Up on the roof went Fritzl once more, this time with loops of heavy rope. He took one end of the rope and tied it around the cow's middle. The other end he dropped down the chimney and pulled through the fireplace. Then he took that end of the rope and tied it around his own middle. "That will keep the cow from falling off the roof," he said, chuckling.

He heaped sticks on the fireplace and set a big kettle of water over it. "We'll soon have a good big soup," he said. He put in the vegetables. He put in the bacon. He started to light the fire—but that he never did, for just then, with a bump and a thump, the cow slipped over the edge of the roof, and Fritzl was whisked up into the chimney. There he dangled, poor man, and couldn't get up and couldn't get down.

Before long, there came Liesi home from the fields. But hulla! What was that hanging over the edge of the roof? It was the cow, half choked, with her eyes bulging and her tongue hanging out. Liesi cut the rope and let the poor cow down.

Now Liesi saw the garden with the gate wide open. There were the pigs and the goats and all the geese, too, full to bursting, but the garden, alas! was empty.

Liesi walked on and saw the churn upturned and Kinndli there in the sun, stiff and sticky with dried cream and butter.

Liesi hurried on and saw the Spitz-dog on the grass, full of sausages and looking none too well.

Liesi looked at the cellar. There was cider all over the floor and halfway up the stairs. Liesi looked in the kitchen. The floor was piled high with peelings and littered with pots and pans.

At last Liesi saw the fireplace. Hulla! What was that in the soup kettle? Two arms were waving, two legs were kicking, and a weak gurgle was coming up out of the water.

"What can this mean?" cried Liesi. Poor Fritzl, for as soon as the cow's rope had been cut, he had dropped down the chimney—crash! splash!—right into the kettle of soup.

Liesi pulled and tugged, and there, dripping and spluttering, with a cabbage leaf in his hair, celery in his pocket, and a sprig of parsley in his ear, was Fritzl.

"Is that the way you keep house?" she asked.

"Oh, Liesi," sputtered Fritzl. "You're right. That work of yours is none too easy."

"It's hard at first," said Liesi, "but tomorrow you will do better."

"Nay, nay," cried Fritzl. "Gone is gone, and so is my house-work from this day on. Please, Liesi, let me go back to my work in the fields, and never more will I say that my work is harder than yours."

"If that's your promise," said Liesi, "we can surely live in peace and happiness forever." And that they did.

What About You?
Ask your child about her chores. If she could trade any of them, what would she trade and why?

The Little Match Girl

This is one of many well-known fairy tales written by Hans Christian Andersen, who lived in Denmark during the 1800s.

It was terribly cold and nearly dark on the last evening of the old year. Snow was falling fast, and yet a poor little girl, with bare head and naked feet, roamed through the streets.

It is true she had on a pair of slippers when she left home, but they were not of much use. They had belonged to her mother, and were so large that she had lost them in running across the street to escape the carriages. She found one, but a boy seized the other and ran away with it. So the little girl went on, her little naked feet blue with the cold.

In an old apron she carried matches. She held a bundle of them in her hands. No one had bought any matches from her the whole day. Shivering with cold and hunger, she crept along. The snowflakes fell on her hair, which hung in lovely curls on her shoulders.

Lights were shining from every window, and there was a fine smell of roast goose in the air. The little girl remembered that it was New Year's Eve. Between two houses, she huddled herself together, but she could not keep out the cold. She dared not go home, for she had sold no matches and could not take home even a penny of money. Her father would certainly beat her. Besides, it was almost as cold at home as here, for the wind howled through, even though the holes in the walls and windows had been stopped up with straw and rags.

Her little hands were almost frozen. Perhaps a burning match might warm her fingers. She drew one out. *Scratch!* How it sputtered as it burned! It gave a warm, bright light, like a little candle as she held her hand over it. It was really a wonderful light. It seemed to the little girl that she was sitting by a large iron stove, with polished brass feet and pretty brass ornaments. It seemed so beautifully warm that she stretched out her feet as if to warm them. But then the flame of the match went out, the stove vanished, and she had only the half-burned match in her hand.

She rubbed another match on the wall. It burst into flame. Where its light fell, the little girl could see through the wall to a table, covered with a snowy-white tablecloth, with splendid dishes and a steaming roast goose, stuffed with apples and plums. What was still more wonderful, the goose jumped down from the dish with a knife and fork stuck into its breast and waddled across the floor to the little girl. Then the match went out, and there remained nothing but the cold wall before her.

She lit another match, and she found herself sitting under a beautiful Christmas tree, with thousands of candles and twinkling decorations. The little girl stretched her hand out. Then the match went out.

At that, the Christmas lights began to rise up into the sky. They rose higher and higher, until they looked to the little girl like the stars in the sky. Then she saw a star fall, leaving behind it a bright streak of fire. "Someone is dying," thought the little girl, for her grandmother, the only person who had ever loved her and who was now dead, had told her that when a star falls, a soul is on its way to heaven.

The little girl struck a match and light shone all around her. In the brightness stood her grandmother, clear and shining, kind and loving.

"Grandmother," cried the girl. "I know you will vanish like the warm stove, the roast goose, and the Christmas tree. Take me with you." She made haste to light the whole bundle of matches. They glowed with a light that was brighter than the noonday sun, and her grandmother appeared more beautiful than ever. She took the little girl in her arms, and they both flew upward in brightness and joy, far above the earth, where there was no cold or hunger or pain.

In the dawn of the morning, there lay the poor little girl with pale cheeks and smiling mouth, leaning against the wall. She had been frozen to death on the last evening of the old year. Now the new year's sun rose and shone upon her. The child still sat, in the stiffness of death, holding the bundle of burned matches.

"She tried to warm herself," said some. No one imagined what beautiful things she had seen, nor into what glory she had entered with her grandmother on New Year's Day.

The People Could Fly

This story was shared among enslaved African Americans for a long time before anyone ever wrote it down. It has many different versions.

They say that these people could fly. Long ago in Africa, some of them would shout a few magic words and lift themselves into the air like crows, flapping their black wings. They say that when these people were put on the ships as slaves, they had to fold those wings. There was no room for flying on those cramped ships. And they say that when these people were put to work in the fields, they lost the freedom to spread their wings. They could not even imagine flying.

But not all of them forgot the magic words.

One afternoon the sun was so hot it seemed to singe the hair on their heads. They had been picking cotton since sunup without a rest. One young woman, Sarah, was carrying her child on her back and was feeling so weary she fainted.

"Back to work," the overseer snarled. "There is no time for rest!" He raised his whip in warning.

All the other slaves stopped to watch him. Sarah staggered to her feet, her child on her back, and began to pick again. Sarah fell again. The overseer snapped his whip at her, and Sarah rose a second time.

An old man came to Sarah through the rows of cotton. He looked both ways, then whispered something in her ear. Sarah looked both ways and passed the message on. The whispering spread from slave to slave as swiftly as a breeze, and the overseer never noticed. The slaves kept working.

But Sarah's baby began to whimper and cry, and Sarah stopped to comfort him. The overseer rode toward her. Just as his whip was about to lash her back, that same old man shouted those magic words, remembered from so long ago.

With those words, Sarah began to rise. She spread her arms. They felt like wings. She rose above the overseer's whip like an eagle.

Wheeling his horse around, the overseer bellowed, "Who shouted? What did he say?" All the other slaves stayed quiet and kept busy, but they knew Sarah had flown to freedom.

The sun was so hot that others began to fall. The overseer cracked his whip at one man, but before that whip made contact, another shout rang out. The

weary slave rose into the air. Then the overseer saw a woman crumpled over nearby, and he raised his whip to strike her. Once again those magic words rang out, and the woman rose up into the air.

As each slave fainted with the heat, the overseer raised his whip. Each time he did, the slave would rise up into the air. Then the overseer saw the old man, his mouth ready to shout.

"Seize that old man," the overseer shouted, raising his whip.

The old man looked the overseer in the eye. "Now," was all he said. With that one word, all the people circled round and joined hands. Chanting the magic words, they slowly rose. They flew above the field and far out of reach of the overseer.

They say those slaves flew back to Africa. We don't really know. But we remember, and we still whisper this story to all those who try, in their hearts and minds, to lift their wings and fly.

Three Words of Wisdom

This story comes from the border territory between the southwestern United States and Mexico.

There were once three men who lived in the country. Two had large families, and one had only his wife and a son who wanted to be a priest. No matter the number of mouths to feed, though, their crops failed year after year. Their families were starving. They decided to find jobs in the city.

Just a few miles from town, they ran into an old man who asked if he might travel with them. They asked if he knew of any work. He answered, "In my lifetime, I have gathered heaps of gold. I don't have a family, so I will share it with you. You may have either my coins or my golden wisdom." The men with large families asked for the money, but the man with the small family asked for the wisdom.

The old man divided his gold coins between the two men. To the third, he said, "Here are my words of wisdom: Don't take shortcuts. Don't ask about what does not concern you. And don't jump too quickly to conclusions."

Two men scolded their friend for his stupidity: "You can't feed your family with wisdom." And they all set off for home.

As they left the main road to take a shortcut through the forest, the third man said, "Remember what the old man said? *Don't take any shortcuts.*" But the two men ignored him and plunged into the woods. There they were attacked by bandits, who took the money and their lives.

Unaware of his friends' fate, the third man traveled on toward the city. As night fell he reached a huge ranch where a rancher lived, starved for good company.

What a feast this man served! Our traveler had never seen more succulent meat, the fruit like gems, candles glistening overhead. Washing down the last sweet mouthful, our traveler began to ask where such riches came from, but then he remembered the old man's words: *Don't ask about what doesn't concern you.* He kept still.

The rancher saw his guest swallow his question. Lifting the cover from the last banquet platter, he revealed the head of a man! "You are very wise," he said, "for this is what happened to the last man who asked how I made my riches. All of my life, I have waited for someone simply to accept me as I am, to share in my gifts without asking how I got them. Now that I have seen your wisdom, I will gladly share them with you!"

The rancher led our traveler to the window, saying, "All of this and all that lives and grows here are yours to use, whenever you are in need."

Our traveler woke the next morning to find a cart and donkey loaded down with more food and money than he could ever ask for. He couldn't wait to get home.

He approached his house quietly, hoping to surprise his wife and son. He peeked into the window and nearly choked with rage! His wife was embracing a priest! He started to howl with anger, but then he remembered the old man's words of wisdom: *Don't jump to conclusions.*

Trying to calm himself, he knocked on the door. His wife turned to the priest and said, "Perhaps it is your father." During the traveler's long absence, his son had become a priest! Our traveler greeted his family as a wise man would, and the three lived happily ever after.

William Tell

The people of Switzerland have told this legend for a long time. No one knows if William Tell was a real man. His story may be a way of telling about an actual rebellion that took place around 1300.

Many years ago a cruel governor named Gessler ruled over the people of Switzerland. He taxed them heavily, so nothing could be bought or sold unless the governor received some of the money. Many people who did nothing wrong were put into prison for a long time. The Swiss people were unhappy indeed.

One day Gessler set up a tall pole in the public square of the town called Altdorf. Atop that pole he put his own cap, announcing that all citizens must uncover their heads as they passed by the cap, or else they would be put to death. Guards stood in the square day and night to see that the order was obeyed.

Now, there lived in a small village not far away a famous hunter by the name of William Tell. No one in all the land could shoot with bow and arrow as well as he could.

One morning Tell took his little son, Walter, with him into Altdorf on business. He heard the news about Gessler's order but could not bring himself to bare his head to a cap atop a pole.

"Take off your hat and bow!" a guard commanded.

"Why should I bow to a cap on a pole?" asked William Tell.

"This man will not uncover his head as he passes by your cap," the guards reported to Gessler.

"You are said to be the best shot in the mountains," said Gessler to William Tell. "I will design a punishment just for you." He sent a soldier to an orchard for an apple. "Place this fruit upon the head of your son," said Gessler. "Then walk a hundred yards away and shoot that apple with your bow and arrow."

Tell begged the tyrant to come up with another punishment.

"Obey my order!" roared Gessler.

Walter took his place, with the apple atop his head. Tell drew an arrow from his quiver. He slowly fit the arrow to the bow and raised them to his shoulder.

"Shoot, Father," said young Walter firmly. "I am not afraid. I am staying still."

Tell pulled back his bowstring. *Ping!* The arrow flew through the air. It pierced the apple, which dropped in two pieces onto the ground. The people watching shouted for joy.

As William Tell rushed to embrace his son, a second arrow fell from under his coat.

"What did you plan for that second arrow?" asked Gessler angrily.

"That arrow was for your heart, you tyrant!" William Tell responded. "If I had hurt my beloved son, you can be sure I would not have missed the mark a second time."

Legend has it that, in the years to come, William Tell did send an arrow through the heart of Gessler—and set the people of Switzerland free.

The River Bank

(adapted from Kenneth Grahame's original)

This episode of The Wind in the Willows *will give you a taste of the wonderful book by Kenneth Grahame, published in 1908. Grahame was born in Scotland in 1859. He worked as a banker and lived in England most of his life. If you enjoy this story, you will like the whole book, full of the antics of little animals in the English countryside, including Toad, who loves his speedy motorcar.*

The Mole had been working very hard all the morning spring-cleaning his little home: first with brooms, then with dusters; then on ladders and steps and chairs, with a brush and a pail of whitewash. He did this until he had dust in his throat and eyes, and splashes of whitewash all over his black fur. Spring was moving in the air above and the earth below, and around him and his dark and lowly little house. Any wonder he suddenly flung down his brush on the floor, said "Bother!" and "O blow!" and also "Hang spring-cleaning!" and bolted out of the house without even waiting to put on his coat.

What About You?

Ask your child, "How do you think Mole felt after cleaning his house all day? Why do you think he threw down his cleaning supplies?"

Mole immediately made for the steep little tunnel, and without a moment's hesitation, he began scraping, scratching, and scrabbling. He worked busily with his little paws and muttered to himself, "Up we go! Up we go!" till at last, pop! His snout came out into the sunlight, and he found himself rolling in the warm grass of a great meadow.

"This is fine!" he said to himself. "This is better than whitewashing!" he added as he jumped with delight at the joy of spring. In this state of happiness, he made his way across the meadow till he reached the hedge on the farther side.

It all seemed too good to be true, as moving hither and thither he observed everywhere birds building, and leaves and flowers bursting forth.

He thought his happiness was complete when, as he meandered aimlessly along, he came to the edge of a full-fed river. There he stood quite mesmerized, as never before had he seen a river. He watched in awe as it shimmered and shined, gurgled and burbled, swirled and curled its way seaward. So bewitched and fascinated was he, that he trotted for a while by the side of it. Eventually, exhausted by this tremendous effort, he sat down on the bank to rest.

As he sat on the grass and gazed across the river, a dark hole in the bank opposite, just above the water's edge, caught his eye. Mole quietly contemplated what a nice snug dwelling place it would make. As he gazed, something bright and small seemed to twinkle like a tiny star down in the heart of it. But it could hardly be a star, and it was too glittering and small for a glowworm. Then, as he looked, it winked at him, and so revealed itself to be an eye; and a small face began gradually to grow up round it, like a frame round a picture.

A brown little face, with whiskers.

A grave round face, with the same twinkle in its eye.

Small neat ears and thick silky hair.

It was the Water Rat!

The two animals stood and regarded each other cautiously.

"Hullo, Mole!" said the Water Rat.

"Hullo, Rat!" said the Mole.

"Would you like to come over?" enquired the Rat.

"Oh, it's all very well to ask," said the Mole, rather grumpily, he being new to a river and riverside life and its ways.

The Rat said nothing, but stooped and unfastened a rope and hauled on it; then lightly stepped into a little boat which the Mole had not observed. It was painted blue outside and white within, and was just the size for two animals; and the Mole loved it immediately. The Rat sculled across. Then he held up his forepaw as the Mole stepped gingerly down. "Lean on that!" he said. "Now then, step lively!" and the Mole to his great delight found himself actually seated in the stern of a real boat.

"This has been a wonderful day!" said he, as the Rat shoved off and took to the sculls again. "Do you know, I've never been in a boat before in all my life."

"What?" cried the Rat, open-mouthed: "Never been in a—you never—well I—what have you been doing, then?"

"Is it so nice as all that?" asked the Mole shyly, though he was quite prepared to believe it as he leant back in his seat and surveyed the cushions, the oars, and all the fascinating fittings.

"Nice? It's the only thing," said the Water Rat solemnly, as he leant forward for his stroke. "Believe me, my young friend, there is nothing—absolutely nothing—half so much worth doing as simply **messing** about in boats. Simply messing," he went on dreamily: "messing—about—in—boats; messing—"

"Look ahead, Rat!" cried the Mole suddenly.

It was too late. The boat struck the bank full tilt. The oarsman lay on his back at the bottom of the boat, his heels in the air.

"—about in boats—or with boats," the Rat went on cheerily, picking himself up with a pleasant laugh. "In or out of 'em, it doesn't matter. Look here! If you've really nothing else to do, what do you say we spend time on the river together?"

The Mole waggled his toes from sheer happiness, spread his chest with a sigh of contentment, and leaned back blissfully into the soft cushions. "What a day I'm having!" he said. "Let us start at once."

"Hold on a minute, then!" said the Rat as he tied fast the boat and

> **New Word**
>
> **Mess** is a word with multiple meanings. Does your child know what the meaning of "messing" is in this story? Your child may be familiar with a dirty or untidy "mess." It can mean "to amuse oneself with." Help your child understand what Rat means when he says that nothing is "half so much worth doing as simply messing about in boats."

climbed up into his hole above. Moments later he reappeared staggering under a fat, wicker luncheon basket.

"Shove that under your feet," he said to the Mole, as he passed it down into the boat. Then he untied the boat and took the sculls again.

"What's inside it?" asked the Mole eagerly.

"There's cold chicken inside it," replied the Rat; "coldtonguecoldham-coldbeef-pickledgherkins-salad-frenchrollscresssandwiches-pottedmeat-gingerbeer-lemonade-sodawater—"

"O stop, stop," cried the Mole. "This is too much!"

"Do you really think so?" enquired the Rat seriously. "It's only what I always take on these little excursions. The other animals complain that I hardly have enough!"

The Mole did not hear a word he said. He was already absorbed in the new life he was entering upon. He trailed a paw in the water and dreamed long, waking dreams. The Water Rat, like the good little fellow he was, sculled steadily on and did not disturb him.

"I like your clothes, old chap," the Rat remarked after some half an hour or so had passed. "I'm going to get a velvet jacket myself someday."

"I beg your pardon," said the Mole, pulling himself together with an effort. "You must think me very rude; but all this is so new to me. So—this—is—a—River!"

"*The* River," corrected the Rat.

"And you really live by the river? What a jolly life!"

"By it and with it and on it and in it," said the Rat. "It's brother and sister to me, and aunts, and com-

Talk and Think
Recite Rat's line, "coldtonguecoldham-coldbeef-pickledgherkins-salad-frenchrollscress sandwiches-pottedmeat-gingerbeer-lemonade-sodawater" aloud with your child. Talk with your child about how having no spaces affects the way the line is read.

pany, and food and drink, and (naturally) washing. It's my world, and I don't want any other."

"But isn't it a bit dull at times?" the Mole asked. "Just you and the river, and no one else to pass a word with?"

"No one else to—well, I mustn't be hard on you," said the Rat. "You're new to it. The bank is so crowded nowadays that many people are moving away altogether. O no, it isn't what it used to be, at all. Otters, kingfishers, dabchicks, moorhens, all of them about all day long and always wanting you to do something—as if a fellow had no business of his own to attend to!"

"What lies over there?" asked the Mole, waving a paw towards a background of woodland that darkly framed the water-meadows on one side of the river.

"W-e-ll," replied the Rat hesitantly, "that's the Wild Wood. We don't go there too often."

"Are there scary creatures there?" Mole asked, trying not to tremble.

"The squirrels are all right," Rat replied. "And the rabbits—some of 'em, but rabbits are a mixed lot. And then there's Badger, of course. He lives right in the heart of it; wouldn't live anywhere else, either. Dear old Badger! Nobody interferes with him."

"Why, who *should* interfere with him?" asked the Mole.

"Well, of course, there are others," explained the Rat in a hesitating sort of way. "Weasels, stoats, foxes, and so on. They're all right in a way; I'm very good friends with them; pass the time of day when we meet, but you can't trust them, and that's a fact."

"And beyond the Wild Wood?" Mole asked.

"Beyond the Wild Wood is the Wide World," said the Rat. "And that's something that doesn't matter, either to you or me. I've never been there, and I'm never going, nor you either, if you've got any sense. Don't ever refer to it again, please. Now then! Here's our backwater at last, where we're going to lunch."

Leaving the main stream, they now passed into what seemed like a little land-locked lake. Green grass sloped down to either edge; brown, snaky tree roots gleamed below the surface of the quiet water. Ahead of them could be heard the foamy tumble of a weir with a restless dripping mill wheel attached to a mill house.

The scene was so beautiful that the Mole could only hold up both forepaws and gasp, "O my!"

The Rat brought the boat alongside the bank and tied it up. Then he helped the still awkward Mole safely ashore, and swung out the luncheon basket. The Mole asked to be allowed to unpack it all by himself. The Rat was very pleased to indulge him. Mole excitedly shook out the tablecloth and spread it. Then one by one he took out the mysterious packets and carefully arranged them, still gasping, "O my! O my!"

When all was ready, the Rat said, "Eat up, old fellow!" and the Mole, who had started his spring cleaning at a very early hour, and had not eaten since then, eagerly set to work.

"What are you looking at?" said the Rat presently, when the edge of their hunger was somewhat dulled, and the Mole's eyes were able to wander off the tablecloth.

"I am looking," said the Mole, "at a streak of bubbles that I see traveling along the surface of the water."

"Bubbles? Oh!" said the Rat cheerily.

A broad glistening muzzle showed itself above the edge of the bank, and the Otter hauled himself out and shook the water from his coat.

"Greedy beggars!" he observed. "Why didn't you invite me, Ratty?"

"This was a spontaneous affair," explained the Rat. "By the way, meet my friend Mr. Mole."

"Proud, I'm sure," said the Otter, and the two animals were friends forthwith.

"Such a rumpus everywhere!" continued the Otter. "The entire world seems to be out on the river today. I came up this backwater to try to get a moment's peace, and then stumbled upon you fellows!"

At that moment, there was a rustling sound behind them. It seemed to come from a hedge wherein last year's leaves still clung. Seconds later, a stripy head, with high shoulders, peered out from within.

"Come on, old Badger!" shouted the Rat.

The Badger trotted forward, then grunted, "H'm! Company," and turned his back and disappeared from view.

"That's *just* the sort of fellow he is!" observed the disappointed Rat. "Simply hates society! Now we shan't see any more of him today. Well, tell us, *who's* out on the river?"

"Toad's out, for one," replied the Otter. "In his brand-new wager-boat; new togs, new everything!"

The two animals looked at each other and laughed.

"Once, it was nothing but sailing," said the Rat. "Then he tired of that and took to punting. Nothing would please him but to punt all day. Last year it was houseboating, and we all had to go and stay with him in his houseboat, and pretend we liked it. It's all the same, whatever he takes up; he gets tired of it, and starts on something fresh."

"Such a good fellow, too," remarked the Otter reflectively: "But no stability, especially in a boat!"

From where they sat they could get a glimpse of the main stream across the island that separated them; and just then a wager-boat flashed into view. The rower was a short, stout figure, who was splashing badly and rolling a good deal, but working his hardest. The Rat stood up and hailed him. However Toad, for it was he, shook his head and concentrated on the task at hand.

"He'll be out of the boat in a minute if he rolls like that," said the Rat.

"Of course he will," chuckled the Otter. "Did I ever tell you that good story about Toad and the lock-keeper?"

"The story happened this way," Otter continued. "Toad—"

At that moment a mayfly swerved unsteadily on the gentle spring breeze toward Otter. There was a swirl of water and a "cloop!" and the mayfly was visible no more. Neither was the Otter.

The Mole looked down. The voice was still in his ears, but the grass whereon he had sprawled was clearly vacant. Not an Otter to be seen.

But again there was a streak of bubbles on the surface of the river.

The Rat hummed a tune, and the Mole remembered that it was considered rude to make any sort of comment about the sudden disappearance of one's friends.

"Well, well," said the Rat, "I suppose we ought to be moving. I wonder which one of us should pack the luncheon basket?" He did not sound overly eager to do it himself.

"O, please let me," said the Mole. So, of course, the Rat let him.

The afternoon sun was getting low as the Rat sculled gently homewards. The Mole was very full of lunch, and self-satisfaction, and already quite at home in a boat (or so he thought). He was, however, getting a bit restless, and presently he said, "Ratty! Please, I want to row, now!"

The Rat shook his head with a smile. "Not yet, my young friend," he said. "Wait till you've had a few lessons."

The Mole was quiet for a minute or two. But he began to feel more and more jealous of Rat. Suddenly he jumped up and seized the sculls from him. Rat, who had been gazing out over the water, was taken by surprise. He fell backwards off his seat. The triumphant Mole took his place and grabbed the sculls with much confidence.

"Stop it, you silly!" cried the Rat, from the bottom of the boat. "You'll have us over!"

The Mole flung his sculls back with a flourish, and made a great dig at the water. He missed the surface altogether, his legs flew up above his

> **Make a Connection**
> After reading this story, ask your child, "How do Rat and Mole move the boat down the river?" Then read the description of how paddleboats travel down the Mississippi River in the geography and history chapter (page 123). Then ask your child, "How do the paddleboats of the Mississippi compare to Rat's boat?"

head, and he found himself lying on top of the Rat. Greatly alarmed, he made a grab at the side of the boat, and the next moment—Sploosh!

Over went the boat, and Mole found himself struggling in the river.

O my, how cold the water was, and O, how very wet it felt. How it sang in his ears as he went down, down, down! How bright and welcome the sun looked as he rose to the surface coughing and spluttering! How black was his despair when he felt himself sinking again! Then a firm paw gripped him by the back of his neck. It was the Rat, and he was laughing.

The Rat got hold of a scull and shoved it under the Mole's arm. Then he did

the same by the other side of him and, swimming behind, propelled the helpless animal to shore.

When the Rat had rubbed him down, and wrung some of the wet out of him, he said, "Now, then, old fellow! Trot up and down till you're warm and dry again, while I dive for the luncheon basket."

So the dismal Mole, wet without and ashamed within, trotted about till he was fairly dry, while the Rat plunged into the water again. He recovered the boat, fetched his floating property, and finally dived successfully for the luncheon basket.

When all was ready to begin again, the Mole, limp and dejected, took his seat in the stern of the boat; and as they set off, he said in a low voice, "Ratty, my generous friend! I am very sorry indeed for my foolish behavior. My heart quite fails me when I think how I might have lost that beautiful luncheon basket. I have been a fool. Will you ever forgive me?"

What About You?
Ask your child, "How would you react in Rat's position? Would you forgive Mole for turning your boat over? Why or why not?"

"That's all right. Bless you!" responded the Rat cheerily. "What's a little wet to a Water Rat? I'm more in the water than out of it most days. Don't you think any more about it; and, look here! I really think you had better come and stop with me for a little time. My home is very plain and rough, but I am sure I can make you comfortable. And I'll teach you to row, and to swim."

The Mole was so touched by his kindness that he had to brush away a tear. But the Rat kindly looked in another direction, and before long the Mole's spirits revived again.

When they got home, the Rat made a bright fire in the parlor. He planted the Mole in an arm chair in front of it. He fetched down a dressing gown and slippers for him, and told him river stories till supper-time. Supper was a most cheerful meal. Shortly afterwards, a sleepy Mole had to be escorted upstairs by his host, to the best bedroom. There he laid his head on his pillow in great peace and contentment. This was just the beginning of their friendship and time together on the river.

Mythology

Gods, Heroes, and Tricksters from Scandinavia

In the world history section of this book, you can read about the Vikings. The Vikings were also called Norsemen, from a word meaning "north." They came from the lands in northwest Europe called Scandinavia, which today includes the countries of Sweden, Denmark, and Norway. Can you find those countries on a map?

Like the ancient Greeks and Romans, the Vikings told stories to explain things like how the world began, or why we have different seasons, or what happens to people after they die. We don't believe these stories, but we still enjoy them. We call these stories myths.

Odin, the greatest of all gods in Norse mythology

Norse Gods and Goddesses

The Norse gods lived in a land called Asgard, ruled by the chief god, Odin (also called Woden). The Vikings believed that the world began when Odin and his brothers fought and killed a terrible frost giant. The earth was made out of the giant's body, the oceans out of his blood, the mountains out of his bones, and the trees out of his hair.

Odin was very wise, but he wanted to be wiser. He once went to the Well of Wisdom and sacrificed one of his eyes to drink of its water. That is why many pictures of Odin show him with only one eye.

Maidens called the Valkyries [VAL-keer-eez] waited on Odin. When a Viking warrior was killed in battle, one of the Valkyries picked up the dead warrior and carried him on her swift warhorse to Valhalla, a great palace in Asgard. In Valhalla, the honored warriors lived forever, fighting by day and feasting by night.

Odin's oldest son, Thor, was the god of thunder. Two goats pulled his chariot through the sky. When he swung his mighty hammer, thunderbolts flew and rain fell onto the earth.

The German composer Richard Wagner [Rick kart VAHG-ner] wrote a series of operas based on Norse myths called *The Ring of the Nibelung* [NEE-beh-loong]. One passage, "The Ride of the Valkyries," has been used in movies and on television.

While the Norse gods lived above the clouds, dwarfs and trolls lived in dark, secret caves. A hag named Hel ruled the underworld, where spirits went after death. From her name comes the word "hell."

Four of the days of the week are named after Norse gods. The day we call Wednesday comes from "Woden's Day." From Tyr, the Norse god of war, comes "Tyr's Day," which is our Tuesday. Friday comes from "Freya's Day," after the Norse goddess of love and beauty. Which day of the week do you think might be "Thor's Day"?

All Together
Repeat the days of the week aloud with your child and explain how they are connected to mythology.

Thor, son of Odin, the Norse god of thunder

The World Tree and the End of the World

The Vikings believed that a giant "world tree" called Yggdrasill [IG-druh-sil] held up the universe. Yggdrasill had three roots. One root stretched to the land of ice. One root reached to Asgard, the land of the gods. And one root stretched to the land of the giants. Three sisters who lived beside the tree controlled everyone's past, present, and future. A giant serpent chewed at the roots of the tree. One day the tree would fall and bring down the world, causing a second great battle between the gods and the giants. The Vikings predicted that the giants would win this battle. The world would be destroyed, then begin again—but this time, everything would be perfect.

Loki and the Gifts for the Gods

Here is a Norse myth about a god named Loki, son of a giant and a god, who loved to cause mischief. Odin invited him to the great feasts of the gods, even though he was always playing tricks on them.

Loki, the trickster god

Thor's wife, Sif, had long golden hair that shimmered like a field of ripe barley grain. Loki knew how much Thor admired his wife's hair. Still, one night as she was sleeping, Loki crept into Sif's room and cut off all of her golden hair!

Imagine Thor's surprise when he awakened the next morning to find his beautiful wife with nothing but fuzz on her head! Thor knew instantly who had played this trick on him. Thunderbolts seemed to shoot out of his angry eyes at Loki.

"Spare me, Thor!" cried Loki. "I know just where to go to ask for long locks of golden hair, even more beautiful than those Sif had before."

Loki traveled beneath the earth, where dwarfs lived in secret caves and hideaways.

The dwarfs were so ugly Loki did not even want to look at them, but they were the best craftsmen in all the world.

"What do you want with us?" the dwarfs grumbled. They were never friendly to anyone.

"Dear dwarfs, I have come with a mission from the gods in Asgard," Loki said. "Only you can work this magic."

The only thing that could turn a dwarf even half friendly was flattery. Loki wondered how much the dwarfs would give him. "First, Odin needs a spear that will never miss its mark," he said. "Second, the gods need a ship that can sail both land and sea." The dwarfs grunted and grumbled, but Loki kept on. "And third, beautiful Sif, wife of Thor, needs hair spun of the finest gold, and magic, so that it comes alive as soon as it touches her head."

The dwarfs could not resist the challenge. They worked all night and day and the next night, too. They made all three of the things that Loki asked for. He tucked the spear under his arm. He folded the ship up and put it in his pocket. He took the hair of pure gold, more beautiful than any human hair could ever be, and draped it across his shoulder. He winked at the dwarfs—that was the only thank-you he gave them—and in a flash he was gone.

On his way back to Asgard, Loki met two more dwarfs, the brothers Brokk and Sindri. "See these gifts?" he said, showing off. "I'll bet you can't make anything better, and you can cut off my head if I'm wrong!"

To answer Loki's challenge, Brokk and Sindri created three more gifts fit for the gods. They made a fierce boar with golden bristles. They made a shining golden ring. Then Brokk worked the bellows and Sindri hammered iron on the anvil and together they made a massive hammer. "We'll put magic into it," one brother told the other, "so it will always hit its mark and return to the one who threw it."

Thor's hammer

Loki worried that he would lose the bet. He turned himself into a gadfly and buzzed around their faces. Brokk swatted the fly away from his eyes as he made the hammer's handle, and it came out a bit too short. Loki grabbed the gifts and fled to Asgard, with an angry dwarf close after him.

When Sif received the golden hair, she was overjoyed. Magically, it attached to her head, just as if it had grown there. Odin, greatest of all the gods and father to Thor, took the spear for his own. Odin also claimed the ring, which had the magic power to make eight more rings every ninth night. Another god claimed the golden boar, believing it better than a horse for riding through the darkness. All the gods of Asgard marveled over the ship, seeing that the wind would fill its sails whenever they wished to travel.

Then Thor picked up the hammer and swung it high above his head. All the gods said it was the best gift of all, because it could defeat the giants. Brokk grinned at Loki, sure now that he had won the bet and getting ready to cut off Loki's head.

"But only my head!" cried Loki. "Not one inch of my neck shall you have!" It was a silly argument, but the gods agreed with Loki.

Enraged, Brokk sewed Loki's lips shut with a leather thong. The gods laughed a deep, thunderous laugh. They were thankful for all Loki had brought them, but they were also happy to have his mouth shut for a little while. As Loki scampered away, struggling to open his lips, Thor forgave him for the mischief that had started this whole adventure.

Myths from Ancient Greece and Rome

Jason and the Golden Fleece

Here is an ancient Greek myth about the hero named Jason. Jason was raised by a centaur, half man and half horse. His adventures fill a whole book, called The Golden Fleece.

One day long ago a centaur sat on the bank of a river, speaking to a handsome young man. "You are now twenty years old," said the centaur, who had raised this man from childhood. "The time has come for you to reclaim the kingdom that your stepuncle, Pelias, stole from your father. Go, and may the gods be with you."

Wearing a leopard's skin and sandals tied with golden strings, Jason set out for the kingdom of his stepuncle. He waded across a river, and one of his sandals came loose. When Jason arrived wearing only one sandal, it worried Pelias. A wise man had long ago predicted that he would lose his kingdom to a man with one shoe.

Pelias kept his worries secret, though. He said that Jason should rule the country. "First there is something that you must do," said Pelias. "Bring me the golden fleece, and I will make you king."

Pelias believed he had given Jason an impossible assignment. Many years before, Hermes, the messenger of the gods, had saved a boy from drowning by sending a large golden ram to carry him across the sea. In thanks, the boy had sacrificed the ram to the gods and nailed its golden fleece high upon an oak tree.

Jason gathered the bravest heroes of the land and set sail in quest of the golden fleece. He named his ship *Argo* and his crew the Argonauts. At every island they passed, they met with danger and adventure. They sailed safely through a narrow strait where two huge rocks moved back and forth in the water and crushed anything between them. They finally arrived at the island where the golden fleece hung.

When the island's king heard what Jason and the Argonauts were after, he said, "I will give you the fleece after you prove your powers. In my fields, you will find two brass bulls. Hitch those bulls to a plow and use them to sow the teeth of a dragon in my fields."

This king, like Pelias before him, felt certain that he had given Jason an impossible assignment. He knew that the brass bulls were wild and strong and difficult to handle. He also knew that when dragon's teeth are planted, iron men spring up out of the earth ready to attack.

The king's beautiful daughter, Medea, had already fallen in love with Jason. She was ready to do anything—even use her magic spells—to help him. "Here is some magic ointment," she said to Jason. "Rub it on your body, your sword, and your shield. Then nothing can harm you. And remember: when you have sowed the dragon's teeth, throw a great stone among the warriors. Then they will destroy each other."

Strengthened through Medea's magic, Jason wrestled the bulls to the ground, yoked them to a plow, and drove them through the field. The plow cut a deep

furrow in the soil. Into that furrow, Jason sowed the dragon's teeth. When the army of iron men sprang up out of the earth, he threw a stone among them. The men turned upon each other, and when the battle was over, Jason was the only man left alive.

The king was furious. "The golden fleece hangs high on a tree, guarded by a giant dragon," he said. "Go and get it for yourself."

Again the king believed he had given Jason an impossible task, but again Medea helped Jason. They approached the fearful dragon, coiled at the foot of the tree. Medea began to sing. At the sound of her voice, the dragon's eyes grew heavy. Slowly, the creature lowered its head and fell asleep.

"Hurry," Medea whispered. Jason reached up and took hold of the precious treasure. As he and Medea fled, they heard a horrible roar as the dragon awoke and found its treasure stolen.

The *Argo* awaited them. With a wild leap Jason and Medea were on board. The Argonauts rowed the ship swiftly, leaving the monster spitting fire behind them.

Jason's stepuncle had never expected to see him again, but the young hero sailed back victorious. Through bravery and magic, he had won the golden fleece.

Perseus and Medusa

This ancient myth describes the Gorgons, who were frightening female monsters with snakes for hair.

There was once a lovely young woman, so lovely that Zeus himself, the king of the gods, fell in love with her. Together they had a son, named Perseus. The father of the young woman was horrified, because it had been predicted that he would be killed by his own grandson. So he put his daughter and her baby boy into a chest and threw them into the sea.

They floated for many days and finally washed up on an island shore, where they made a home. Perseus grew up to be a strong and handsome young man.

Now, the king of the island was also cruel. He wanted Perseus's mother all to himself. He assigned Perseus to a great adventure, but he really intended a task so difficult that Perseus would not survive.

> **New Word**
>
> Have your child focus on the word **furrow**. Explain that the word "furrow" can be a noun (plowed land for planting seeds) and a verb (to make wrinkles or lines).

"Bring me the head of Medusa," said the king.

"Medusa?" asked Perseus in wonder. Medusa was a Gorgon, a hideous monster with a head full of snakes. She turned a man to stone the minute he looked her in the eye. No one could approach Medusa, let alone cut her head off! But Perseus accepted the challenge.

Zeus sent his messenger, Hermes, with gifts for Perseus.

"Your father has sent me from Mount Olympus, home of the gods, with three things," said Hermes. "From Athena, the goddess of wisdom, here is a bright brass shield. From Hades, the god of the underworld, here is a helmet to make you invisible. And from me, here is a sword that cuts through anything with one stroke." Then Hermes took the winged sandals off his feet and gave them to Perseus.

With gifts from the gods, Perseus felt even braver. He thanked Hermes, and through him all the gods, including great Zeus. "But where will I find this monster Medusa?" he asked.

"You must put that question to the Three Gray Sisters," said Hermes. "These three women share a single eye. They live together in a deep, dark cave at the western edge of the world."

Perseus traveled for days and nights until he came to a twilight land. There he stood at the opening of a deep, dark cave and listened as the Three Gray Sisters mumbled among themselves.

"Someone is coming," said the first sister. "I can feel him."

"Someone is coming," said the second sister. "I can hear him."

"Someone is coming," said the third sister. "I can see him with my eye."

"Give me the eye," said the first.

"No, me," said the second, "so I can see, too!"

As they struggled over the one eye they shared, Perseus grabbed it. A howl shot up from all three sisters when they realized that not one of them had the precious eye anymore.

"Never fear, good women," said Perseus. "I will return your eye as long as you tell me where I will find the Gorgon Medusa."

The sisters told Perseus how to find Medusa. With Hermes's sandals on his feet, he flew over land and sea to the land of the Gorgons. There they were, three massive monsters, lying asleep. The biggest and most horrible one was Medusa.

Perseus put on the helmet of invisibility so that Medusa would not see him coming. He held up the bright shield so that his gaze would not meet hers and yet he could see her face, reflected as in a mirror. Aided by Hermes's winged sandals, he approached the Gorgon, raised the sword, and with one swing cut the head off the horrible Medusa. The snakes on her head hissed in pain. Perseus shoved her head into a goatskin pouch and instantly flew away.

Returning to the island where the cruel king kept his mother, Perseus approached the throne.

"Just as I suspected," said the king with a smile. "You have come back empty-handed."

"On the contrary," said Perseus. "I have done what you commanded." He pulled Medusa's head out of the goatskin bag. Even in death, with her eyes wide open, the Gorgon had her powers. The evil king looked her straight in the eye and turned to stone.

Cupid and Psyche

Have you ever seen Cupid, that little boy with wings, on a Valentine's Day card? To the ancient Romans, Cupid was a god. Here is a myth about how he fell in love with a woman.

Once there was a king who had three daughters. The youngest, named Psyche [SY-kee], was the most beautiful of all—so beautiful, in fact, that people began to say she was even more beautiful than Venus, the goddess of beauty.

When Venus heard these claims, she was filled with jealousy. She went to her son, Cupid, and said, "Shoot the girl with one of your arrows and make her fall in love with the ugliest man on earth."

Obediently, Cupid took his bow and arrow and flew down to earth. Just as he was taking aim to shoot Psyche, his finger slipped. He pricked himself with his own arrow and fell in love with Psyche.

Cupid sent a message to Psyche's family, saying that the gods wished her to climb a mountain and marry the husband that they had chosen for her—a terrible monster. Psyche bravely climbed the mountain, feeling a warm wind surround her. Suddenly, she found herself in a magnificent palace. She saw no one, but she heard friendly voices, promising her that her every desire would be satisfied. She fell asleep, surrounded by sweet music. While she slept, Cupid visited her. She knew her husband only in dreams. He stayed all night, but left before morning's light. Night after night, Psyche felt her husband come to her in the darkness and leave before morning's light.

One night Psyche asked her husband why he came in darkness. "Why should you wish to see me?" he answered. "I love you, and all I ask is that you love me." Still, Psyche grew more curious. Who was her husband? What did he look like? Why did he hide? Was he indeed a terrible monster?

One night she stayed awake. She waited until she felt him lying by her side, then she lit a lamp. What she saw was no monster, but the lovely face of Cupid himself. Her hand trembled with delight, and a drop of hot oil fell from the lamp onto Cupid's shoulder and awoke him.

"I asked only for your trust," he said sadly. "When trust is gone, love must depart." And away flew Cupid, home to Venus, who scolded him for falling in love with a mere woman.

The moment Cupid flew away, the magnificent palace vanished. Night and day Psyche wandered, searching for her lost love. At last she went to the temple of Venus herself. "You dare to come seeking a husband, you ugly girl?" Venus cried. She showed Psyche a huge pile of grain—wheat, millet, barley, and lentils. "Separate this grain by morning." Venus laughed, then disappeared.

Psyche knew the task was impossible. Then, looking through her tears, she noticed a seed moving, then another, and then many more. An army of ants had come to her aid, each carrying a seed and dividing the seeds into separate piles.

Venus was furious to find the work done. "Your next task will not be so easy," she said. "Take this box into the underworld and ask the queen of that realm, Proserpina [pro-SUR-pi-nah], to send me a little of her beauty."

The underworld? No mortal could return. Suddenly a voice spoke to her. "Take a coin to the boatman who will carry you across the river to the underworld. Take a cake to calm the mean three-headed dog who guards the underworld. And this above all: once Proserpina has placed beauty in the box, do not open it."

Following the mysterious voice, Psyche journeyed safely to the underworld, and Proserpina sent a box of beauty back with her to Venus.

But Psyche could not help wondering what was inside the box. She lifted the lid and peeked inside. A deep sleep came over her, and Psyche fell senseless to the ground.

Meanwhile, Cupid's love for Psyche had grown stronger than ever. Finding her lying on the ground, he took the sleep from her body. "See what curiosity gets you?" Cupid said, smiling, as she awoke.

While Psyche delivered the box to Venus, Cupid begged Jupiter, the king of the gods, to bless their marriage. Jupiter invited Psyche to drink the **ambrosia** of the gods, and she became immortal. In the marriage of Cupid and Psyche, love and the soul (which is what the word "psyche" means today) were united at last and forever.

The Sword of Damocles

This story comes to us from ancient Rome. Many people still use the phrase "sword of Damocles" to speak of danger that is always present.

Damocles [DA-mo-klees] looked with envy on his friend Dionysius [die-oh-NIS-ee-us], the king of Syracuse. He believed that the king had a very good life—all the riches and all the power that anyone could imagine.

"You think I'm lucky?" Dionysius said to him one day. "If you think so, let's trade places. You sit here, on the throne, for just one day and see if you still think I'm lucky."

Damocles eagerly accepted his friend's invitation. He ordered servants to bring him fine robes and a great banquet of food. He ordered expensive wine and fine music as he dined. He sat back, sure that he was the happiest man in the world.

Then he looked up. He caught his breath in fear. Above his head, a sword dangled from the ceiling attached by a single strand of horse's hair. Damocles could not speak, could not eat, could not enjoy the music. He could not even move.

"What is the matter, my friend?" asked Dionysius.

"How can I conduct my life with that sword hanging above me?" Damocles said.

"How indeed?" answered Dionysius. "And now you know how it feels to be king. That sword hangs over my head every minute of every day. There is always the chance the thread will break. An adviser may turn on me, or an enemy spy may attack me. Even I might make an unwise decision that brings my downfall. The privilege of power brings dangers."

Damon and Pythias

Here is a story told by the ancient Roman writer Cicero as an example of true friendship.

Dionysius, the king of Syracuse, heard rumors that a young man named Pythias [PITH-ee-us] was making speeches and telling people to question whether he, or any king, should have so much power. He called Pythias before him. The young man arrived with his best friend, Damon, by his side.

"You dare to stand before the king without bowing?" barked Dionysius when he saw the two men before him.

"I believe that all people are equal," Pythias boldly stated. "No man should have absolute power over another."

"Who do you think you are, to speak such a philosophy and spread it among my people?" Dionysius raged.

"I speak the truth," Pythias answered bravely. "There can be nothing wrong with that."

Dionysius was outraged. "You risk punishment, even death, by speaking like that."

"My philosophy teaches me patience. I have no fear of punishment, or even death."

"We shall see what your philosophy provides you in prison," roared Dionysius. He commanded his soldiers to seize Pythias and lock him in the caverns of Syracuse until he promised never to contradict the king again.

Pythias stood strong and tall. "I cannot make that promise, and so I will accept that punishment," he said. "But may I first go home and tell my family and put my household in order?"

"Do you think I'm stupid?" shouted the king. "If I let you go, you will never return!"

Then up stepped Damon. "Put me in the cell until he returns."

"I will agree to this plan," said the king, "but if Pythias does not return in three days, Damon will be executed."

"I trust my friend," said Damon.

So Pythias traveled to his home, and Damon sat in the deep, dark cell alone. Two days came and went. On the morning of the third, Dionysius ordered Damon brought before him.

"Your friend has not returned," he bellowed. "You know what that means? It means your death!"

"I trust my friend," Damon repeated. "Something has delayed him. He will come back. I am sure of it."

At sundown, the soldiers led Damon to the place where he would be put to death. Dionysius watched with a sneer on his face. "What do you say of your friend now?" he asked.

"I trust my friend," Damon replied.

Just then Pythias rushed in, his clothing torn and his face bruised and dirty. "Thank the gods you are safe," he said to Damon. "My ship was wrecked in a storm. Thieves attacked me on the road. But I did not give up, and I finally made it here. Now I am ready to take my punishment."

Seeing such friendship, Dionysius learned an important lesson. He revoked Damon's death sentence, freed Pythias, and asked the two men to teach him how to be such a good friend, too.

Androcles and the Lion

The ancient Romans thought it was great sport to watch men fight wild animals to the death. This fight has a surprise ending.

Androcles [AN-droh-clees] was a Roman slave who escaped his master and ran away. He was delighted with his freedom but uncertain how he could make it on his own. As night fell, he found a cave carved naturally out of the hillside. He crept into the cool darkness, lay down, and fell asleep.

Suddenly he awoke, hearing the loud roar of a lion nearby. It was no dream—it was a real lion, looking straight into the cave. Androcles shrank back, fearful for his life, watching the lion's every move.

Then he noticed that the lion was suffering. It was roaring in pain. The great beast limped into the cave and flopped down. It lifted its right front paw and licked it.

Androcles took a step toward the lion. The big cat gave him a sad look, as if asking for help. Androcles crouched next to the lion. He saw a thorn stuck in the middle of its paw. Gently he pulled the thorn out. The lion looked him in the eye again and purred.

That was the beginning of a warm friendship between Androcles and the lion. They lived together in the cave and slept side by side, keeping each other warm.

But one day Roman soldiers discovered Androcles. The law of Rome said that runaway slaves must be punished, so Androcles was captured and shut into a prison cell in the city of Rome.

For ten days, Androcles sat alone in prison, fed nothing but water and crusts of stale bread. Then a soldier announced that he was to meet his death in the Colosseum.

Androcles knew what that meant. Runaway slaves were often made to fight vicious lions before crowds of Roman citizens. He knew, as he walked the path from the prison to the Colosseum, that he would soon die.

The crowd cheered as Androcles stepped into the arena. They cheered even more loudly as the lion appeared on the other side. Androcles walked into the ring and bravely faced his death.

Then he and the lion recognized each other. To the amazement of the crowd, instead of attacking, the lion began licking the slave's face—and the slave began stroking the lion!

The crowd cheered even more. "Free the slave! Free the lion!" they were yelling, and the emperor agreed. Androcles and the lion lived a long life together in the city of Rome.

> **Make a Connection**
> Read "Androcles and the Lion" with your child. Then turn to page 147 to teach your child about the real-life Colosseum.

Horatius at the Bridge

The famous story about a Roman hero has stayed with us in part because the English poet Thomas Macaulay wrote a book called Lays of Ancient Rome, *which included a poem about Horatius's acts of heroism. In the telling of this story, we quote some of the best verses from the poem.*

Lucius Tarquinius, the last of the Roman kings, was so cruel that the people called him "Tarquin the Tyrant." Finally they banded together and sent him out of Rome. Forced out of power, Tarquin visited Lars Porsena, king of the Etruscans, who lived to the north of Rome. Tarquin convinced Lars Porsena to assemble a huge army, much larger and more powerful than the Roman army, and attack Rome.

There was only one way for them to enter the city of Rome: over a small wooden bridge across the Tiber River. A soldier named Horatius [he-RAY-she-us] guarded that bridge. When he saw the Etruscans preparing to attack his city, he came up with a plan.

He and two others would cross the bridge and fight off the Etruscans as they came down the narrow path toward the bridge. As they fought, Horatius suggested, the Romans could tear apart the bridge, making it impossible for the Etruscans to cross and storm the city.

"Horatius," quoth the Consul,
"As thou sayest, so let it be."
And straight against that great array

Forth went the dauntless Three.
For Romans in Rome's quarrel
   Spared neither land nor gold,
Nor son nor wife, nor limb nor life,
   In the brave days of old.

While the three soldiers held the Etruscans back, others chopped away at the wooden bridge. Just before the bridge fell into the river, Horatius commanded his two helpers to cross to the Roman side. He remained, fighting off the Etruscans until he could do so no longer. Then, praying to the Tiber River to take good care of him, Horatius dove into the water.

Every Roman soldier held his breath, afraid he had seen the last of brave Horatius. Then the crest of his helmet surfaced above the river, and all cheered. The current was high, the river was fast, and Horatius, wearing heavy armor, had to struggle to survive.

And now he feels the bottom;
   Now on dry earth he stands;
Now round him throng the Fathers
   To press his gory hands;
And now, with shouts and clapping,
   And noise of weeping loud,
He enters through the River-Gate,
   Borne by the joyous crowd.

Thanks to Horatius at the bridge, Tarquin and the Etruscans could not enter Rome. For many generations after, men and women told the story of how Horatius saved the city of Rome in the brave days of old.

Learning About Literature

Biography and Autobiography

A biography is the true story of a person's life.

Suppose you wanted to write the life story of someone you know. You could talk to her and ask her questions about what happened in her life. You could find out about her from her parents, relatives, and friends who know her well. If she had old letters and scrapbooks, you could learn from them, too.

But suppose you wanted to write the life story of someone who lived 200 years ago. You could use writing that she and other people left behind, like old letters, diaries, and newspaper articles. You would have to read carefully and remember all that you learned. You would most likely have to take notes about the facts you learned about the person's life. Then you could turn that information into a story about the person's life.

A person is likely to tell her own life story differently than someone else would tell it. When a person chooses to write her own life story, it is called an autobiography. The prefix "auto-" means "self." An autograph is your name written by yourself. Something automatic works by itself. So an autobiography is a biography you write yourself.

We read autobiographies to learn about what people did and about the times in which they lived. For example, you might read the famous autobiography of a Jewish girl named Anne Frank, who wrote about what happened when she and her family hid from the Nazis by living in a tiny attic room. Or you could read the famous autobiography by Frederick Douglass, who wrote about his experiences as a slave.

Fiction and Nonfiction

Fiction is a story that did not actually happen, such as a fairy tale, a myth, or a made-up story like *Alice's Adventures in Wonderland* or *Charlotte's Web*. Fiction can be so close to the truth that it seems real, or it can be so fantastic that it could never happen. When you make up a story, you are creating fiction.

Nonfiction, on the other hand, is all about true things—people who really lived and the things they really did. A biography is nonfiction. An autobiography is nonfiction. History is nonfiction. Articles in the newspaper and science reports are nonfiction, too. When you tell someone what you did on your summer vacation, you are creating nonfiction.

There is an old saying that "truth is stranger than fiction." Do you think that's true?

Familiar Sayings and Phrases

PARENTS: Every culture has some sayings and phrases that make no sense when carried over literally into another culture. To say, for example, that someone has "let the cat out of the bag" has nothing to do with setting free a trapped kitty. Nor—thank goodness—does it ever "rain cats and dogs"!

In this section, we introduce a handful of common English sayings and phrases and give examples of how they are used. The sayings and phrases in this section may be familiar to many children, who hear them at home. But the inclusion of these sayings and phrases in the *Core Knowledge Sequence* has been singled out for gratitude by many parents and by teachers who work with children from home cultures that are different from the culture of literate American English.

Actions speak louder than words

This saying reminds us that what people say does not always show what they think, while what people do reveals their thoughts or beliefs more clearly.

"Dad says he hates cats—even Jojo!" Stewart shook his head.

"But last night," Tracy said, "I saw Dad kiss the top of Jojo's head when he thought no one was looking."

"Maybe he really loves Jojo, but he keeps it a secret. Actions speak louder than words!"

His bark is worse than his bite

People use this saying to describe a person who speaks angrily or threatens but may not be truly dangerous.

"Mr. Kreckle is scary," Jason said.

"Yeah," Mickey said. "I heard he threw a stapler at my cousin's friend's sister because she couldn't remember the names of all 50 states!"

"You two are so silly," Miyaka said. "Mr. Kreckle would never hurt anybody. He might get mad easily, but he's really a nice man. His bark is worse than his bite!"

Beat around the bush

People use this phrase to mean that someone is avoiding direct discussion of a difficult subject by talking instead about related subjects that are less important.

"So how'd you do on your math test, Carlos?" Mr. Ramos asked.

Carlos cleared his throat. "Three kids were late for class, so the teacher didn't start the test until 10 minutes after the hour began."

Carlos's father looked at his son, waiting for an answer to his question.

"I was supposed to bring in three pencils," Carlos said. "I forgot."

"Didn't you say you were going to grade the test in class, Carlos?" said Mr. Ramos. He was getting impatient.

"I don't know how that teacher expects us to finish 20 problems when we only have 40 minutes."

Mr. Ramos got up and put his arm around Carlos's shoulder. "Come on, Carlos. Stop beating around the bush. Tell me how you did on your math test."

Beggars can't be choosers

People use this saying to mean that when you are in a weak or disadvantaged position, you shouldn't be picky about the help that may be offered—even if it isn't exactly the sort of help you want.

"I didn't have time to eat breakfast," Janel said, "and I'm starving. But the only thing left in the cafeteria is spinach salad—yuck!"

"Beggars can't be choosers, Janel," Nikki said. "Looks like you'll have to eat something healthful for a change."

Clean bill of health

People use this phrase to express that something is in perfect shape.

Latasha worked for an hour on her math homework. She went over every problem and did her best to make sure every answer was correct. When she was finished, she showed it to her mother, who said, "You've certainly improved in math, Latasha. You did all of these equations perfectly! This homework gets a clean bill of health!"

Cold shoulder

People use this phrase to mean that someone is acting unfriendly.

"Ever since I told Daryl his solo in the talent show was pitchy, he pretends he doesn't know me," Christina said. "I said hi to him at recess, and he just walked away."

"Maybe it's the way you said it," Sara said. "If you told me I sounded like a dying cat when I sang, I'd give you the cold shoulder, too!"

A feather in your cap

This expression indicates a person has done something to make her proud.

Camille loved to play the violin. She practiced every day. One day during orchestra rehearsal, the string section was playing a piece that Camille had practiced carefully.

"Camille, let me hear that measure again," the orchestra conductor said.

Camille played the measure perfectly.

"Beautiful!" the conductor said. "You deserve to be first chair in next week's concert. That will be a feather in your cap."

Last straw

This phrase describes the moment when things have gone too far one way and just have to change. It comes from a legend about a man who piled straw on his camel's back, one piece at a time. Even though each piece of straw was light, one piece was the "last straw" that broke the camel's back.

"What's wrong, Paul?" Lenny asked. "Do you need any help?"

Paul was kneeling down next to his bicycle, trying to remove his front tire, which had gone flat. "Just leave me alone," he snapped. "First I fell off my bike on the way to school and skinned my elbow. Then, once I got to math class, I remembered that I left my homework at home. Then Bob Banks tripped me when we were playing basketball, and I bruised my knee. And now I have a flat tire. This is the last straw!"

Let bygones be bygones

People use this saying to mean letting go of whatever is bothering you so it becomes a thing of the past.

"I can't believe the teacher gave me a C on my science homework last week!" Tyrone banged his desk with his fist. "It makes me so mad!"

"Come on, Tyrone, that was last week! You just got an A on this week's homework," Janine said. "Let bygones be bygones!"

One rotten apple spoils the whole barrel

This saying means that one bad thing can spoil everything connected with it.

Mr. Small's class was known as the best-behaved class in the school. One day a new boy joined the class. He was noisy and rude, but he was also funny. Soon the other kids in Mr. Small's class started talking and laughing and becoming rowdy. Mr. Small just shook his head and said, "One rotten apple spoils the whole barrel!"

On its last legs

People use this phrase to say that something is about to die or is too worn out to be repaired.

"This has been a good old truck," Mr. Johnson said to his grandson, Vincent. They drove down the bumpy dirt road, and the truck sputtered and groaned. "I've had it for nearly 20 years."

Vincent was amazed to hear that the truck was older than he was.

"But you hear those noises it's making, Vincent?" The old man shook his head. "I'm afraid this truck is on its last legs."

Rule the roost

People use this phrase to describe a person who bosses other people around. It comes from the way a rooster acts in a chicken house, or "roost."

Katie and June were watching television in their living room. When Janice came in from playing, she ran in front of her sisters and changed the channel.

"Hey!" Katie said. "We were here first."

"Too bad," Janice said. "I'm the oldest."

"You may be the oldest," June said, "but that doesn't mean you rule the roost!"

The show must go on

This saying means that no matter what happens, things will continue as planned.

"We can't play in the championship next Saturday," Karen said to her coach. "Lisa sprained her ankle, Cecilia has the mumps, and Jenny has to go away for the weekend. They're the best soccer players on the team. We'll lose without them."

"We've been practicing all season," her coach answered. "We're not giving up. The show must go on!"

Touch and go

This phrase describes a situation that is so difficult that no one knows how it will turn out.

Harold had been training to be a tightrope walker, but today was his first day to perform for an audience. He took his first steps steadily and slowly, using a long pole to keep his balance. When he got to the middle, he looked down for a moment. He felt himself teeter. The crowd gasped. Then, just in time, he regained his balance. The rest of his steps were strong and sure.

Later, Harold said, "Everything was fine until I looked down. For a few seconds there, it was touch and go."

When in Rome, do as the Romans do

This saying suggests that when you are in an unfamiliar situation, it's good to behave like others around you.

After a day at her new school, Clarisse called Morgan, her best friend from her old school. "You're not going to believe this, Morgan," she said. "They all pile their backpacks up outside the classroom door."

"They do?" Morgan said. "We never do that here at our school."

"I know," Clarisse said. "I wanted to keep mine with me, but when I saw what everyone else was doing, I took out my books and left it outside. When in Rome, do as the Romans do."

Learning About Language

Let's Write a Report

What if you had to write a report about box turtles? You know some things about turtles, but you need to learn more to write a good report. So where do you go? For a start, you can go to books.

Say you are at the library. What kinds of books would you look for to learn more about box turtles?

Let's say you look up box turtles in a book called *Reptiles of the World*. Open to the front of the book and you will find the table of contents. The table of contents tells all the subjects in the book, listed in the order that they appear.

CONTENTS

What page will you turn to in order to learn about turtles? For the chapter on turtles, you will go to page 26. Because turtles are reptiles, you might also want to read the chapters on reptiles. On what pages can you find those chapters?

You can also use a part of a book called an index to look up subjects that interest you. The index is always at the back of the book, and it gives an alphabetical list of everything in the book. Indexes help you find the subjects that might not be named in the table of contents.

> **Do It Yourself**
>
> Your child can practice using an index right now! Have your child go to the index in this book and use the skills he just learned to look up the section "Native Americans" or "fractions."

INDEX

To do some reading for your report on box turtles, what page will you turn to?

There are other books that can give you information about box turtles. One very helpful kind of book is an encyclopedia. Encyclopedias give information about famous people, places, things, ideas, events in history, and more.

Some encyclopedias are printed in volumes; others are available for use on the Internet. With these, you just type in a word—like "turtle"—and the computer helps you search for information.

Encyclopedias provide information on topics. Dictionaries, on the other hand, explain words. They show how to spell a word correctly, how to divide it into syllables, how to pronounce it (using symbols that stand for sounds), and what it means. Dictionaries also tell what part of speech a word is.

If you were reading a book and saw the word "flabbergast," where would you look to find out what it means? In a dictionary, under the letter "F." Say—what *does* "flabbergast" mean? Why not look it up?

After you have read about box turtles, you'll need to plan your report. Let's say you have three big ideas you want to write about:

1. What box turtles look like
2. Where box turtles live
3. What box turtles eat

You could write one paragraph about each of these big ideas.

A paragraph is a group of sentences all written about the same idea. It's a good idea to start a paragraph with a sentence that states the topic, or the main idea, of the paragraph. Then you can write a few more sentences to explain the idea and give examples.

Every time you start writing about a new idea, you should begin a new paragraph. How do you show that it is a new paragraph? You indent. See the space at the beginning of this paragraph, before the word "Every"? When you make a space like that, you're indenting.

a paragraph

indent

topic sentence

Box turtles are omnivores, which means they eat both plants and animals. Box turtles eat leaves and fruit. They also eat insects, earthworms, and slugs.

examples

Let's Write a Letter

Today most people use computers to send email, but there are times when you will want to write a letter—to thank someone for a present, to send someone an invitation, or to make a formal request or statement, such as a letter to your city's mayor suggesting your idea for a name for the new city park.

Writing a letter is different from writing a report. It's a lot more like talking. Still, there are a few rules to follow.

123 Main Street
Columbus, Ohio 43240
June 10, 2015

Dear Tooth Fairy:

I have had a loose tooth for almost a month. Yesterday when I was playing soccer, I bumped into my friend really hard and fell on the ground. When I stood up, I noticed my tooth was missing!

We looked all over the ground. All my teammates looked with me. We still didn't find my tooth.

I'm putting a drawing of my missing tooth under my pillow anyway.

Sincerely,

Amelia

- Begin by writing a **heading**, which tells your address and the date.
- Write a **greeting** to the person you're addressing. The greeting is like saying hello.
- Write the body of your letter in **paragraphs**. Indent each new paragraph.
- End your letter with a **closing** (such as "Sincerely" or "Your friend").
- Then write your **signature**—your name in handwriting.

Sentences

What Is a Sentence?

You know sentences. You speak and write them all the time. A sentence is a group of words that expresses a complete thought. Every sentence has a subject and a predicate.

Is this a sentence?

Four fresh figs

No, something is missing. Is this a sentence?

Grow in my grandmother's garden

No, something is missing here, too. But if you put them together, you can make a complete sentence. In the sentence below, the **subject** is in bold and the predicate is underlined.

Four fresh figs <u>grow in my grandmother's garden</u>.
 └─ subject ─┘ └────── predicate ──────┘

Now look at the subject and predicate in this sentence:

Six silly spiders <u>sing songs in the shower</u>.
 └─ subject ─┘ └──── predicate ────┘

Can you find the subject and predicate in this sentence?

Sammy the small sea horse swims south in summer.

Here's a sentence with something missing. This has a predicate, but it needs a subject.

Eight enormous _____ *eat doughnuts every morning.*

What's the predicate? It's *eat doughnuts every morning.* Now you make this a complete sentence. Choose a subject. *Eight enormous* whats?

> Every sentence begins with a capital letter. Do you remember other times when you use a capital letter? Capital letters start proper nouns, like names of people and places: for example, *George Washington* and *United States.* You capitalize the main words in titles of books: for example, *Little House in the Big Woods.* You capitalize holidays, days of the week, and months of the year: for example, *Hanukkah, Wednesday,* and *January.* And you always use a capital letter for the word that stands for yourself: *I.*

What Kind of Sentence Is It?

Now let's find out about three different kinds of sentences. You make up these kinds of sentences every day. The three basic kinds of sentences are:

- Declarative
- Interrogative
- Imperative

Let's start with this sentence:

Julia took her pet bear for a walk.

That's called a declarative sentence because it declares or makes a statement about Julia and her pet.

If Julia's friend visited and found her not at home, she might use an interrogative sentence, which is a sentence that asks a question.

Did Julia take her pet bear for a walk?

Interrogative sentences end with a question mark.

If Julia was sleeping late and had been ignoring her pet, then Julia's mother might use imperative sentences, which are sentences that make requests or give commands.

Wake up! Take your pet bear for a walk.

Both of these are imperative sentences. Look at the first one again: "Wake up!" Where is the subject in that sentence? You don't see a subject, but we say that the subject, "you," is understood. In most imperative sentences, the "you" is understood, such as in "Stop!" or "Please sit down."

If Julia took her pet bear for a walk to the park, then the people who saw her might use exclamatory statements, which are incomplete sentences that show strong feeling:

Wow! A pet bear! What a crazy girl!

Exclamatory sentences often end with exclamation marks!

Do It Yourself

This page describes the three basic kinds of sentences: declarative, interrogative, and imperative. Ask your child to write an original sentence for each type.

Parts of Speech

Let's review the parts of speech you already know and find out about some new ones.

Nouns

Can you find the nouns in this sentence?

My brother put on his snorkel, mask, and fins, but he forgot to bring a beach umbrella.

Remember, a noun names a person, place, or thing. Here is the sentence again with the nouns printed in color.

My brother put on his snorkel, mask, and fins, but he forgot to bring a beach umbrella.

Adjectives

Do you remember what adjectives do? Here's a hint. Look at this sentence, with the adjectives printed in color:

On cold mornings, Carla likes to cuddle up in her soft, fuzzy, pink blanket.

Adjectives are words that describe. Adjectives include words like "cold," "soft," "fuzzy," and "pink," as well as "long," "big," "scary," and "beautiful." Can you think of three adjectives to describe a puppy? How about an elephant?

There are three special adjectives you use all the time, called articles (or determiners). The articles are:

a   an   the

You might say, "Please hand me a glass," but if you wanted a certain glass, you would say, "Please hand me the glass." If you felt hungry for an apple, just any old apple, you might say, "I would like an apple." But if you wanted to eat a certain apple—the big juicy red one on the counter—you might say, "I would like the apple." Notice that you use "a" before words that begin with a consonant but "an" before words that begin with a vowel. You say "a glass," but "an apple."

Verbs

Can you think of a good word to fill in the blanks in each of these sentences?

José _____ fast.
Alison _____ the basketball.

For the first sentence, did you come up with something like "runs," "walks," or "eats"? For the second sentence, did you say something like "shot," "dribbled," or "passed"?

Words like "runs," "walks," "shot," and "dribbled" show actions. Words that express action are "verbs." Can you find three verbs in this sentence?

Henry carries his backpack and shouts to his friends while he rides his bicycle to school.

Adverbs

We use adverbs to add something to a verb. Adverbs describe the verb. For example, you could say,

Liz showed us her trophy.

What is the verb in that sentence? It's "showed." So *how* did Liz show us her trophy? You could say,

Liz secretly showed us her trophy.

"Secretly" is an adverb. It tells us something about the verb, "showed." Most adverbs end with the letters "-ly," such as:

quickly   slowly   suddenly
quietly   politely   carefully

Here are two sentences. First find the verb. Then think of a good adverb to tell something more about the verb.

The cat crept toward the mouse.
I asked for permission to leave the room.

Now, can you find the adjectives and the adverbs in this sentence? Adjectives first, then adverbs.

Melanie proudly showed her mother the fuzzy pink petunias that she had carefully planted in the garden.

Pronouns

Do you like to talk about yourself? Most people do! What do you call yourself when you do? Sometimes you use your name, but most of the time you use words called pronouns. You call yourself "I" and "me," depending on what you are saying. "I" and "me" are both pronouns.

Pronouns are words that stand for nouns. "He," "she," "it," and "they" are pronouns. Here's a sentence without any pronouns:

James asked Sarah to tell James when Sarah was going to come over to James's house.

Would you ever say or write a sentence like that? No! You would use pronouns, like this:

James asked Sarah to tell him when she was going to come over to his house.

When you read that sentence, you understand that the pronouns "him" and "his" stand for "James" and the pronoun "she" stands for "Sarah."

More About Verbs

Some words help express action. They are called helping verbs, like:

does ride	*will* shout	*have* brought	*is* diving
has carried	*had* broken	*was* throwing	*am* thinking

More Grammar

. . . .

Let's Punctuate!

Writing isn't just words and letters. All those little squiggles and symbols like **, ? ! .** " and — mean something, too.

Some punctuation marks come at the end of a sentence.

That last sentence ended with—what?—a **period**.

What other punctuation marks can end a sentence?

That last sentence, which was a question, ended with—what?—a **question mark**.

There is one more punctuation mark that can end a sentence!

What punctuation mark ended that sentence? It ended with an **exclamation mark**. When a sentence ends with one of those, you know it's about something exciting.

The **comma** is a punctuation mark that comes inside a sentence. Consider the comma in these sentences.

What About You?

Review these four sentences with your child. Ask your child to write his own version of each sentence, stating his birthday, hometown, likes, and an imagined response. Each sentence should use commas correctly!

I was born on March 30, 1995.

A comma always comes between the date and the year.

I live in Oshkosh, Wisconsin.

A comma always comes between the names of a city and a state.

My favorite animals are earthworms, moles, and eagles.

Commas always separate words in a series.

Yes, I know that my favorite animals are strange!

Commas always come after the words "Yes" or "No" at the start of a sentence.

The **apostrophe** is a punctuation mark that comes inside a word. It has two different jobs.

An apostrophe can show possession.

Emily's scarecrow costume
my puppy's name

When the word is plural and ends in "-s," you just add an apostrophe to the end to make it possessive:

five crabs' claws

An apostrophe is also used to make contractions, when two words come together to make one.

did not –> didn't
it is –> it's
is not –> isn't

In contractions, the apostrophe stands for a letter that has been dropped. In the contractions above, what letters do the apostrophes stand for?

Just Say No Once

Here are two good, easy-to-understand sentences.

I didn't eat lunch today.
I ate no lunch today.

But what would it mean if somebody said:

I didn't eat no lunch today.

Would it mean that the person ate *no lunch*, or that the person *did* eat lunch? It's confusing, isn't it?

The third sentence has what is called a double negative: both "didn't" (which stands for "did not") and "no lunch" are negatives. If you say you did not not do something, that can only mean you really did it. Double negatives are confusing, and it's best not to use them.

Prefixes and Suffixes

Prefixes attach to the beginning of words to change their meanings.

re- means "again":
refill means "fill again"
reread means "read again"

un- means "not":
unfriendly means "not friendly"
unpleasant means "not pleasant"

un- can also mean the opposite or reverse of an action:
untie means the reverse of "tie"
unlock means the reverse of "lock"

dis- means "not":
dishonest means "not honest"
disobey means "not obey"

dis- can also mean the opposite or reverse of an action:
disappear means the opposite of "appear"
dismount means the reverse of "mount"

See if you can find an example of your own for each of these prefixes.
Suffixes attach to the end of words to change their meanings.

"-er" and "-or" change verbs to nouns naming people:
sing + er –> *singer*
paint + er –> *painter*

"-less" makes an adjective meaning without that noun:
hope + less –> *hopeless*
fear + less –> *fearless*

"-ly" turns an adjective into an adverb:
quick + ly –> *quickly*
calm + ly –> *calmly*

Can you find another example for each of these three suffixes?

They Sound Alike, but They're Different

Can you solve this riddle?

Why was six afraid of seven?
Answer: Because seven eight nine!

This riddle works because the words "eight" and "ate" sound alike, even though they mean different things.

Words that have the same sound but different spellings and meanings are called homophones. "Eight" and "ate" are homophones. Can you think of some others? What is the word for a female deer, and what word is its homophone? "Doe" and "dough." Here's a silly sentence with two pairs of homophones:

We went *by* the store to *buy* a *whole* doughnut *hole*.

Can you make up a sentence with a pair of homophones?
Sometimes you just have to memorize the different words and their spellings. Here are a few to memorize.

Where are the bears? *They're there*, in *their* cave.
they're –> "they are"
there –> "in that place"
their –> "belonging to them"

You're sure *your* hair is three feet long?
you're –> "you are"
your –> "belonging to you"

Look at that polar bear. I wonder if Ice Cube is *its* name and if *it's* cold in that icy water.
its –> "belonging to it"
it's –> "it is"

Do It Yourself

After reading this page, your child will have learned some basic homophones. Ask your child to think of a few more and use them in sentences.

Here are two more sentences. Can you find the homophones?

Come over here so you can hear the bird better.
Those two tortoises are creeping too slowly to win the race.

Shorten Up with Abbreviations

Sometimes it's useful to find a short way to write a word that is used often. For instance, we use the word "Mister" so often that we abbreviate it as "Mr." When you see the abbreviation "Mr.," you still say the whole word, "Mister." Here are some common abbreviations.

Abbreviations for Addresses

125 Main **St.** (street)   99 Prairie House **Rd.** (road)

Abbreviations for Places

Born in the **USA**   Charlottesville, **VA** (Virginia)
(United States of America)

Abbreviations for Measurements

99 **ft.** (feet)   66 **in.** (inches)   500 **lb.** (pounds)

Abbreviations for Titles

Mr. Magoo   **Mrs.** Piggle-Wiggle   **Ms.** Manners   **Dr.** Gizmo (doctor)

Suggested Resources

· ·

Poetry

A Child's Book of Poems, by Gyo Fujikawa (Sterling, 2007)
Favorite Poems Old and New, selected by Helen Ferris (Doubleday, 1957)
Spider, Cricket, and *Muse* magazines (Cricket Magazine Group)

Stories

Alice in Wonderland, by Lewis Carroll (Bantam Classics, 1984)
A Thousand and One Nights, illustrated by Gustaf Tenggren (Golden Books, 2003)

Mythology

Classic Myths to Read Aloud, by William F. Russell (Crown Publishers, 1992)

D'Aulaire's Book of Greek Myths, by Ingri d'Aulaire and Edgar Parin d'Aulaire (Delacorte Books for Young Readers, 1992)

D'Aulaire's Book of Norse Myths, by Ingri d'Aulaire and Edgar Parin d'Aulaire (NYR Children's Collection, 2005)

II
History and Geography

Introduction

Have you ever seen a child who was fascinated by dinosaurs, knights in armor, or pioneers on the prairie? Young children tend to be interested in distant people, places, and times. The goal is not for the child to achieve deep historical knowledge, but to become familiar with diverse people, words, and ideas. The hope is that, years later, the child can say, "Oh, yes, I know something about that."

Learning history does not mean recalling facts—although getting a firm mental grip on certain dates, such as 476 CE, 1492, and 1776, is important. Dates reinforce a sense of chronology and historical context, establishing a foundation for more sophisticated understanding in years to come.

By third grade, children are ready to make more subtle connections among historical facts. They are beginning to understand how ideas cause change and how changes have effects. Still, the best history lesson emphasizes the story. In some cases, it can be hard—and perhaps not really necessary—to separate history from legend, like the story of Romulus and Remus. We encourage you to find art, drama, music, and literature that help your child learn more about the stories in history.

A special emphasis should be placed on learning geography in third grade. The elementary years are the best time in which to establish a lasting familiarity with the main features of world geography, such as the continents, the larger countries, major rivers and mountains, and major cities. Especially when connected to interesting stories, these features and places can stay with a person throughout life. Knowledge should be reinforced through working with maps by drawing, coloring, and playfully practicing place names. Maps offer children a foundation for understanding how geography influences world politics and economics.

World History and Geography

Let's see how many geographical facts you already know.

- What continent do you live on?
- What country do you live in?
- What state do you live in?

Was that easy? Well, we're just getting started. Now look at this map.

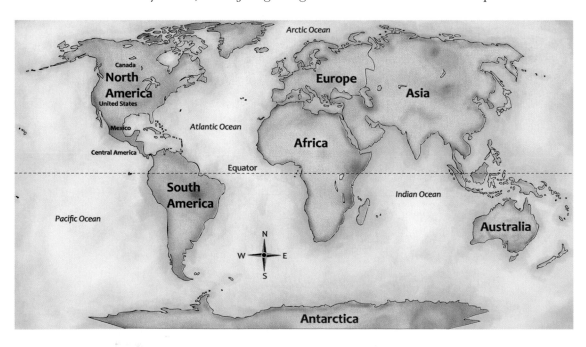

- Where is the compass rose located on this map?
- What do N, E, S, and W stand for?
- Can you point to and name the world's seven continents?
- Can you point to and name the world's four big oceans?

Now, can you point to the following areas on the map?

- Canada
- United States
- Mexico
- Central America

- The equator
- The Northern Hemisphere
- The Southern Hemisphere

Do you have a globe? If you do, see if you can find the North Pole and the South Pole. How do you know which is which? Don't worry—that's the end of the quiz. How well did you do?

Look at the Legend

Look at the map of Canada below. See the box in the corner? That's the map's legend. The legend explains the symbols used on the map. For example, it shows

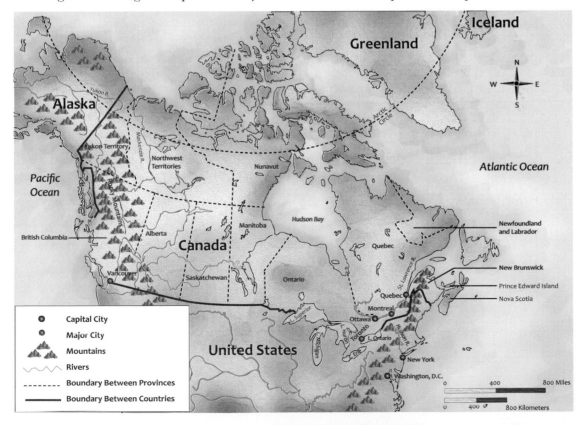

that a dotted line marks the boundary (or dividing line) between provinces, while a solid line marks the boundary between countries.

Maps also have bar scales to help you read distances. For example, the scale on this map shows that 1 inch on the map equals a little less than 800 actual miles. If you traveled the full length of the boundary between Alaska and the Yukon Territory, how far would you travel? You can estimate your answer by using this map and a ruler. It's a little more than an inch, right? This distance on the map represents about 800 miles in real life.

Great Rivers of the World

Many of the world's great civilizations—ancient Mesopotamia, Egypt, India, and China—started near rivers. When rivers flood and recede, they leave behind nutrients that make the soil rich and good for planting. By providing water and building rich soil, rivers help people grow lots of food. Where plenty of food can grow, civilization develops.

Rivers make a difference in the lives of everyone who lives near them. People travel on rivers, bathe in rivers, drink water from rivers, and use river water in their fields and orchards. The water in most rivers is fresh. Ocean water is salty, so people cannot drink it or use it to water crops.

Rivers flow through every continent of the world. Every river begins as a little stream, at a starting point called the river's source. Several streams called tributaries flow together and join to make a river. A really big river might have a tributary that is also big enough to be considered a river on its own. For example, the Mississippi River has many tributaries, and some of them are called rivers. The Missouri River, the Ohio River, the Tennessee River, and the Arkansas River (to name just a few) all flow into the Mississippi and make up a "river system."

When it rains or snows, some water soaks into the ground, but some runs into rivers. In other words, rivers "drain" the land. The area of land drained by a river system is called a drainage basin or, for short, a basin. The word "basin" is another way to say "sink." The drainage basin of a large river like the Mississippi is massive. With so many tributaries flowing into it, the Mississippi River drains almost half the land of the United States.

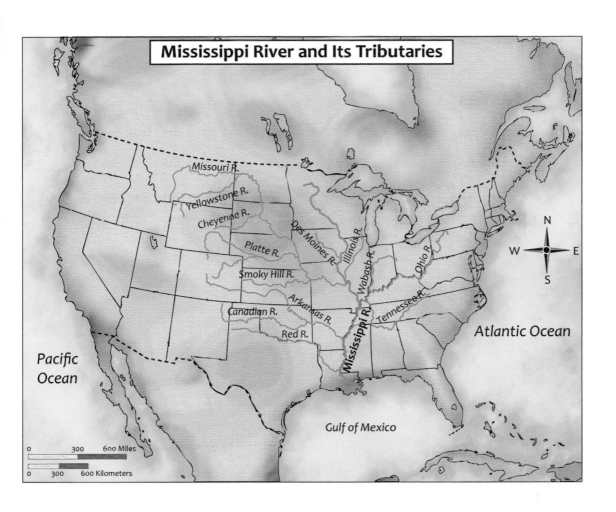

Mississippi River and Its Tributaries

Missouri R.
Yellowstone R.
Cheyenne R.
Platte R.
Des Moines R.
Smoky Hill R.
Illinois R.
Wabash R.
Ohio R.
Arkansas R.
Canadian R.
Mississippi R.
Tennessee R.
Red R.

Pacific Ocean

Atlantic Ocean

Gulf of Mexico

N
W
E
S

0   300   600 Miles
0   300   600 Kilometers

Some Geography Words

channel = a body of water connecting two larger bodies of water. The Yucatán Channel connects the Gulf of Mexico and the Caribbean Sea.

delta = a fan-shaped deposit of sand and mud at the mouth of a river. The Ganges River widens into a broad delta as it flows into the Indian Ocean.

isthmus = a narrow strip of land connecting two larger areas of land. The Isthmus of Panama connects Central America and South America. Today ships pass through the Panama Canal, which was dug through the Isthmus of Panama.

plateau = a high, flat area of land. Some Native American tribes made their homes on plateaus in western North America.

reservoir = a lake created by humans for storing water. The ancient Egyptians, living near the Nile River, built some of the world's first reservoirs.

strait = a narrow body of water connecting two larger bodies of water. The Strait of Gibraltar connects the Atlantic Ocean and the Mediterranean Sea.

What About You?
Ask your child: "Do you live near a body of water? What kind is it? Use the geography terms provided. What other bodies of water have you visited? What kind were they?"

At its mouth, a river pours out into the ocean or another large body of water. For instance, the Mississippi River empties into the Gulf of Mexico.

Let's visit the great rivers of the world. Use the map here to locate each river, but also check out their locations on a world map or globe.

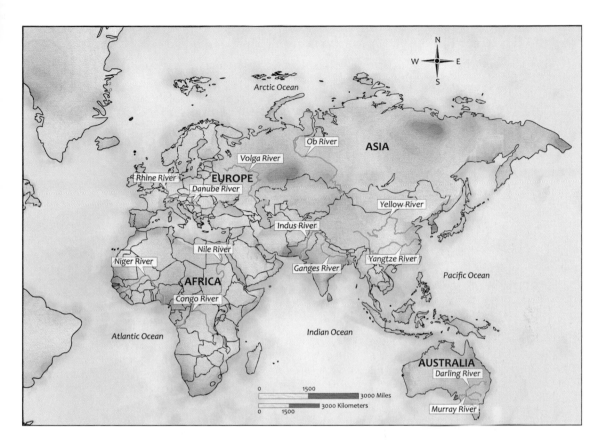

Rivers of Asia

In China, people call the two main rivers by different names. The **Yellow River** is called the Huang He. The **Yangtze River** is called the Chang Jiang, which means "long river." The Yangtze is nearly 4,000 miles long, flowing from the high mountains of Tibet all the way across China into the East China Sea.

If you go to Siberia in northern Russia during winter, you will find

This boat, called a junk, sails along the Yellow River in China.

the **Ob River** frozen solid. If you go in springtime, you might see the Ob River overflowing its banks. Its drainage basin fills up when the snow and ice melt.

The **Ganges River** flows through India and Bangladesh. The source of the Ganges is in an icy cave high in the Himalaya Mountains. The river is fairly short compared to the other great rivers in Asia, although it is very important to the Indian people.

The Ganges is the holy river of Hinduism. Every year, many thousands of Hindus come to bathe and pray in its sacred waters.

Thousands of years ago, the great civilization of ancient India started along the **Indus River**. The Indus is still an important river, but the country through which it flows is now called Pakistan. Along the Indus River valley, people grow corn, rice, and dates.

The Aswan High Dam, which controls the flow of the Nile River, was built during the 1960s.

Rivers of Africa

Do you know what the longest river in the world is? It's the **Nile River**. The Nile flows from south to north through Egypt, emptying into the Mediterranean Sea. Egypt's climate is hot and dry, so most Egyptians live close to the Nile. In southern Egypt, the huge Aswan High Dam creates a reservoir and controls the flow of the Nile.

Imagine traveling on the **Congo River** through the rain forest of central Africa. You could not travel on some stretches of the Congo because of dangerous waterfalls. But the river has many tributaries, forming a large network of waterways. The path of the Congo makes a big loop before emptying into the Atlantic Ocean. This river was also formerly known as the Zaire River. The **Niger River** travels through four nations in West Africa: Guinea, Mali, Niger, and Nigeria. It forms an unusual boomerang shape before emptying into the Gulf of Guinea. Some of the great West African kingdoms developed near the Niger.

A River by Any Other Name

The Congo River was first called the Zaire River when Europeans learned of its existence in the late 1400s. The word "Zaire" was a mispronunciation of a word in local African languages that means "river." For about 300 years, the river was known as the Zaire River. In the early 1700s, people began calling the river the Congo, after the kingdom of Kongo, which was built along the river. Although the government of the Democratic Republic of the Congo renamed the river Zaire between 1971 and 1997, the river was still known locally and around the world as the Congo River. It is still called the Congo River to this day.

Rivers of Europe

The **Volga River** is the longest in Europe, beginning north of Moscow, Russia's capital city, and flowing into the Caspian Sea. The Russian people call it "Mother Volga." All along the Volga, people have built canals and reservoirs, making it easier to travel and use its water.

The **Danube River** flows through Eastern Europe, from the mountains of Germany to the Black Sea. If you visit in winter, you can

Do It Yourself

Play the waltz "On the Beautiful Blue Danube." Recordings of the waltz should be available on the Internet. Ask your child to close her eyes as she listens and describe what the song makes her think the Danube River may be like. Then show your child the image, and have her compare what she imagined to the photograph.

The Danube River runs past farms and villages in Austria.

ice-skate on the Danube's frozen surface. In 1867, the Austrian composer Johann Strauss composed a lovely waltz about this river, called "On the Beautiful Blue Danube."

The **Rhine River** starts high in the Alps in Switzerland and then flows north through (or along the borders of) Liechtenstein, Austria, Germany, France, and the Netherlands. It eventually empties into the North Sea. Parts of the Rhine have been dug wide and deep to make canals for large barges that carry timber, iron, coal, and grain.

Rivers of Australia

Let's go "down under" and visit the continent (and country) of Australia.

In the southeastern part of the nation, the **Darling River** joins the **Murray River**. The Murray then flows south into the Indian Ocean. The people in southeastern Australia use the Murray's water for irrigation, or watering their crops. Sometimes they use so much water that the river dries up.

Do you recognize this animal with webbed feet, fur, and a bill like a duck? It's a duck-billed platypus, which lives in Australia, along the banks of the Darling and Murray Rivers.

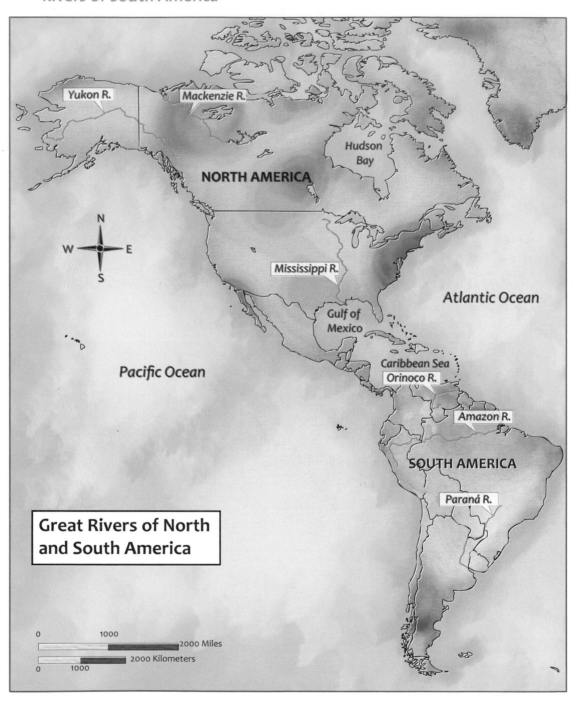

Great Rivers of North and South America

Look how well this family balances their canoe as they fish in the Amazon River in Brazil.

The world's second-longest river, the **Amazon River**, starts in the Andes Mountains in Peru and flows through the rain forest in Brazil. It has the largest drainage basin in the world: more than 2.7 million square miles of land drain into the Amazon!

If you go to Buenos Aires, the capital of Argentina, you will find yourself at the mouth of the **Paraná River**. The Paraná is so wide and deep that massive cargo ships can travel 400 miles up the river. The Paraná begins high up in the mountains and spreads into a wide delta as it empties into the Atlantic Ocean.

The **Orinoco River** flows through Venezuela into the Caribbean Sea. Christopher Columbus probably sailed into the mouth of the Orinoco in 1498. Today you can travel up one of the tributaries of the Orinoco and visit Angel Falls, the world's highest waterfall.

Rivers of North America
All aboard! Let's ride this big paddleboat down the **Mississippi River**, the most important river in the United States. Big tributaries flow into the Mississippi, in-

cluding the Missouri River from the northwest and the Ohio River from the northeast. The Mississippi spreads into a wide delta in the state of Louisiana.

Native Americans called the Mississippi "gathering of waters" because so many tributaries flow into it. This is probably the original meaning of the name we use.

The paddle wheel turns to make the *Creole Queen* move down the Mississippi River.

Canada's **Mackenzie River** flows north into the Arctic Ocean. It was named for Sir Alexander Mackenzie, the first explorer to travel from its source in the mountains to its mouth.

The **Yukon River** begins in the Canadian Rocky Mountains, just as the Mackenzie does, but it flows west through Alaska. The entire river stays frozen from October to June. Salmon like to swim through its cold, fresh water.

Salmon swim almost 2,000 miles upstream on the Yukon River to spawn, or lay their eggs.

Ancient Rome

Have you ever heard the saying, "When in Rome, do as the Romans do"? It's a saying in the language and literature section of this book. When people use this saying today, are they really talking about the great city in Italy? Consider another saying, "Rome wasn't built in a day." Again, when people use that saying, they aren't really referring to Rome. Instead, they mean, "Be patient. It takes time to complete a great task."

These sayings and others about Rome exist today because ancient Rome is still important in Western culture. Like the civilization of ancient Greece, ancient Rome influences many aspects of our lives today. In our laws and government, in the design of our buildings, in our calendar, and even in many English words, ancient Rome lives on.

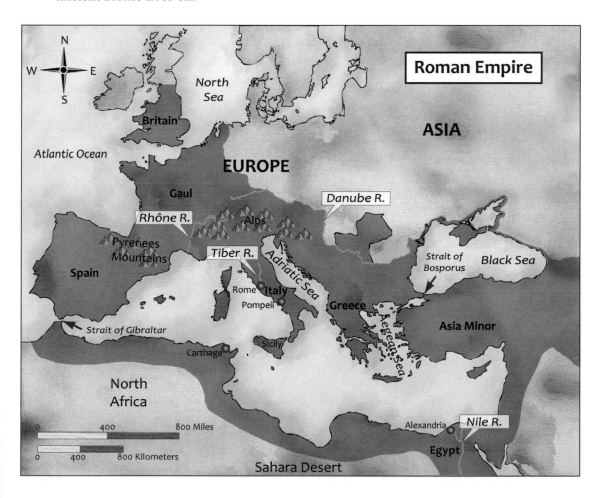

The Legend of How Rome Began

Almost 3,000 years ago, people chose seven hills above the Tiber River in Italy as a good place to farm and build their huts. Those villages grew together into the city called Rome. As Rome's population increased, its army conquered other countries. The boundaries of Rome's empire expanded. At its biggest and strongest, the Roman Empire included most of modern Europe and some of Africa and the Middle East. Sixty million people lived under Roman rule, many of them far from the city of Rome, in places that we now call the United Kingdom, Germany, France, Spain, Greece, Egypt, and Turkey.

The ancient Romans believed their empire was created to rule the world. They traced their history back to a story about how their city was founded by two brothers, Romulus and Remus.

In the legend, there was a jealous king who feared that if his niece had children, they might grow up and overthrow him. To make sure she never had any children, the jealous king made his niece become a priestess. This way she would devote herself to the gods only and never marry any man.

Imagine the king's surprise (and anger) when his niece gave birth to twin boys, Romulus and Remus. She explained that the father of these two boys was not a man, but Mars, the Roman god of war. The angry king put the babies into a basket and threw them into the Tiber River to drown.

Legend has it that Rome was founded by two brothers, Romulus and Remus, who were raised by a wolf.

But Romulus and Remus were rescued from the river by a mother wolf. She took the infants back to her lair and fed them as if they were her own. When a shepherd happened to find the boys, he took them to his village and cared for them until they grew into men.

Romulus and Remus agreed that they should start a city. As brothers will do, though, they argued over many things. Where would they put the city? Who would be its ruler? During one extreme argument, Romulus killed Remus.

Romulus went on to build his city on the seven hills overlooking the Tiber River. He named it Roma after himself. He ruled as king for many years. Then one night, in the midst of a huge thunderstorm, Romulus disappeared. The Romans believed that he became a god.

As with most legends, there is some truth in the story of Romulus and Remus. Almost 3,000 years ago, around 950 BCE, shepherds and farmers lived on those seven hills overlooking the Tiber River. About 200 years later, around 750 BCE, those communities joined to form the one city of Rome.

Talking About Time in History

When we talk about ancient history, we must go back a long time, sometimes more than 2,000 years. This means going back even further than the year with the number 1. How do we number those years more than 2,000 years ago?

The traditional calendar eras are based on the life of Jesus, whom Christians call Christ, by using the year when Jesus was born. The years before Christ was born are called *BC*, which stands for "before Christ." If we say Rome was founded in the year 753 BC, we mean 753 years before Jesus was born. Every date after Jesus's birth is called *AD*, which stands for *anno Domini*, or "in the year of Our Lord" in Latin, the Roman language. "In the year of Our Lord" is another way of saying "after Christ." If you were born in 1995, then another way to name your birth year is AD 1995, meaning that you were born 1,995 years after the birth of Jesus.

The secular, or nonreligious, system BCE (Before Common Era) and CE (Common Era) is popular today, but the two systems are equivalent—for example, "1995 CE" is the same thing as "AD 1995."

Religion, Roman Style

Like the ancient Greeks, the ancient Romans worshiped many gods and goddesses. The Romans believed that they looked and acted like normal people but held powers greater than any human. Like the Greeks, the Romans built temples in which they worshiped their gods. They carved beautiful statues to show what their gods looked like and what they did. Today we can see those statues in some museums and the ruins of those temples in the city of Rome.

Also like the Greeks, the ancient Romans believed the gods ruled different parts of their world. The king of all the gods, who ruled the sky, was named Jupiter by the Romans. He was based on the Greek god Zeus. The Romans believed Neptune ruled the sea, just as Poseidon did for the Greeks.

Romans performed ceremonies to please the gods. They would pray, offer food and wine, and sacrifice animals, such as sheep or goats. These ceremonies would take place at home, led by the head of the household, or at temples, led by the priests and priestesses.

The ancient Romans also believed that godlike spirits lived in nature. When birds flew overhead, Romans saw them as messengers from the gods. Priests would watch the way the birds flew and decide what message the gods were trying to send.

Some Roman Gods

Jupiter: king of the gods and the god of the sky

Juno: Jupiter's wife, the goddess of women and marriage

Apollo: the god of the sun, medicine, music, and knowing the future

Diana: the goddess of the moon and hunting

Venus: the goddess of love and beauty

Mars: the god of war

Neptune: the god of the sea and horses

Pluto: the god of the underworld

Mercury: the god of commerce and luck

Minerva: the goddess of wisdom and crafts

Jupiter, king of the gods, carries a lightning bolt.

Rome's Powerful Location

What made Rome so powerful? One answer is its location. Let's look at the map on page 125. First, find the country we call Italy. It is a **peninsula**, shaped like a boot, sticking into the Mediterranean Sea. Its long eastern coastline touches the Adriatic Sea. Now find Rome. What are the advantages of this location?

Rome sits at a crossroads of land and sea. It is on a river, so boats can leave Rome and reach the Mediterranean Sea. It is far enough south in Europe to provide a mild climate. Farther north, the mountain range called the Alps runs from one edge of the boot shape to the other. The Alps protected the ancient Romans from northern invasions. Their rocky, snow-covered peaks kept out most invaders—but not *all*, as you will see.

Rome's Early Republic

For 250 years, kings ruled Rome. Some were powerful, some were caring, but the last king was so mean and proud that the people drove him away (as

New Word

Focus on the word **peninsula** and what kind of landmass it is. Explain to your child that a peninsula is an area of land that is surrounded by water on almost all sides and connected to a mainland. Ask the student to identify another example of a peninsula, looking at the map on page 115.

Talk and Think

Ask your child if she is familiar with the word "veto" and its meaning in U.S. government today. Ask your child what rules she would like to veto. Discuss why that would or wouldn't be a good idea.

you read in "Horatius at the Bridge," page 80). To be sure no cruel kings came to power again, the Romans developed a new form of government. They called it a "republic," from the Latin words for "a thing of the people."

The wealthy men of the Roman Republic selected two leaders, called consuls, to lead them. Every year, they chose a new pair of consuls so that no single person was likely to grab all the power. In times of war, the consuls led the army. In times of peace, they ran the business of the city. To make decisions, both consuls had to agree. If one disagreed, he would say "**veto**," which means "I forbid" in Latin.

The Romans also had a Senate, which advised the consuls. The Roman Senate was a group of as many as 300 wealthy landowners. Once a man became a Roman senator, he held that position for life.

Roman senators.

Who's Got Class?

Some people who lived in Rome were considered citizens, but many were not. Enslaved people, foreigners, and, in early times, the people living in conquered lands were not considered citizens. Women were never considered citizens, no matter how intelligent or wealthy they were.

Among the citizens, there were two classes: the patricians [puh-TRISH-uns] and the plebeians [pluh-BEE-ans]. Patricians were wealthy men who owned a lot of land. They could become consuls or senators. Plebeians were ordinary people who perhaps owned a little property but were still poor.

The plebeians wanted the power and riches of the patricians. As Rome conquered more lands, the patricians needed the plebeians more, because it was the plebeians who fought in the army. Over time, the plebeians gained rights and freedoms nearly equal to those of the patricians.

Rome and Its Provinces

Rome expanded by taking over territory in every direction. Any area the Roman army conquered became a province of Rome. A Roman ruler was assigned to each province, governing the people and reporting back to Rome. The ruler collected taxes, either food or money, from the people in the provinces and sent them to Rome.

Some of the conquered people became enslaved. In other provinces, the Romans allowed the conquered people to follow their own customs and religions. They even let wealthy men from the provinces become Roman citizens. Those who did business in the provinces had to speak Latin, the language of Rome.

These men are dressed as Roman soldiers.

Latin Lives!

Do It Yourself

Help your child look up the Latin roots for a selection of words (e.g., *impossible, disappear, agreement, unknowable*) by using a dictionary. This activity will help him remember and recognize common Latin roots and affixes.

Today, some people call Latin a dead language, because no one speaks or reads it in everyday life. However, many scholars study Latin, because it has played an important part in the history of many languages spoken today. In this way, Latin is far from a dead language.

Ancient Romans spoke and wrote Latin. As Rome conquered its provinces, Latin became the official language used throughout the Roman territories. Foreign merchants and local town rulers used Latin to communicate with the Roman soldiers, businessmen, and governors. Over centuries, as the language spread, Latin words influenced the words spoken in other languages from those regions.

Look at these Roman letters chiseled into stone and see how many letters in the Roman alphabet are the same as ours today. Can you find the name "Caesar" on the stone?

Conquering Carthage

By 265 BCE, Rome had conquered most of the peninsula of Italy. Next the Romans decided to conquer lands that were farther away. To the north, they invaded by land. But to the south, they had to invade by sea, and there they faced the biggest threat to Roman power, the strong and wealthy city of Carthage. (Find Carthage on the map on page 125.)

Carthage was a city on the north coast of Africa in the country we call Tunisia. The Phoenicians [fuh-NEE-shuns], who were seafarers and traders from the Middle East, founded the city of Carthage around the same time that Rome was founded. By 265 BCE, Carthage controlled much of North Africa. The Carthaginians [car-thuh-JIN-ee-uns] were great shipbuilders and sailors. One of the lands they had conquered was the island of Sicily.

Take a look at the map on page 125 to find Sicily. Which is closer: Italy or Carthage? Sicily is less than 10 miles from Italy, while Carthage is across the Mediterranean Sea. Now you can see why Rome considered Carthage a threat.

Carthage and Rome went to war over who controlled Sicily. Many battles were fought at sea. Who do you think had the advantage? Not the Romans! They could easily win battles on land, but on the water, it was another story.

Yet the Romans believed they were destined to rule the world, so they didn't just give up and go home. They found a wrecked Carthaginian warship and, with the help of Greek shipbuilders, made 100 copies of it in 60 days.

Even with those improved ships, the Romans could not outsail their enemies. They could win in hand-to-hand combat, though, so they added a new feature to their ships: a way to board enemy ships at sea. When a Roman ship pulled alongside the enemy, the sailors lowered a drawbridge with a hook that attached to the

Once the Romans learned to build ships, as shown in this drawing of a Roman galley warship, they began waging battles at sea.

enemy ship's deck. Roman soldiers crossed the drawbridge and attacked the Carthaginians on board their own ships, wielding swords and spears. As a result, the Romans started winning many battles.

After more than 20 years of struggle, Rome won its first war against Carthage, called the First Punic [PYOO-nick] War. The proud Carthaginians did not want to be conquered by the Romans. One man was so upset that he made his son promise to battle Rome for the rest of his life. This promise begins the next chapter in ancient Roman history.

> Rome's wars against Carthage were called the Punic Wars because the Romans used the Latin word "Punicus" to mean a person from Carthage.

Hannibal Keeps His Promise

New Word
Does your child know all of the meanings of the word **scale**? Explain that it has multiple meanings. It can refer to a piece of a snake or lizard's skin, to climb up something, a device used for weighing things, or a system of measurement. What is the correct meaning for "scale those icy slopes"?

Hannibal was only nine years old when his father, angry at the Roman conquest of Carthage, took him to a temple. He demanded that Hannibal place his hand on the sacrificial animal and swear to be an enemy of Rome forever. The young boy agreed, and from that day forward, this promise shaped Hannibal's life. By the age of 25, Hannibal had already led an army of Carthaginians across the Mediterranean Sea and into Spain, capturing a city that was friendly with Rome. This attack began the Second Punic War.

When word arrived in Rome that Hannibal had attacked the city in Spain, the Senate sent soldiers to find him. It took those soldiers a long time to reach Spain, and when they got there, Hannibal was nowhere to be found.

"He's headed east," everyone told them.

"East?" questioned the Romans. "Across the dangerous Alps? Even if he were foolish enough to **scale** those icy slopes, his men would die trying."

The Romans had no idea how courageous Hannibal was. He did lead his army across the Alps—and what an army it was. Hannibal started out with about 70,000 soldiers, marching all the way from Spain, through France (then called Gaul), across the Alps, and into Italy. At least 37 massive beasts marched along with those men. These animals frightened the Romans, who had never seen them before. They were huge and heavy, much taller than a human, with big ears, thundering feet, spiked tusks, and long trunks. Hannibal had a cavalry of elephants!

Hannibal and his soldiers crossed the Alps on paths not much better than goat tracks. They marched across icy streams and over snow-covered slopes. Many soldiers and most of the elephants died, but this didn't stop Hannibal. He was devoted to his boyhood promise.

At last, he and his soldiers made it into Italy. They camped in the villages and countryside outside of Rome. They befriended villagers who hated Rome and banded together to raid Roman villages. Hannibal stayed in Italy for more than 16 years, tormenting the Romans but never actually capturing the city of Rome. Yet the Romans could not defeat Hannibal, no matter what tactic they tried.

The Romans decided that if they could not defeat Hannibal on their own soil, maybe they could defeat him in his territory. They sent a mighty army across the Mediterranean Sea to Carthage while Hannibal was still camped outside Rome. They thought that if Hannibal's own city was under attack, he would rush home to defend it.

The plan worked. Hannibal returned to Carthage, but he was too late. In 202 BCE, Rome defeated the Carthaginians, ending the Second Punic War. The Romans demanded large sums of money and made the Carthaginians promise to keep a smaller fleet of ships.

However, the Romans failed to capture Hannibal. He lived in hiding for years, refusing Roman rule because of his promise. When it looked like Roman soldiers were going to capture him, Hannibal poisoned himself, choosing to die rather than to live under Roman rule.

Imagine leading thousands of soldiers and dozens of elephants along the narrow, icy paths of the Alps, as Hannibal did.

The Final Defeat of Carthage

Rome and Carthage did not stop fighting after this war. Fifty years later, they fought the Third Punic War. Rome won this time and burned Carthage to the ground. The Carthaginians who survived were sold into slavery. Soldiers poured salt over the farmlands so that no crops would ever grow again. With this victory, Rome extended its rule to North Africa, Spain, and the islands of Corsica, Sardinia, and Sicily.

All Roads Lead to Rome

This is one of the many ancient roads that lead to Rome.

Many roads were built to connect the city of Rome with its provinces. As soon as Rome took over a new territory, the soldiers and enslaved people would build roads from there to Rome.

Imagine building a road where there are only trees, rocks, and dirt. There were no trucks or bulldozers! The Romans wanted their roads as level and straight as possible. They dug tunnels through hills. They built bridges over rivers. Even today, more than 2,000 years later, people still use the roads and bridges the Romans built.

Good roads and strong bridges helped Rome become powerful. The Romans had no cars, trains, or planes, yet they controlled an enormous area. This network of roads helped the Romans travel rapidly among the faraway provinces. Because of this network, you could travel from Rome to Great Britain or to the edge of the desert in North Africa. If there was a foreign uprising, the system of roads and bridges meant that messages got to Rome more easily. Roman soldiers could reach the province more quickly to crush the rebellion.

Well-constructed roads and bridges also helped business. Romans carried what they grew or made to the provinces to sell, and they brought back goods from the provinces to Rome. We know that the Romans traded many things with their provinces, such as pottery, wool, gold, silver, olive oil, wheat, copper, tin, and iron. The farther the Roman roads reached, the more materials could be brought back to Rome, helping the city grow wealthier over time.

By 100 BCE, Rome had greatly expanded its territory. Taxes poured in from the provinces. Rich Romans conducted business with the conquered peoples. Thousands of foreign enslaved people built roads, bridges, and buildings. It may sound like a time of prosperity, but, in fact, it was a time of war and discontent. Then a man named Julius Caesar came on the scene, changing the course of Roman history forever.

Julius Caesar Shows the Pirates Who's Boss

Julius Caesar was born in 100 BCE. He was the son of a wealthy patrician who believed the goddess Venus was one of his ancestors. In those days, if a rich young man wanted to be successful, he would serve in the Roman army and fight in foreign lands. Julius Caesar did just this.

Often Roman ships carried gold from conquered territories back to Rome. Young Julius Caesar was assigned to protect the gold from pirates. During one mission across the Aegean Sea, he was captured and held prisoner. Rome paid a high ransom to set him free. Later Caesar tracked down those same pirates and killed them.

Gaius Julius Caesar (100–44 BCE).

Julius Caesar became a great hero to the Romans. The consuls and Senate valued his leadership, and many soldiers under his command fought in Gaul. Eventually Caesar conquered Gaul and led his soldiers into lands that are now part of Germany and Great Britain.

Pompey, Caesar's Rival

While Julius Caesar was away from Rome fighting in the north, a man named Pompey rose in power. Like Caesar, Pompey was a spectacular military leader. He helped put an end to a huge slave rebellion. He led Roman soldiers into Sicily and Africa. He was put in charge of more than 250 ships and assigned to take control of the whole Mediterranean Sea from the pirates. In three months, Pompey managed to clear the sea of most pirate ships.

At first, Pompey and Julius Caesar believed they could rule Rome together. But Pompey grew jealous of Caesar's power and popularity. While Caesar was fighting in Gaul, Pompey convinced some senators that Caesar was a dangerous man who might try to take over Rome. The Senate ordered Caesar to give up his leadership, disband his army, and return home, or else be labeled an enemy of the people.

Crossing the Rubicon

On horseback, Julius Caesar leads his soldiers across the Rubicon.

Can you imagine how Julius Caesar felt? If he obeyed the Senate's command and gave up his army, he lost all power. But if he chose not to obey their orders, he would be charged with treason.

Caesar thought over his decision as he and his troops camped along the Rubicon River, on the border between Gaul and Italy. He and his army had left Rome to conquer new territories. If they turned back and crossed the Rubicon, it would be like invading their own country. He made his decision, and there was no going back. "The die is cast," Caesar said. He marched his army across the river in 49 BCE and on to Rome. Ever since then, people have used the phrase "crossing the Rubicon" to mean making a choice you cannot undo.

Soldiers fought against the approaching army, but Julius Caesar took control of the city and became ruler of the Roman Republic. Later, he named himself **dictator** for life, governing the army and all the provinces. Elections continued, but only people Caesar chose stayed in office. The consuls became less important over time, and Rome's republic came to an end.

Caesar Meets Cleopatra

When Julius Caesar seized power, Pompey decided to flee Rome. He had turned the Senate against Caesar, after all. First he fled to Greece. Caesar's troops followed his path and defeated his army. From there, he fled to Egypt, where he hoped the king, Ptolemy XIII, would protect him. But Ptolemy's army refused and instead killed him. Ptolemy wanted the powerful Julius Caesar on his side.

Caesar invaded Egypt anyway. There he met Ptolemy and his sister, Queen Cleopatra. Cleopatra was very attractive to Caesar—her beauty, her power, the way she spoke her mind. Whatever it was, Caesar fell in love with her. He ordered his army to overthrow her brother, making her the one and only ruler of Egypt. She had succeeded in uniting her country with the power of Rome.

> Even though Ptolemy and Cleopatra were brother and sister, and teenagers, these two Egyptians were married. They were the king and queen of Egypt. But they kept fighting over who should be in charge.

Back home, the Romans worried about Egypt's influence. What if their leader, Julius Caesar, married Cleopatra? What if he brought her home and made her queen of Rome? Had Caesar lost his mind? He even ordered a gold statue of Cleopatra placed in a Roman temple! What would the gods think?

Julius Caesar stayed with Cleopatra in Egypt for a year. Then, when an uprising

Cleopatra of Egypt (69–30 BCE) and Julius Caesar (seated).

Talk and Think

Ask your child why she thinks the Romans were so nervous about trusting one man's leadership.

occurred in an eastern province, Caesar rushed his troops there and defeated the enemies. Back in Rome, Caesar celebrated his victory with a grand parade and a big sign that said, "Veni, vidi, vici" [WAY-nee, WEE-dee, WEE-kee]. These Latin words mean "I came, I saw, I conquered." It was Caesar's way of saying, "It was no big deal to win that battle. I'm awesome."

Pride Comes Before a Fall

Julius Caesar's behavior as an army general and a dictator scared many Romans. The people did not want one man to rule the city and its territories. They especially didn't want Caesar to be dictator for life, nor did they want Cleopatra as queen. They liked the old system of government, and they wanted their republic back. Some of the senators thought Caesar had gone too far, so they plotted to kill him.

They planned the assassination for the Ides of March, which was the Roman name for March 15. On that day in 44 BCE, as Julius Caesar walked out of the Roman Senate, a group of men jumped out from the shadows and stabbed him many times. Caesar tumbled down, right at the feet of a statue of Pompey. When

As Julius Caesar walked through the Roman Senate, Brutus and others attacked and murdered him.

he looked up, he saw his old friend Brutus, who had helped plot his death. As he died, Caesar said, "Et tu, Brute?" [et too broo-TAY]—Latin for "You too, Brutus?" This phrase has come down in history as Caesar's famous last words.

All for Love—and Power

Those who killed Julius Caesar thought they had rescued the Roman Republic, but they were in for a big surprise. Many people, including soldiers in the army, did not support the senators' decision. They supported two men who had been close to Julius Caesar: Marc Antony, one of Caesar's best friends, and Octavian, Caesar's grandnephew and adopted son. Marc Antony and Octavian took control of Rome and divided the responsibilities for governing its territories.

Octavian ruled the west. Marc Antony ruled the east and moved to Alexandria, Egypt's capital city. There, he met the famous Cleopatra. Like Caesar, Marc Antony fell in love with her. Soon, they were married. Back in Rome, there was a problem, though. Marc Antony was already married to Octavian's sister! The Romans cried out against Antony marrying a foreigner. This brought an end to Octavian's friendship with Marc Antony.

Octavian went to the Roman Senate and warned that Marc Antony planned to make Cleopatra queen of Rome. The senators had heard that story before, and they certainly did not want a non-Roman ruler this time, either. The Senate removed Antony's powers as consul and declared war on Egypt.

Marc Antony's army fought Octavian's navy near Greece. In the end, Octavian won. Marc Antony went back to Egypt with Cleopatra. Soon, after believing that he had lost all hope of restoring his power in Rome, Marc Antony killed himself.

Cleopatra still did not give up on her quest to unite Egypt with Rome. Next she tried to make Octavian fall in love with her. But Octavian announced that he would capture Cleopatra, drag her back to Rome, and parade her through the streets like a trophy. When she heard that, Cleopatra lifted an asp—a poisonous snake—to her chest, let the animal bite her, and died.

Talk and Think
Caesar's last words are the subject of debate. The Roman historian Plutarch records that Caesar said nothing and pulled his toga over his head when he saw Brutus, while "Et tu, Brute?" comes from William Shakespeare's play *Julius Caesar*. Why might Shakespeare have included this question instead of nothing?

Our Calendar: A Gift from Rome

We have the Romans to thank for developing the names for the calendar months we use today.

January—from Janus, the Roman god of entrances and exits
February—Latin for "the month for cleaning"
March—from Mars, the Roman god of war
April—from the Latin word "aperire," meaning "to open"
May—from Maia, the Roman goddess of spring
June—from Juno, the queen of the gods
July—from Julius Caesar, the Roman dictator
August—from Augustus Caesar, the Roman emperor
September—from the number 7 in Latin
October—from the number 8 in Latin
November—from the number 9 in Latin
December—from the number 10 in Latin

Talk and Think

Ask your child about the meaning behind the names of the months. For example, ask questions such as, "Why might the Romans have named so many months after gods and goddesses? Why might the Romans have chosen to name April after a word meaning 'to open'?" Then ask, "If you had to come up with new names for the months, what names would you choose?"

Octavian Becomes Augustus Caesar

When Octavian defeated Marc Antony in 31 BCE, he became the sole ruler of Rome. The senators welcomed him and soon gave him a new name of honor. They called him Octavian Augustus, which was like calling him "Your Majesty." From 27 BCE on, this great Roman leader was known as Augustus Caesar. Because of the power granted him by the Roman Senate and the people, Augustus Caesar is considered the first Roman emperor. His name also has stayed with us in another way, because the Senate decided to honor him by renaming a month after him.

Augustus Caesar, Rome's first emperor (63 BCE–14 CE).

As Rome and its provinces expanded, people in the cities needed more water than nearby streams and rivers could provide. The Romans built aqueducts, which were stone troughs that carried water many miles from a spring or river to the city. The Romans built their aqueducts so well that you can still see some today. In France, cyclists now bike over the Pont du Gard [pohn dyoo GAR], which was built as an aqueduct by the Romans in 19 BCE.

Bicyclists still use the Pont du Gard to cross the river.

With plenty of water brought into the cities, Romans could enjoy public fountains and baths. For them, taking a bath was something you did in the middle of town with a lot of your friends. How would you feel taking a bath like that?

Pax Romana

Nowadays, we often think that an emperor is cruel and selfish. But that was not the case with Augustus Caesar. He ruled for more than 40 years, establishing peace and prosperity that lasted 200 years. Historians call those 200 years the Pax Romana, Latin for "Roman peace."

Augustus improved soldiers' lives by increasing their pay and taking care of them when they retired. He created an active police force in the city of Rome, which meant less crime and fewer riots. Life in the provinces changed, too. Augustus appointed governors to oversee the provinces and found ways to tax more fairly. He made sure the tax collectors stopped stealing money, and he insisted that tax money be spent to help citizens by building new roads, bridges, and public buildings.

During the Pax Romana, no large-scale wars disturbed the people. Cities and roadways were safer than ever. Trade increased, and both Rome and its provinces prospered. Everyone felt the benefits of Augustus's rule, but the Romans were still uneasy about one man making so many decisions.

Augustus Caesar was also concerned with how people behaved toward each other. Family and marriage were important to him. He encouraged people to participate in religious festivals. He constructed temples and other great buildings dedicated to the gods. He bragged that he found Rome a city of bricks and left it a city of marble. In this time of plenty, Rome was called the "Eternal City" because it seemed like the good times might last forever. Due to the city's lasting influence, people still use this name for Rome today.

Downtown in the Roman Empire

Does your hometown have a downtown or a place where people go to shop, eat, and work? The city of Rome did, too. Rome's downtown area was called the Forum. You can still visit the ruins of the Forum in the city of Rome today.

Let's walk through the Forum and see what it was like to live in ancient Rome. Look at all the people buying and selling goods. There's a merchant selling pottery, and another selling woven cloth. Mmm—there is the smell of cinnamon in the air. This shop must sell spices from Africa and the East.

Here is a shop selling food. I see grapes, apples, and olives. There are also dried fish hanging from the ceiling. In the corner, there's a big pot filled with wheat. You can grind it yourself into flour. And there's the delicious aroma of bread baking. Look, next door—the baker is pulling round brown loaves out of a stone oven.

The busy Roman Forum

Now that we have experienced the shops, let's visit the temple around the corner. Is that someone shouting in Latin? There's a man debating an issue on the steps of the courthouse. People listen to his arguments and respond to them. It seems everyone has an opinion on how the government should be run. Now we're at the entrance to the beautiful white marble temple to Saturn, the god of farming. I bet those two men in togas, carrying pitchers toward the temple, are bringing gifts of wine for the god.

Where's the Spaghetti?

As we stroll through the Forum, we might see a vendor cooking pieces of meat over an open fire and selling them to people passing by. Most Roman houses were built of wood and very close together, so household ovens were fire hazards. Many Romans bought their cooked food from street vendors. Along with meat or fish, they might eat bread, cheese, onions, garlic, and fruit.

A Roman family with plenty of money could build a large, spacious house with enough room for an oven. These Romans often hosted big banquets. Enslaved people prepared enormous amounts of fancy food. Guests usually began arriving in the late afternoon. They wore fancy clothing and expensive jewelry. They took their shoes off as they entered a home. When they ate, they leaned back on couches near tables low to the ground, picking up food with their fingers. A servant would stand by the couches, ready to pour wine and wipe clean their hands. Guests also brought cloths to wrap leftovers and take them home for later.

Take a Look
Look at the picture of a Roman banquet and compare it to the mealtime customs in your household.

What do you think the Romans ate? You might picture mounds of spaghetti covered with tomato sauce, but this wasn't the case! Pasta and noodles were not made in Italy at that time, and the ancient Romans never saw a tomato (which originated in South America). They ate some foods we still eat today, like bread and fruit, but they also ate many things we would never dream of eating. Ancient Romans ate everything from pig udders to stuffed jellyfish to flamingo. Can you imagine a dinner party where the menu might consist of roasted parrot, boiled ostrich, stuffed dormice, snails, fig wine, and dates

A platter full of escargots, or snails, would not be unusual at an ancient Roman dinner party.

stuffed with chopped apples and spices? If you went to a dinner party in ancient Rome, you might have been presented with any one of these dishes.

Roman Sports: Play at Your Own Risk

The ancient Romans loved sports, and they preferred violent and bloody spectacles like gladiators fighting to the death. From Greek architects, they learned to build amphitheaters, which were huge sports arenas with a field in the middle and seats raised all around it. The most famous Roman amphitheater, the Colosseum, was so massive that 50,000 people could sit on its marble seats and watch athletic events. Today you can visit the remains of the Colosseum in Rome.

Crowds entered the Colosseum through any one of 76 doorways. Canvas awnings stretched above the seats to shield spectators from the sun. The field was covered with sand, which would become soaked with the blood of men and animals. Complicated stairways and even mechanical elevators brought people up

The Roman Colosseum still stands today.

> **What About You?**
> Consider the description of the Colosseum and other Roman amphitheaters. Have you ever been somewhere with similar features, like a sports stadium?

to their seats. Wild animals, caged in dens below, were brought up to the field when an event was due to begin. There is also evidence that it was possible to fill the arena with water to stage sea battles.

A typical day at the Colosseum might start out with a wild-animal fight. Roman officials paid lots of money for fierce, exotic animals, including lions, tigers, rhinoceroses, elephants, ostriches, and leopards. Sometimes the sport was to hunt and slay the beast, unless the animal killed the hunter first.

Gladiators were typically enslaved people or criminals who had been trained to fight. A gladiator who was skilled and continually victorious might win his freedom. Some fought animals, but more often two gladiators would fight each other to the death. Sometimes the spectators might become fans of a certain gladiator. If they thought he was putting up a good fight, they might yell and point their thumbs up in the air, which meant "Let him live!" But if they didn't like him, they would point their thumbs down, meaning "Death to the loser!" We still use thumbs up and thumbs down to signal that we agree or disagree with someone or some action.

The Roman patricians signal thumbs down to show that they believe the gladiator on the ground ought to die.

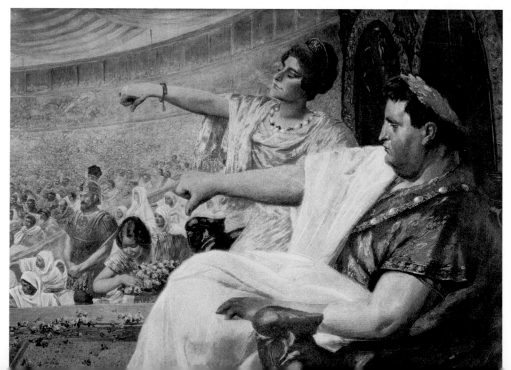

A Day at the Races!

The Romans also loved watching chariot races. Each racer drove a chariot by holding the reins and driving a team of horses at top speed around a huge racetrack. In Rome, the main racetrack was called the Circus Maximus, which means "very big circle" in Latin. Today we use the word "circus" to describe the festivities that happen in a big, round tent.

Chariot races at Rome's Circus Maximus

The racecourse at the Circus Maximus was more than 650 yards long, longer than six football fields. Can you imagine the noise and excitement of all those chariots, pulled by snorting, stomping horses?

Roman Games

Children in ancient Rome played with dolls made of cloth rags, marbles made of glass, and dice made of ivory. They also played knucklebones. They tossed the knucklebones on the ground, as we do in the game of jacks today, and guessed how the bones would land.

Game pieces, such as dice, counters, and knucklebones (top left).

Pompeii: A City Frozen in Time

How do we know so much about ancient Rome and how the early Romans lived? For one thing, the Romans did a good job of writing down who did what and when. They built their statues, buildings, bridges, and aqueducts very well, and we can study the remains of these ancient Roman structures today.

We also have a volcano to thank for much of what we know about ancient Rome. Mount Vesuvius erupted one summer afternoon in 79 CE near Pompeii. Pompeii was a little town about 100 miles south of Rome on the coast of Italy. Romans would visit there to enjoy the sea breezes and beautiful view of nearby Vesuvius. Imagine their surprise that day when they felt the rumble, heard the blast, and looked out to see the volcano erupting! Mount Vesuvius spewed gas, stones, and hot lava all over Pompeii.

Some lucky people escaped to tell the tale, but many in Pompeii met their end. Intense heat from the eruption and poisonous gases smothered some, while others were buried under layers of hot ash. People considered the eruption of Vesuvius to be a punishment from the gods. They believed that Vulcan, the god of fire, caused the smoke, flames, and ashes. As a result, they were afraid to return to Pompeii. It took many years before anyone returned to build a new city on the ruins.

Mount Vesuvius, a volcano near the town of Pompeii, erupted in 79 CE.

A Firsthand Account of the Eruption

(written by a Roman named Pliny)

By now it was dawn, but the light was still dim and faint. The buildings round us were already tottering.... We also saw the sea sucked away and apparently forced back by the earthquake.... On the landward side a fearful black cloud was **rent** by forked and quivering bursts of flame, and parted to reveal great tongues of fire, like flashes of lightning magnified in size.... Many besought the aid of the gods, but still more imagined there were no gods left, and that the universe was plunged into eternal darkness for evermore.

> **New Word**
>
> The word **rent** has multiple meanings. In Pliny's firsthand account, it means "to tear apart." "Rent" can also mean "to pay money to use something that belongs to someone else."

Over time, people forgot about the city of Pompeii. Then in 1748, archaeologists began digging in the area and discovered an astounding fact. The molten lava that destroyed Pompeii had also preserved it. Hot ashes had hardened around people's bodies, preserving the exact positions they were in when they died. The bodies had long since rotted, but by pouring plaster into the holes in the hardened ash, archaeologists could make out the shapes of men, women, children, and even a dog. In some cases, they could even see the expression on the person's face. Inside the houses, they found impressions of a cake on a table, a half-eaten loaf of bread, an egg, and a kettle. These foods have provided a valuable insight into what the Romans ate and how they cooked and preserved food.

The hot lava also preserved much more: shops, temples, a theater, and paintings on the walls. Today you can visit the ancient city of Pompeii. In the

Victims of Mount Vesuvius were preserved as they were when they died.

paved streets, you can see the tracks made by the wheels of chariots. In the hall-way of one house, you can see a sign, written almost 2,000 years ago, that says "Cave Canem"—Latin for "Beware of dog."

Columns still stand from houses in Pompeii, which the eruption of Mount Vesuvius destroyed. See the volcano in the distance?

A Long Line of Emperors

Now that you have learned a little about life in ancient Rome, let's go back to Augustus Caesar. Augustus ruled for a long time. When he died in 14 CE, millions of people across the empire grieved. His stepson Tiberius became the next emperor, ruling until 37 CE. Tiberius lived simply and saved lots of money for the empire. He was a skilled general and wise ruler, but the people did not like him. If they had known who was coming next, they probably would have appreciated Tiberius better.

After Tiberius, Augustus Caesar's great-grandson became emperor. As a boy, he spent most of his time in the army camps. The soldiers called him Caligula, which means "little boots" in Latin. Caligula hated his nickname, but it stuck.

What kind of emperor was Caligula? Here's a hint: When Caligula died, people ran through the streets cheering. All that money Tiberius saved for Rome? Caligula spent it! He once spent 10 million sesterces (more than one million dollars) on a single banquet!

Caligula thought the Romans should worship him as a god. He dragged statues of Jupiter out of the temples and replaced them with statues of himself. He also appointed his horse a consul. You can imagine that these decisions did not go over well with the Romans. Finally, one of Caligula's own bodyguards killed him in 41 CE. One Roman historian joked that this was the day Caligula found out he *wasn't* a god.

After Caligula, a man named Claudius became emperor. Both the citizens and soldiers liked Claudius. Under Claudius's rule, the Romans built more roads, aqueducts, and buildings. They also conquered more territory to the north and east. However, Claudius did not reign long. His fourth wife, Agrippina, poisoned him in 54 CE.

Nero: Not a Hero

Agrippina placed Nero, her son from another marriage, on the throne. This was a dark day for Rome. Just as Caligula had done, Emperor Nero wasted public money on fancy parties. He built an enormous golden palace filled with precious jewels. He called it his Golden House and decorated it with a statue of himself, more than 100 feet tall! But Nero did even worse things to the people. He tortured his enemies and killed anyone who seemed a threat to his power. He even ordered the deaths of his teacher, his mother, and his wife.

Nero thought he was extraordinary. He considered himself a brilliant actor and poet. Whenever he performed, the audiences were so scared of him that they cheered even if they didn't like the performance.

In 64 CE, a terrible fire burned down half of Rome. Some claimed Nero started it, just for a dramatic backdrop as he recited his poetry or to clear space for his Golden House. The Romans cried out that Nero fiddled while Rome burned, meaning Nero did not care that his people had suffered.

However, we don't know the exact truth. Historians don't know how the fire

One artist's depiction of what Rome looked like while it burned in 64 CE.

Talk and Think

Discuss with your child how the reigns of Caligula and Nero explain why the officials of the Roman Republic had felt nervous about having a single ruler with total authority.

started, or whether Nero played music or recited his poems while Rome burned. Nero blamed the Great Fire on Christians living in Rome, and he began to kill and torture them.

Leaders in the Roman army hated Nero. When the military named someone else to be a new emperor, Nero knew he had lost control of the people. He ordered his personal secretary to stab him to death. As he died, Nero supposedly said, "What an artist the world is losing!"

Christians During the Days of Ancient Rome

Augustus Caesar became emperor of Rome in 27 BCE, or 27 years before the birth of Jesus. Rome burned during Nero's reign in 64 CE, or 64 years after

Jesus's birth. Between those dates, a major event had happened. A Jewish man named Jesus had lived, died, and inspired a new religion. He lived in the area of the Middle East that we now call Israel. Jesus's ideas changed many people's minds about religion, but Jewish and Roman leaders of his time considered these ideas to be dangerous.

Jesus taught that there was one God. He said people should love God more than anyone or anything else, even the Roman emperor. He also said people should love others as much as they love themselves. Jesus said he was the son of God and that those who believed in him would live forever.

Jesus often talked about a kingdom in heaven. Some people got excited, mistakenly thinking that Jesus planned to overthrow the Romans and set up a kingdom on earth. Jesus's popularity worried the leaders where he lived. They worked out a plan to kill Jesus by crucifying him, which means hanging him on a cross to die.

However, Jesus's death did not stop his followers. They claimed Jesus came back to life three days after his crucifixion. They also claimed that before Jesus went up to heaven, he told them to spread his teachings and invite other people to follow them. These believers, called disciples, traveled all through the Roman Empire, preaching about Jesus. During the reign of Nero, many Christians had come to live in Rome.

Usually the Romans let conquered people in the provinces practice their own religions. But Christian beliefs presented a problem. Romans wanted all people to believe the emperor was a god, but the followers of Christ disagreed. They worshiped only one god and refused to worship any human, especially an emperor.

Some Romans were willing to allow the Christians to practice those beliefs, but others, like Nero, were angered by their rejection of Roman authority. After the Great Fire of Rome, Nero ordered Christians to be jailed, tortured, and killed. He persecuted the Christians, which means that he cruelly made them suffer, all because of their beliefs.

The Beginning of the End

For more than 100 years after Nero, Rome was ruled by much kinder emperors than him. The fifth good emperor, Marcus Aurelius, arranged for his son Commodus to take his place, but Commodus wasted lots of money and killed people and animals for fun. The empire was struggling with other problems, too. A terrible disease called a plague had killed many people. With fewer people to buy and sell goods, Romans could not make enough money. Farmers went out of business and could not grow enough food. The government became poorer, and the army became weaker.

At the same time, fierce foreign warriors began attacking along the borders of the empire. At first, the Roman army fought successfully, but then the Romans began to fight among themselves. The invaders moved closer, and the Roman Empire began to shrink.

Constantine Sees a Burning Cross

In 306 CE, a man named Constantine became emperor of Rome. He grew up worshiping the Roman gods and goddesses. But one night before leading his army to battle, Constantine claimed he had a vision—like a daydream. A flaming cross appeared to him with the words "In hoc signo vinces," Latin for "In this sign, you will conquer."

Constantine knew that the cross was a symbol for Jesus. He ordered his soldiers to paint crosses on their shields. When they won the battle, Constantine took it as a sign from the Christian God that his army should wear this symbol.

Constantine declared that all religions could be practiced in Rome and ordered an end to the persecution of Christians. Constantine may have become a Christian himself, and he is known as the first Christian emperor. Christianity eventually became the official religion of the Roman Empire.

In this engraving, Constantine sees a glowing cross in the sky, representing the vision that inspired him to become a Christian.

Take a Look

Although we say he saw a cross, historians say what he actually saw was a Chi Rho, which looks like ⚹. This symbol is formed from the Greek capital letters "chi" (which looks like an "X") and "rho" (which looks like a "P"). It stands for the first two letters of the Greek word for Christ.

Constantinople: A City Full of Art

During his reign, Constantine moved the capital of the Roman Empire from Rome to Byzantium, an ancient Greek town. The city became known as Constantinople, which means "Constantine's city" in Greek. Today this city, located in the country of Turkey, is called Istanbul.

Try to find Istanbul on a map. Notice how the city sits right on the Bosporus Strait, which is a long, narrow water passage between the Black Sea and the Mediterranean Sea. This city connected Europe and the western part of Asia, called Asia Minor. It had pleasant weather, good soil, and a safe harbor. Constantinople was the perfect center for trade.

A later emperor divided the empire into two halves: the western half, called the Western Roman Empire, and the eastern half, called the Byzantine Empire, named after the old city of Byzantium. The people of the Byzantine Empire blended Roman traditions with Greek and Asian cultures.

The Byzantine Empire continued for another 1,000 years. Constantinople became one of Europe's most beautiful cities, and its churches and palaces were filled with art. It became especially famous for its mosaics, which are artworks made by arranging small colored tiles, pieces of glass, stone, or other materials, on walls or ceilings. You can see a Byzantine mosaic in the visual arts section of this book.

Take a Look
Ask your child to compare the architecture of the Hagia Sophia to the architecture they see in the Roman street scene on page 145.

This is the Hagia Sophia [HAY-ja so-FEE-a], the most famous building from the Byzantine Empire. The Hagia Sophia was built as a Christian church. Fires and earthquakes damaged it, but the people of Constantinople rebuilt it. Later the Hagia Sofia became a mosque, an Islamic holy building. Today it is a museum.

The Fall of the Roman Empire

It took a long time to build the Roman Empire, and the fall of the empire occurred over many **decades**. Warriors called Huns came from the north, attacking the Germanic tribes who lived north of Rome. The people in the Germanic tribes, scared of the Huns and eager for the safety of Rome, moved south toward Italy. Slowly these tribes began to conquer other parts of the Roman Empire as well, moving into Britain, Spain, France, and North Africa.

Some of these tribes settled peacefully. They farmed, used the roads, and took control of the public buildings. When invaders moved peacefully into a province, the people did not bother to fight. They preferred the Germanic invaders to the Romans, who had demanded high taxes and governed harshly sometimes.

Other tribes did not arrive so peacefully. In 410 CE, after a two-year battle, the Visigoths marched into Rome. They stole from the temples, killed many people, and burned everything in sight. Romans had not experienced any invasion like this since Hannibal's attempt 600 years before.

The days of Rome's glory were over. Historians name 476 as the year when the Roman Empire finally collapsed. In that year, the German general Odoacer forced the emperor to give up his power. That emperor was a 16-year-old boy named Romulus Augustulus.

Do you recognize his first name? Oddly enough, the last emperor of Rome had the same name as the city's legendary founder.

> **New Word**
> Does your child know how many years there are in a **decade**? Explain to him that a decade is a period of 10 years.

Roman History: A Brief Timeline

753 BCE	Legends claim that Romulus founded Rome.
509	The Roman Republic begins.
300s–200s	Rome expands throughout Italy and begins foreign conquests.
100s	Rome conquers territories in Greece, Spain, North Africa, and the Middle East.
44	Julius Caesar dies, and the Roman Republic ends.
27	Augustus becomes emperor, which marks the beginning of the Roman Empire.
About 1 CE	Jesus is born.
54 CE	Nero becomes emperor.
64	The Great Fire of Rome rages; much is destroyed and rebuilt.
79	Mount Vesuvius erupts and destroys Pompeii.
306	Constantine becomes emperor.
380	Christianity becomes the official religion of the Roman Empire.
395	The Roman Empire splits into the Byzantine (Eastern) and Roman (Western) Empires.
410	Visigoths sack Rome.
476	Germanic invaders take over Rome; the Western Roman Empire ends.
527	Justinian becomes emperor of the Byzantine Empire.

The Justinian Code: A Gift from the Byzantine Empire

Although the Western Roman Empire had collapsed, the Byzantine Empire in the East continued to prosper. People built magnificent buildings and made beautiful art, which we study and can appreciate today. They also wrote important books about philosophy and law, and we continue to use some of these ideas today.

A man named Justinian ruled the Byzantine Empire for almost 40 years, from 527 to 565 CE. He borrowed the law of the Romans and organized it into 10 books, called the Justinian Code. Some of the laws in the Justinian Code were:

1. A person is innocent until proved guilty.
2. Above all, the court should consider the rights of the individual.
3. No one should be punished for what he or she thinks.
4. When deciding a punishment, you should consider the guilty person's age and experience.

Talk and Think

Can your child point out any resemblances between the Justinian Code and modern U.S. legal and constitutional rights?

These ideas, still regarded as important rules of law, were first written down by Justinian in the Byzantine Empire.

Can you guess which person in this picture is the emperor Justinian? (He's the one in the middle.) This picture is one of the mosaics in a chapel in Ravenna, Italy. You can see another mosaic from Ravenna in the visual arts section of this book, on page 238.

The Vikings: Raiders and Traders from the North

The Long, Dark Winter Nights

The year is 753. You are a Viking child, living on a small farm in Norway. It is late at night, and the winter wind howls outside. You squat on a dirt floor by a smoky fire, trying to warm your freezing hands. Your mother, brother, and two sisters sleep huddled near the wall on pillows stuffed with chicken feathers. You wonder where your father is. He is late getting back from hunting.

You try not to worry, but your stomach growls. There is not enough food. There is never enough food. An early frost last fall destroyed most of the vegetables. An ice storm in February killed the cow and two goats. Every night your family goes to sleep with empty bellies.

Your mind wanders to the sea. Yes, that is where you would like to be: on a ship sailing away swiftly from these cold, hungry, and dark winter nights.

If you were a Viking child, you might live in cottages like these, with thin walls and roofs made of thatched straw.

Did you use any Viking words today? Here are some English words that began as Viking words: anger, die, happy, husband, sky, ugly, window, wrong.

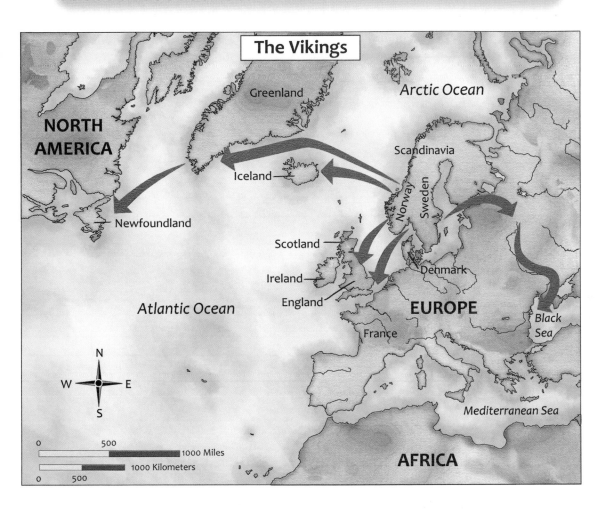

Who Were the Vikings?

The Vikings, or Norsemen, came from an area of Northern Europe called Scandinavia. This area includes the countries we call Norway, Denmark, and Sweden. These lands are cold and rocky with not much good farmland. Near the end of the 700s CE, there was not enough farmland to support the large number of

Viking families, so they traveled by sea to other lands. Sometimes they would barter, trading what little they had for what they needed. Other times they would raid a village and steal what they needed instead.

Beginning in the 790s, Viking raiders began attacking their neighbors in Western Europe. They stormed villages, castles, and monasteries. They stole valuables, such as gold, silver, and silk. They burned houses and killed people. Sometimes they enslaved their prisoners. A wealthy person could pay the Vikings to be left alone. People were so terrified of these raiders that they prayed, "A furore normannorum libera nos domine," or "From the fury of the Norsemen, protect us, O Lord."

In Norway, the ocean cuts into the coast in many places, making fjords [fee-YORDS]. A fjord is a narrow, deep inlet between steep, rocky cliffs, as shown here.

Good Guys or Bad Guys?

Much of what we know about the Vikings comes from writings in monasteries, where devout Christian men called monks lived. The Vikings attacked monasteries, stole from them, and burned them down. So naturally, monks did not have many good impressions of the Vikings. Maybe if the Vikings had written down their own history, it would be different. Instead of writing it down, they tended to

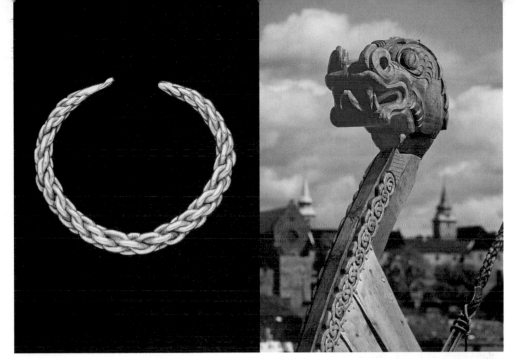

The Vikings made beautiful objects, like this gold bracelet (above left) and dragon's head (above right) carved at the top of a wooden post on a Viking ship.

tell their stories by word of mouth. These Viking stories are called sagas, and have since been captured in writing.

The Vikings began to question why they should go home to icy winters and rocky farmland. Other places seemed to have better weather and soil. Often when they found a good new territory, they sent for their families and settled there. They started colonies in many places across Europe, including the places that we now call England, Ireland, Scotland, France, and Russia. They even sailed to North America, 500 years before Columbus!

To record their sagas, Vikings carved picture stones like this one. See the letters that curve across the stone? They are called runes, and they are different from the alphabet that the Romans used.

Make a Connection

Read the Viking myth "Loki and the Gifts for the Gods" on page 66. Notice that one of Loki's gifts was "a ship that can sail both land and sea."

Men of the Sea

What made these Vikings so powerful? How could they take over one area after another? For one thing, Vikings were excellent sailors and the best shipbuilders of the time. Viking boats were fast because they used both sails and oars.

If you lived close to a coast or river, you were not safe from Vikings. Viking ships could sail up most rivers. The boats were light enough to be carried across land to another river if necessary. Even kings with strong armies had trouble defending themselves. They never knew exactly where or when the sly Vikings would show up.

The Vikings were also fierce warriors. Have you ever heard the word "berserk"? It means "to get crazy and out of control." It comes from a Norse word meaning "bear shirt." Before battles, Viking warriors threw bearskin cloaks over their shoulders and worked themselves into a frenzy like angry bears. They went berserk. No wonder all of Europe was terrified of them!

A Viking helmet with eye holes and a nose shield.

Eric the Red

One of the fiercest of all Vikings was Eric the Red, named for his red hair, red beard, and possibly his red-hot temper. Eric and his father got into trouble and had to leave Norway. So, Eric fled to Iceland, where his temper flared again, and local officials declared him an outlaw. An outlaw could be killed by anyone without fear of punishment.

So, Eric headed west to an island covered with ice and snow. He lived at the southern tip of the island, where there were good pastures. After a few years, Eric wanted to attract settlers to the new place, so he cleverly named it Greenland. Eric knew that a more accurate name like "Frozen Toes Land" would not attract anyone. His plan must have worked, because in 982 more Vikings traveled to settle in Greenland.

Eric the Red sailed west past Iceland and discovered Greenland, a land of ice and snow. Can you find Iceland and Greenland on a map or globe?

Leif the Lucky

Eric's oldest son, Leif [LEEF], often called "Leif the Lucky," turned out to be an adventurous explorer. Sometime around 1000, Leif sailed south and west from Greenland. He reported visiting a place with a mild climate. He saw grass for grazing, wild grapes growing on vines, and salmon swimming in the rivers. Leif named the place Vinland and spent the winter there.

Where was Vinland exactly? Some historians say Newfoundland in Canada; others say New England in the United States. Still others suggest Florida. Perhaps Leif was the first European to come to the

> **Talk and Think**
> Leif's full name was Leif Ericson. He got that name because he was the "son of Eric." Do you know anybody with a family name that ends in "-son," like Johnson, Jackson, or Jacobson? Those names were made up long ago for people who were the sons of John, Jack, or Jacob.

What About You?

Based on the sights he saw, do you have any guesses or theories about where Leif landed?

Americas, but no one knows for sure. During the 1960s, archaeologists found the ruins of Viking buildings in Newfoundland. So we know that Vikings lived there, but we can't be 100 percent positive that is the place Leif described.

Do you want to know why Leif was nicknamed "Leif the Lucky"? After the winter in Vinland, he and his crew sailed home. Near the coast of Greenland, Leif spotted survivors of a shipwreck clinging to some rocks. He rescued 15 people. He took such a chance that people considered him lucky. It seems like the people he rescued were the lucky ones!

A statue of Leif Ericson.

American History and Geography

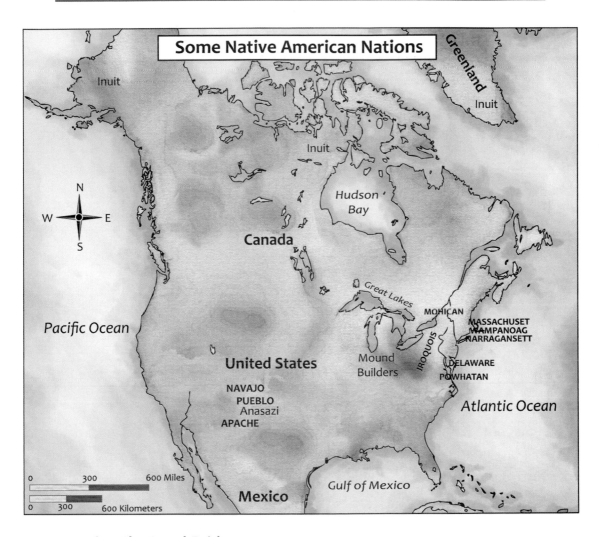

Some Native American Nations

Crossing the Land Bridge

For thousands of years, men and women hunted for their food. They followed roaming herds of animals, such as woolly mammoths and caribou. When those animals moved from Asia to North America during an ice age, it is possible people followed them, walking across a strip of frozen land called a land bridge. Different groups of people came from and went in different directions. Each developed its own way of living. Some groups became the people called Native Americans today.

The Native Americans of those prehistoric days did not write, so we must learn about them from their art and the objects they left behind, such as baskets, pottery, and buildings. Let's learn about some of these people and their ways of life.

We learn about Native Americans from the art they made. The symbols on this rock wall are called petroglyphs. Do you see the shapes of animals and humans among other objects?

The Inuits

Some of these Native Americans live in the northern regions of Canada and Alaska. They have been called Eskimos, which means "raw-meat eaters." But these Native Americans should be called by their own name, Inuit [IN-oo-it], which means "the people."

Way up north in the land of the Inuit, the weather is extremely cold. Snow and ice cover the ground for 10 months of the year. Even after the snow has melted, the weather is cold.

Lots of animals used to live in these northern lands. Polar bears, seals, walruses, and sea otters all have thick fur that protects them from the cold. The Inuit people hunted these animals. They made clothing from their furs and skins. They ate their meat and used their bones to make tools. They also burned their fat for light and heat.

The Inuit people learned to drill through the ice to fish in the water below. They built houses using blocks of snow or animal skins. Today people often call these dome-shaped snow houses igloos, but to the Inuit people, "igloo" simply means "house," no matter how the house is made. To travel along the snowy ground, the Inuit drove sleds pulled by a team of dogs. In the water, they paddled kayaks, or covered boats made from the skins of animals.

Today, many Inuit drive snowmobiles or motorboats. They may travel faster, but now they have to worry about where to buy oil, gasoline, and parts in their often remote locations.

Take a Look
What does this photograph reveal about how the Inuit deal with harsh living conditions?

This Inuit boy and his father, who live in the far north of Canada, stand in front of their home. They show off a fox skin from a recent hunt.

The Mound Builders

Imagine you're flying in a plane over the state of Ohio. While gazing out the window, you look down and see a huge, strange shape in the landscape. It looks like a giant serpent is coiling up a hillside! Then you realize it's not a real snake. It's a snake-shaped mound of dirt more than 1,000 feet long. Who made this giant mound and why?

This is a bird's-eye view of a snake-shaped mound made by Native Americans almost 2,000 years ago.

Do It Yourself

Have your child create mounds like the Mound Builders using clay, sand, or other materials. Ask him to imagine making the mound more than 1,000 feet long. That's more than three football fields.

Thousands of years ago, Native Americans built this mound and others like it. Today we call these people the Mound Builders. The mounds were burial places like the pyramids of ancient Egypt.

In the early 1800s, farmers discovered dirt mounds shaped like flat-topped pyramids all over their farms in Ohio. They called on archaeologists to study the objects left behind by these ancient cultures. The archaeologists dug carefully into the mounds and found artifacts like seashells, pearls, and shark's teeth. But there is no ocean in Ohio. How did these objects get into the mounds?

Archaeologists think the Mound Builders must have traded for the seashells, pearls, and shark's teeth. Perhaps they traveled to the ocean and brought the unusual items back to their homes.

Cliff Dwellers: The Anasazi

Around the same time that the Vikings crossed the Atlantic Ocean to North America, the Anasazi people lived in what is now the south-western United States. The Anasazi lived where the states of Utah, Arizona, New Mexico, and Colorado meet. But they lived there long before there were any states.

Another tribe gave the Anasazi their name, which means "ancient other people." We don't know what they called themselves. The Anasazi made their homes out of rock. An overhanging cliff served as a roof. About 1,000 years ago, hundreds of Anasazi people lived in the many rooms of these cliff dwellings.

Today, at Mesa Verde National Park in Colorado, you can visit the cliff dwellings that the Anasazi people built. They almost look like apartment buildings, don't they?

Many Anasazi homes included an underground room with a fireplace in the middle. You can almost imagine the people sitting around the fire on a cold desert night, telling stories or praying for their crops to grow well.

What happened to the people who lived in these cliff dwellings? We don't know for sure. We do know that the Anasazi lived in the same area for hundreds of years, building their homes, planting their crops, and making beautiful pottery and baskets. Then, about 700 years ago, they disappeared, leaving behind their cliff dwellings and belongings. Some historians think that another tribe attacked them. Others think their crops failed, perhaps because of droughts, or long periods without rain.

The Pueblo People

Today, Native Americans called the Pueblos are related to the Anasazi of long ago. The Pueblos call the Anasazi "the Ancient Ones."

During the 1500s, Spanish explorers first encountered these Native Americans, who built their homes out of adobe [uh-DOE-bee], a mixture of clay, sand, and straw. Some adobe buildings were several stories high. The Spanish called these people Pueblos because "pueblo" is the Spanish word for town.

The Pueblo Indians built houses like these out of adobe bricks. They built small steps but also used ladders to climb from one floor to the next. They built brick chimneys, too, so that they could have fires inside their houses.

Because they lived in the desert, the Pueblos had to work especially hard to grow food. They held a special ceremony called the Corn Dance every year. They wore special hats and costumes. They used red clay to draw designs on their hands and faces. They believed doing the Corn Dance helped make the rain fall and their crops grow.

Many Pueblo Indians believed in spirits called kachinas. They believed that each kachina had a different power to help the people. During important ceremonies, the men dressed up as kachinas. People danced and hoped the ceremonies would bring them good luck and good crops. When Pueblo children were given kachina dolls, they learned about the ceremonies and their meaning.

The descendants of the Pueblos, such as the Hopi and Zuni, still live in the American Southwest and follow many of their traditional customs.

Each kachina doll represents a different spirit being.

The Apaches and the Navajos

Some Native Americans, like the Pueblos, lived in the same place all year around, but other Native American groups hunted, traveling long distances to search for deer and bison. They were nomadic, which means they moved from one place to another.

When Spanish explorers met these people, they called them Apaches, which may have been their version of a Native American word for "enemy." These people did not call themselves "Apache," but it is the name we use today.

Young Apache boys learned to be warriors by playing games. The Apaches had to learn how to go long distances without water. In one game, an Apache boy would fill his mouth with water and then run for miles—without swallowing a drop!

Because they were nomadic, the Apaches needed to build houses quickly wherever they traveled. Some houses, called wickiups, had a dome-shaped frame of sticks covered by thick grass or brush. Other Apache people built tepees by stretching animal hides over poles. These structures could be easily taken apart, carried to a new place, and reassembled.

Another Native American tribe, the Navajo [NAH-vuh-ho], started out as nomadic people. They traveled across the land now called New Mexico, Utah, and Arizona. The Navajo considered the boundaries of their territory to be four mountains. By praying to those four mountains, they spoke to their ancestors.

The Navajo people called themselves the Diné [dih-NAY], which means "the people." From the Pueblos, the Diné learned how to grow crops, raise sheep, and weave beautiful blankets.

The Diné built round homes called hogans. A simple hogan was built of trees and mud, but others were more like log cabins with wooden frames covered by brush, clay, and mud. Most hogans had a hole to let out smoke from a fire burning inside on the floor.

This hogan was built with logs, rocks, and clay.

Today, the Navajo (or Diné) are the largest Native American nation in the United States. Many live on the Navajo Nation, which is land the U.S. government reserves for them. This reservation is located near the Four Corners, where Utah, Colorado, Arizona, and New Mexico meet. The Navajo Nation elects its own government and passes its own laws.

Eastern Woodland Peoples

The Native Americans who lived east of the Mississippi River are often called the Woodland tribes, because they lived near thick forests of oaks, maples, birches, and pines. For food, they hunted deer, bears, and wild turkeys. They fished in rivers and streams. They gathered berries, nuts, and fruits. Later, they began to plant and harvest crops, such as beans, squash, and pumpkins. But their most important crop was corn, or maize.

You can see the names of some of the largest Eastern Woodland tribes on the map on page 169. Can you find two names that later became the names of two U.S. states?

In what is now the upper part of New York, five Native American nations made an important agreement. They promised not to fight each other. Instead, they agreed to come together in a council and talk over their differences. They promised to follow the same laws that they all knew and shared. These five nations were called the Iroquois Confederacy. Later, another tribe joined the confederacy, and the whole group became known as the Six Nations.

The people of the Iroquois Confederacy recorded their ideas and memories by weaving. They would weave pictures into belts with beads made out of shells. During ceremonies when council leaders talked together and made decisions, they shared these special belts and read the stories told on them.

What About You?

After reading about how Native Americans used weaving to keep records, ask your child what she does to remember things.

A Day with Little Thunder

When the Pilgrims and other early English colonists landed on the east coast of North America, they met Native Americans of different tribes who all spoke the language called Algonquin. Let's imagine what it was like to be an Algonquin child in the time when the first Europeans were settling in North America. We're going to spend a day with a 10-year-old boy named Little Thunder.

Early Morning

As the morning sun rises, Little Thunder wakes up on a warm, cozy bearskin. He walks outside to see his father smearing a reddish paste on his body. Little Thunder knows that his father has mixed mud with bear fat to make it. He watches his father cover his arms, chest, face, and legs. The paste will help keep away mosquitoes while they hunt.

Little Thunder sees his mother cooking breakfast over a fire. How good the food smells! Today he will eat a stew of maize and deer meat, which his father and uncle brought home two days ago.

As he eats his stew, Little Thunder admires the way his father's hair is shaved. Only a stripe of shiny black grows from the middle of his forehead to the back of his neck. When Little Thunder turns 16, he will wear his hair as the men do. He will also get a tattoo on his arm, just like his father, using porcupine needles and berry juice. It will hurt, but he will not let the pain show. He will proudly wear the sign of the wolf, showing that he is a man and a member of the Wolf Clan.

Algonquin men sharpened a bone against a stone to make a razor. They shaved their hair so that when they lifted a bow and arrow and took aim, no hair got in the way.

The Day's Work

Each member of Little Thunder's family has work to do today. His father will go hunting with the other men. His mother will break up the earth for planting, and

The towne of Pomeiock and true forme of their howses, couered
and enclosed some wth matts, and some wth barcks of trees. All compassed
abowt wth smale poles stock thick together in stedd of a wall.

Here is a drawing of a village like Little Thunder's.

his sister will work alongside her, preparing to sow the seeds. Later they will gather fresh roots to boil for dinner.

Little Thunder will spend the morning outside the tall wooden fence that surrounds the village. He will check his traps to see if he has caught any squirrels or rabbits. As he leaves the village, he passes the home of an elderly man who lies close to death. Little Thunder hears the deep voice of the village shaman, a medicine man, who sings over the sick man and shakes a rattle made of tortoiseshell. Little Thunder remembers how his mother gathered herbs to help heal the sick man. Sometimes the herbs help, but not this time. Now the shaman chants to drive away the evil spirits that are making the old man so sick.

A snake slithers across Little Thunder's path—a sign of good luck, because the snake is the spirit animal that watches over Little Thunder. He thinks about the one Great Spirit, whom all Algonquins believe will greet them after death. The Great Spirit may not be watching him this morning, but the snake will protect him from harm.

Little Thunder finds a rabbit in one trap and carries it home to skin it. At the edge of the forest, he meets his father, who is proud to see that his son is becoming a hunter. They pass by the older boys repairing the longhouses. Last year, Little Thunder helped cut cedar saplings to build a longhouse. Men worked the saplings into the ground and then bent them into a rainbow-shaped frame. His mother and grandmother used sharp knives to strip the bark from the birch trees. The girls sewed together the sheets of bark with wood twine, making a roof to keep out the wind and rain.

> Some of the Woodland nations built homes called longhouses. The biggest longhouses were 25 feet tall and more than 100 feet long, with room for many families to live together inside.

Lacrosse is our modern version of the Algonquin stickball game.

Let the Games Begin

Today is an exciting day in Little Thunder's village. The chief sachem, the highest and most respected leader among many Algonquin tribes, is coming to watch the games. Little Thunder hears men cheering in the village center. He finds them standing in a circle, surrounding two strong boys, about 10 years older than Little Thunder, who are wrestling. When one boy pins down the other, the chief sachem declares him the winner.

Next there is a game of stickball.

Two teams of young men run up and down the field, tossing and catching a ball with long-handled nets of woven leather strips. Little Thunder shouts when his favorite team wins.

The Chief Sachem Speaks

When the games are over, the chief sachem stands to speak. Everyone falls silent. With a frown, the chief sachem announces, "We face the threat of war from another tribe. We must be strong. We must prepare." The men let out a loud whoop of support. Little Thunder sees his mother and knows from her sad eyes that she is worried.

That night, under a sky full of stars, Little Thunder and his family gather with others around the big campfire in the village center. The sound of beating drums fills Little Thunder with excitement, but he feels worried, too. Many of Little Thunder's relatives have died recently, though not in battle. Little Thunder has heard the adults say that since the white man has arrived, asking to buy furs, the Algonquins are suffering diseases they never knew before. The shaman cannot always frighten away these evil spirits.

With so many of his people dying, Little Thunder wishes they would not fight other tribes. He wishes the tribal leaders would sit together, work out their disagreements, and make peace instead.

The drums beat louder as the chief sachem calls men to a war dance. A man from the village sings about the brave deeds of their ancestors. Shadows from the campfire flicker on his face. He raises his arms like bird wings, pointing to the sky. More men join the dance. Caught up in the excitement of the drums, dancing, and singing, Little Thunder is proud of his people. One day he will join the adults in the war dance and fight for his people.

The drums beat louder as the chief sachem calls men to a war dance.

Early Explorers in North America

A "New World" for Europeans

In 1492, Columbus sailed the ocean blue.

And what did he find? He discovered a "new world" for the Europeans. After crossing the Atlantic Ocean, he landed on an island in what we now call the Bahamas (in the Atlantic Ocean), and named it San Salvador. He met the native people living there, the Arawak [AR-uh-wahk] people, whom he mistakenly called Indians. He thought he had landed on islands near Asia, which Europeans used to call the Indies. He did not know that he had landed on a different continent.

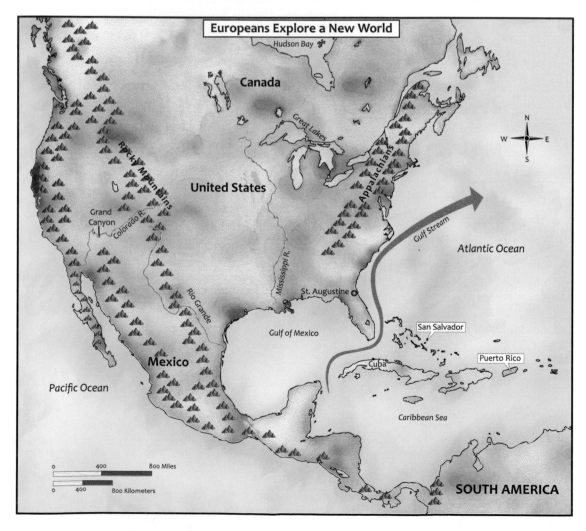

Why are the continents called America instead of Columbia? Columbus thought he had reached Asia. Soon other explorers realized they actually found a continent that Europeans had not yet discovered. Around 1500, an Italian named Amerigo Vespucci [ah-MARE-ee-go ves-POO-chee] explored the coast of what we call South America. A mapmaker used Vespucci's descriptions to make a map of the new continent. He called the southern continent America, after Vespucci's first name. Later, people used that name to refer to both continents in the New World.

European explorers were eager to discover new land territories and ocean passages. The desire to get rich from trade drove many explorers to seek out new lands and ocean pathways. Some explorers were careless and cruel in the way they treated the native people, who had already lived on these lands for generations. For instance, the Spanish conquistadors Hernán Cortés and Francisco Pizarro conquered the Aztecs and destroyed the Inca civilization. Was it all for gold and silver?

A Fountain of Youth?

King Ferdinand and Queen Isabella of Spain paid for Columbus to make four voyages to the New World. During these voyages, Columbus never landed on the continent of North America, though he did visit many islands in the Caribbean Sea, including Puerto Rico and Cuba. Ferdinand and Isabella wanted to claim ownership of the new lands being discovered, even though Native Americans already lived there. The king named one of his men, Juan Ponce de León [hwahn PON-seh deh leh-OWN], the governor of Puerto Rico.

Ponce de León found gold in Puerto Rico. This discovery made him rich, but he kept exploring. Some say he believed he could find a "Fountain of Youth" in the West Indies. One sip of its water would restore the person's youth, making them young forever. Of course, he never found a Fountain of Youth, but he did find other lands.

Ponce de León thought he had landed on another island. He landed during the Easter season, which the Spanish called "Pascua Florida." As a result, they called the "island" Florida, which means "full of flowers." What Ponce de León thought was an island was really a peninsula. We still call that peninsula Florida.

A few years later, Ponce de León returned to Florida, this time with soldiers and horses to conquer the land. He was sure he would find cities of gold even greater than the Aztec city that Cortés had conquered. But the Native Americans were ready to defend their land—they had seen their people captured or killed by explorers before. They shot poisoned arrows at the soldiers. One of the arrows hit Ponce de León in his leg. The Spaniards sailed back to Cuba, where Ponce de León died.

> Ponce de León noticed that near Florida his ship had a hard time sailing south, but if he sailed north, his boat went fast. Why? The reason is because a strong current, like an underwater river, moves through the Atlantic Ocean near Florida. It is called the Gulf Stream. After Ponce de León's discovery, Spanish ships used the Gulf Stream to sail home faster.

De Soto's Cruel Quest

The king of Spain made Hernando de Soto [air-NON-doe day SO-toe] the governor of Florida and Cuba. De Soto had already traveled with Francisco Pizarro in Peru and had seen the great Incan cities. He hoped that he could find cities with just as much gold and silver in Florida. In 1539 he arrived in Florida with about 10 ships, 700 men, 200 horses, and many weapons. He also had some enslaved Africans and native guides with him.

Like Ponce de León, de Soto thought Florida was an island. He traveled north to the Appalachian Mountains, then west. One of the men who traveled with him wrote this description of walking through Florida:

They came at noon of the fourth day to an extensive swamp which was difficult to cross . . . and skirting the edge of this swamp, was a jumble of tall, thick trees, intertwined with a great undergrowth of brambles and other low bushes, so dense that they looked like a strong wall. Through this entanglement and mud there was no passage except that of a small footpath made by the Indians, so narrow that two men could hardly walk along it abreast.

New Word
Ask your child to think about the double meaning of the word **skirt** based on the use of the word "skirting" in the quotation. In the quotation, "skirting" means "going around the edge."

This is how one artist imagined de Soto and his men looked when they first saw the Mississippi River.

De Soto stopped at nothing in his quest for gold. He and his men killed many Native Americans along his journey. The native people fought back, but the Spanish soldiers had both guns and horses. The Spanish lost many supplies after a fire in their camp, but they pushed on over mountains, through forests, and across rivers for almost two years. They finally came to the banks of a huge river—the Mississippi. They were the first Europeans to see it.

But de Soto had not yet found enough gold. His men built boats, crossed the river, and continued to trudge westward. Soon, however, de Soto caught a fever. Within a week, he died. His men wanted to bury his body in a place where the Native Americans would not find it. According to one source, they secretly took his body, filled a blanket with sand, and then sank the wrapped corpse in the waters of the Mississippi River.

The First Lasting European Settlement

In 1565, more Spaniards landed on Florida's eastern shore. They found a safe harbor where a river flowed into the Atlantic Ocean. Their leader, Pedro Menéndez de Avilés [meh-NEN-dez day ah-vee-LACE], was a very religious man. He named the place where they landed St. Augustine after the Catholic saint. When he met the Native Americans nearby, he invited them to eat with him. He wanted to tell them about his Christian religion.

Soon, the Spanish built a fort in St. Augustine to defend themselves against soldiers from other European countries, who were coming in search of land and riches. You can still visit St. Augustine today, the oldest permanent European settlement in the United States.

The Castillo de San Marcos still stands in St. Augustine, Florida. This Spanish built this fort built between 1672 and 1696.

In Search of the Cities of Gold

Back in Europe, stories buzzed about Seven Cities of Gold. Rumors had spread that there was a place where the people ate off gold plates with gold knives and forks and the streets were paved with gold!

Coronado led soldiers from Mexico north into the territory we call Arizona and New Mexico, looking for cities of gold.

Many men set off, seeking the legendary Seven Cities of Cíbola [SEE-bow-lah]. One explorer was Francisco Vásquez de Coronado [co-ro-NAH-doe]. The king of Spain had made Coronado governor of Spanish territories in Mexico. Coronado kept hearing that the golden cities lay somewhere to the north in the area that is now Arizona and New Mexico.

Native American guides led Coronado and about 300 followers to the town called Cíbola. They expected to find riches, but, as Coronado wrote back to Spain, "The Seven Cities are seven little villages." He found Native American pueblos—"very good houses, three and four and five stories"—but no gold. So Coronado sent explorers in different directions to continue the search for gold.

The Grand Canyon is about a mile deep, more than 250 miles long, and in some places 18 miles wide from one edge to the other.

One group traveled for many days. Eventually they came to a river canyon so wide and deep they could not cross. They had found what we call the Grand Canyon. The sight of it must have taken their breath away. For days Coronado's men searched for a way to get down to the river, but the canyon walls were too steep and dangerous, so they had to give up.

Another band of Coronado's men marched past a city of pueblo buildings, where they met friendly Native Americans who grew maize, beans, and melons and raised chickens. Then they came to a big river, which they named Nuestra Señora, which means "Our Lady," in honor of the Virgin Mary. Today we call that river the Rio Grande, which means "big river." Can you find this river on a map? It forms the boundary between Texas and Mexico.

Take a Look
Look at the map on page 182 and trace the route that Coronado's men took.

Coronado's men may not have found gold, but they did find one North American natural wonder: the Grand Canyon.

Spanish Missions

Coronado marched as far north as today's state of Kansas, but eventually the Spanish gave up their search for gold. They still moved into the lands where Native Americans lived, but they did so because they wanted to spread their religion, Catholic Christianity, among the native people. Christian priests built churches and schools, called missions, near villages. They taught classes and held worship services, wanting the Native Americans to become Christian.

Some Native Americans pray with a Spanish missionary.

The missionaries thought they were doing God's work, but their actions made some Native Americans angry. These native people did not want to give up their traditional religions. The missionaries were not aware of it, but they also brought disease from Europe. Many native people, who had no natural defense against European diseases, got sick and died.

Up North

Make a Connection

As you found out on page 167, Viking sailors had visited this part of North America, but they did not stay.

At the same time the Spanish were exploring the southwestern United States, other Europeans explored the northern regions.

In 1497, not long after Columbus made his first voyage, John Cabot and his crew of only 18 men bravely sailed the small ship *Matthew* across the Atlantic Ocean. Cabot was an Italian sailor, but the English paid for his voyage. Cabot landed on what is now called Newfoundland in Canada. Because of Cabot's voyage, the English claimed that they owned the whole North American continent.

King Henry VII of England paid for the voyages that John Cabot (pictured here) made to North America.

Make a Connection

Compare the impression that the Vikings had of Greenland with that of Cabot's sailor.

One of Cabot's sailors wrote that in the waters off Newfoundland there were "fish swarming so thick" that the boat could not sail. They were in the waters called the Grand Banks, one of the best places in the world for catching fish, such as cod, haddock, herring, and mackerel.

Seeking a Northwest Passage

If you look at a map or globe, you can see it is a long way from Newfoundland to Asia. The Europeans wanted to find a quick route to Asia without going over land. They enjoyed many fine goods from Asia, like tea, perfumes, spices, and silk. Trading companies wanted to bring more of those goods to Europe more quickly, but unknown lands kept getting in the way.

People thought there must be a strait, or water passage, through the North American continent that would lead to Asia. They called this hoped-for shortcut the Northwest Passage.

If you have a map or globe handy, see whether you think the Europeans could find a Northwest Passage to Asia. What sort of waters would they go through if they did? A ship would have to pass through the frigid, icy waters of the Arctic Ocean, not far from the North Pole. Even in summer, these waters are clogged with ice—but the explorers did not know this.

The Sad Story of Henry Hudson

After Cabot, an Englishman named Henry Hudson tried four times to find the Northwest Passage.

First, in 1607, he tried sailing north from England. If you look at a globe, you can see what he was trying to do. He understood that the earth was round and thought he could sail across the North Pole. However, he was not aware that solid ice covers the Arctic Ocean. "I hoped to have a clear sea between the land and the ice," Hudson wrote of this first journey, but that proved impossible.

Hudson tried again in 1608. He sailed northeast and again found icebergs and freezing weather. He turned his boat and tried sailing northwest. When his crew realized they were not heading home, they rebelled against Hudson, saying they would stop working unless they sailed to England. So, they went home.

In 1609, Henry Hudson sailed west. This time he was working for a group of businesspeople called the Dutch East India Company. On this trip he reached North America and claimed the land for the Netherlands.

People who come from the Netherlands are called Dutch. Another name for this country is Holland.

Hudson saw many Native Americans when he landed. One sailor wrote in his journal, "They go in deer-skins loose, well dressed." The Native Americans traded their crops for knives and beads, and they also gave the sailors bread made of maize.

Hudson sailed past a piece of ground with a white-green cliff on the side of a river. This area was called Manna-hata. It was the island we call Manhattan, the center of New York City today. Next, Hudson sailed up a river that still bears his name. You can find the Hudson River on a state map of New York.

In 1610, Henry Hudson tried once more to find a shortcut from Europe to Asia. He sailed a ship called *Discovery* into a wide expanse of water in the northern part of Canada. Today this body of water is named the Hudson Bay after him.

On a map, the Hudson Bay looks like a big open body of water. But in many places, the water gets too shallow for sailing. In many other places, it is frozen solid almost all year long. Once again, Henry Hudson had sailed into icy waters, just as winter was coming.

Hudson and his crew spent the winter aboard the *Discovery*, which became frozen in the ice. They ran short of food and water. Some of the crew got sick, and some died. The sailors blamed Henry Hudson for caring more about finding the Northwest Passage than about keeping his crew safe and healthy. When the ice began to melt, the crew rebelled. They forced Hudson, his son, and a few crew members loyal to Hudson to get into a small boat with few supplies. Then they sailed the *Discovery* back to England, leaving Hudson and the others behind. No one ever heard from Henry Hudson again. He had given his life to find the Northwest Passage.

Angry at their leader for forcing them through a winter without enough food and water, Henry Hudson's crew rebelled. They took over the ship *Discovery* and left Hudson, his son, and a few others adrift in a rowboat.

Canada Today

In terms of land area, Canada is the largest nation in the Western Hemisphere and the second-largest nation in the world. (Only Russia is bigger.)

Canada stretches from the Atlantic Ocean in the east to the Pacific Ocean and Alaska in the west. It shares a long boundary with the United States in the south and extends all the way north to the Arctic Ocean. While the United States is divided into states, Canada is divided into provinces.

The province of Québec used to be called New France. People in Québec speak French, while people in other provinces speak English. Farmers in Manitoba, Saskatchewan, and Alberta grow so many crops that these provinces have been nicknamed "the food basket of the world."

In the west, the Canadian Rocky Mountains connect with the Rocky Mountains of the United States and stretch all the way north through the Yukon Territory, where Canada meets Alaska. The biggest river in western Canada is the Yukon River, which starts in the Rockies and flows through Alaska into the Bering Sea.

The farther north you go in Canada, the colder it gets. Above the Arctic Circle, snow covers the land, and the water stays frozen almost all year long. Only a few trappers and fishers live in the forests around Hudson Bay. About 9 out of every 10 Canadians live in the south, near the border with the United States. All of Canada's large cities, such as Québec, Montréal, Toronto, and Vancouver, are found in the south. Ottawa, in the province of Ontario, is the capital of Canada.

Fur Trade in New France

A Frenchman named Samuel de Champlain [shawm-PLAIN] made many voyages across the Atlantic Ocean, getting to know the land that is now Canada.

Champlain sailed down the river we call the St. Lawrence. He met Native Americans who shared a stew of moose, beaver, and seal blubber. He met others who ran footraces to celebrate when they won a battle.

Champlain was in North America looking for furs, not gold. Europeans paid high prices for the soft pelts of bears, beavers, and foxes. He eventually arrived in a place where the river turned and the land jutted into the water. He called that place Kebec, after an Indian word for "narrows in a river." In 1608, Champlain built a trading post there. Over the years, the trading post grew into a town, and the town grew into one of Canada's biggest cities: Québec.

After that, Champlain sailed along the coast of Newfoundland and traveled back and forth to France. He spent one winter with the Huron Indians. He liked their meals of cornmeal bread, red beans, and roasted ears of corn. The Hurons told him stories of the big lakes that we call the Great Lakes. Champlain visited three of the five Great Lakes—Lake Ontario, Lake Erie, and Lake Huron, but not Lake Superior or Lake Michigan. He hoped one of them might lead to Asia, but he finally realized there was no Northwest Passage.

Samuel de Champlain always came home to Québec. He brought his wife from France to live with him there, even though not many European women lived in the fur-trading settlements. Champlain is often called "the Father of New France." The region he settled is now called French Canada.

Samuel de Champlain established a trading post with fences and gardens at a site on the river's edge. He named the place Kebec. Today we call it Québec, the capital of one of Canada's provinces.

English Colonies in North America

Thirteen Colonies

July 4, 1776.

Why is this date so important? On July 4, you can wish a happy birthday to the United States of America. On this day in history, American leaders signed the Declaration of Independence. This was the day when America said, "England will no longer rule us. We will be our own country."

Before 1776, America was not its own nation but a cluster of English colonies. After the American Revolutionary War, those colonies became the first 13 states in the United States (which is why the U.S. flag has 13 stripes).

People often use the words "English" and "British" to mean about the same thing. A long time ago, the country called England took over the neighboring lands of Scotland and Wales. The English used the name "Great Britain" to refer to their country combined with the lands they had taken over in the British Isles.

A colony is a place that another country owns and rules. In the 1600s, many European nations had claimed parts of the world as colonies. Spain had colonies in the West Indies and in Central and South America. The Netherlands and Portugal had colonies in Brazil. France had colonies in North America and the West Indies.

Take a look at the map on page 196. It shows that in 1750, Great Britain had 13 colonies in North America:

- The New England colonies: New Hampshire, Massachusetts Bay, Connecticut, and Rhode Island, founded mainly by Puritans
- The Middle Atlantic colonies: New York, New Jersey, Delaware, and Pennsylvania, started by the English and the Dutch

- The southern colonies: Maryland, Virginia, North and South Carolina, and Georgia, started by the English; these colonies made their wealth from growing tobacco, rice, a blue dye called indigo, and (later on) cotton

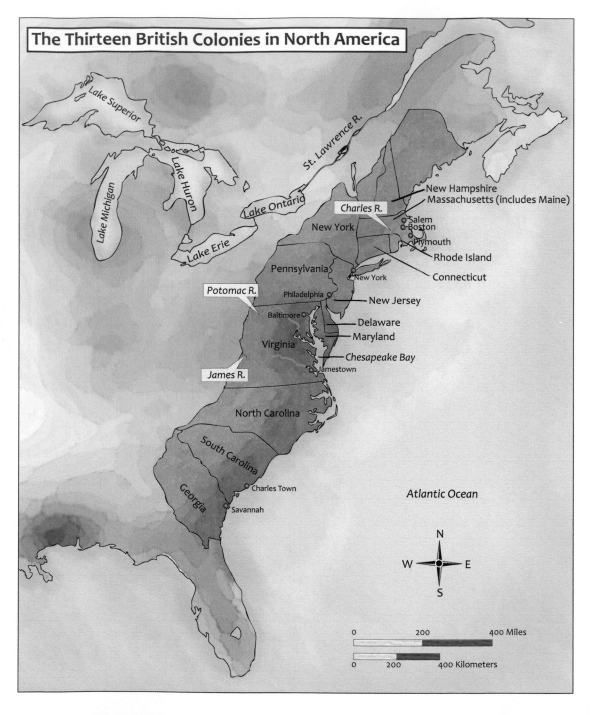

The Thirteen British Colonies in North America

The first English colonists crossed the Atlantic Ocean on creaky wooden ships that pitched and rolled in the waves. The trip took more than two months at sea. When they finally landed, there were no houses, churches, schools, or shops—just deep forests of wilderness. Native Americans made their homes in and around these forests, hunting the animals, fishing in the streams, growing food, and raising their families. Sometimes the colonists tried to understand and trade with the native people. But more often they saw them as "savages" and fought them to take over their land.

The colonists chopped down trees and mowed the fields. They sawed and hammered together rough lumber to build structures. They worked, prayed, and fought, but all too often they were sick, hungry, and cold. Many died, but many more kept coming, bringing their different dreams and desires for a new life.

The colonists worked hard to clear land and build homes in the New World. Most of the tools and materials they used came with them on sailing ships from Europe.

Jamestown: Dreaming Big

Gold, silver, jewels, silk—don't those sound like treasures fit for royalty? These are some of what King James I of England hoped to find in the New World. In the early 1600s, King James and many English people were sure these great treasures awaited them in America. They heard stories about Spanish explorers who found jewels and gold scattered on the ground. As Spain grew rich and powerful after Columbus's explorations, the leaders in England asked, "Why not us? We want our share of the New World!"

So the king of England wrote charters, or documents that gave permission to settle in parts of North America. A group of businessmen called the Virginia Company received one of the charters in April 1606. They paid for a voyage to the New World in the hopes of getting much richer in return.

Smith Lays Down the Law

"He that will not work shall not eat!" Captain John Smith shouted. He glared angrily at the men, who scowled back at him. A hardened soldier, Smith meant serious business. January 1608 was bitterly cold, and the colony of Jamestown faced disaster.

Captain John Smith of the Jamestown Colony.

The mission had begun only about a year earlier. The Virginia Company had prepared three ships for the voyage: the *Susan Constant*, the *Discovery*, and the *Godspeed*. In December 1606, these three ships loaded with 105 men and boys set sail from England. From the start, things did not work out as planned. Strong winds forced them back toward London. It took weeks before the winds changed and the ships could sail away from the coast.

Once they were on the open seas, the crew must have thought those winds were trying to warn them. Rough waves tossed the little boats. Supplies of food and drinking water ran low. The men grew hungry, tired, and afraid. Some considered mutiny—rebelling against the ship's captain.

By April 1607, they had arrived at the Chesapeake Bay. The voyage had taken longer than expected, and one of the colonists had died on the way. Looking for a good place to start a colony, they sailed up a river, which they named the James River in honor of the king. After some searching, in May they chose a grassy peninsula and called their settlement Jamestown. The spot they picked seemed green, pleasant, and easy to defend.

The Jamestown Colony was founded in Virginia in 1607 and named for King James I of England. John Smith created this map.

However, they found no gold or jewels. "We could find nothing worth the speaking of," wrote one of the men, "but fair meadows and goodly tall trees." They also found freshwater, plenty of oysters, and strawberries "four times bigger and better than ours in England."

But the spot they picked turned out to be a terrible place. Building on the swampy ground was difficult and slow. Stale, dirty water made the men ill, and the humidity was overwhelming. Mosquitoes buzzed everywhere, carrying a deadly disease called malaria. Many Jamestown colonists did not survive to see the fall.

Winter came, and still they found no gold. Because finding gold was their main mission, they had not stored enough food or built enough strong shelters. Men continued to die of hunger and pneumonia. At last, John Smith took charge, thinking, "There is treasure here, but it's not gold. If we're going to survive, we need to concentrate on fish, timber, and fur. We must make the Indians fear us or they'll attack. We can't keep wasting our time looking for gold."

After the terrible winter and another difficult summer, John Smith took charge of the Jamestown colony in September 1608. Not many of the original English colonists remained alive. Yet Smith put them to work. They chopped trees and dug wells. They drove posts into the ground and built forts. Many of the colonists were upper-class Englishmen, used to having servants do the work. These colonists had never used an ax before in their lives. They complained about having to chop wood, dig holes, and carry supplies. Smith sternly replied with his no-work, no-food policy: "He that will not work shall not eat!"

The men grumbled, but they were hungry enough to keep working. They built forts for defense, fished in the rivers, and combed the forest for nuts and berries. They had some good luck, too. "It pleased God to move the Indians to bring us corn, when we rather expected they would destroy us," John Smith wrote. He got to know some of the Powhatan [POW-uh-tun] tribes around Jamestown. He traded blankets and tools for food. He gratefully accepted the gift of corn, which would help his hungry men survive the winter.

The Powhatan and the English

Relations between the English and the Native Americans were never simple. Sometimes they traded peacefully, and at other times they fought. The ruler of the Powhatan tribes near Jamestown was named Wahunsenacawh [WA-hun-SEN-a-co], though he was honored by the title of "Powhatan." He ruled over thousands of Native Americans called the Powhatan people.

Most likely you've heard the story of Powhatan's favorite daughter, Matoaka, but you probably know her by her nickname, Pocahontas, which means "playful one." According to John Smith, Pocahontas saved his life. Smith wrote how he was captured by the Powhatan Indians:

Their clubs were raised, and in another moment I should have been dead, when Pocahontas, the King's dearest daughter, a child of 10 years old, . . . darted forward, and taking my head in her arms, laid her own upon it, and thus prevented my death.

This painting recreates the story of how Pocahontas saved John Smith from death. Do you see Chief Powhatan in the background?

Smith wrote that Pocahontas risked "the beating out of her own brains to save mine." Is this truly what happened? Some historians think not, but the story has been told this way ever since. Smith said the Powhatan treated him "with exceeding great courtesy." He also wrote that if, during that first winter, the Native Americans "had not fed us, we directly [would have] starved."

How did the Powhatan people feel about the English? They were both curious and suspicious. They admired the English for their tools, metal, and swords, wanting to trade for them. But they did not fully trust these people, who dressed strangely, talked differently, and built their forts on lands where the native people had once hunted freely.

The "Indian Princess" in London

When Pocahontas was 17 years old, she was kidnapped by the English. They wanted to trade her for English prisoners held by the Powhatan, but instead, she stayed among the colonists. She became a Christian and took a new name, Rebecca. When an Englishman named John Rolfe proposed, she agreed to marriage, which took place at the Jamestown church in April 1614. Soon they had a baby boy, Thomas, and the family set sail for a visit to England. The English were delighted by "Lady Rebecca, the Powhatan princess."

Sadly, Pocahontas did not live long. In England, she became ill and died when she was only about 21, far from her homeland. She never knew whether her people and the colonists could ever make peace, but her marriage marked the beginning of eight years of friendly relations between the English and Powhatan. Those eight years are called the Peace of Pocahontas.

Talk and Think

Has your child heard or seen other versions of the Pocahontas story? How does he think it compares to the one presented in this book?

The Starving Time

In September 1609, an explosion of gunpowder injured John Smith. His wounds were so bad that he was sent back to England, never to return to Jamestown.

That winter, the Jamestown colonists suffered even worse than before. There were no gifts of corn from the Powhatan. In fact, the colonists were so afraid of surprise attacks from the surrounding tribes that they stayed locked inside their fort. Soon hunger and disease began to spread. By winter's end, they resorted to eating horses, dogs, cats, and rats—anything they could find. Nearly all of the settlers died during the awful winter of 1609–10, also called the Starving Time. There had been about 500 colonists when the winter began. Only 60 survived to see the spring, many of them sick or dying.

A Cash Crop

If they couldn't find gold, how else could the colonists make money? Some Englishmen said they should plant mulberry trees to feed silkworms and start producing silk in Jamestown. But several attempts failed. Some merchants suggested planting grapes to make fine wines. This didn't work, either.

Then in 1614, the colonists found the answer: tobacco. The Native Americans smoked tobacco in their peace pipes. John Rolfe, the colonist who married Pocahontas, brought premium tobacco plants from the Caribbean. The Europeans enjoyed smoking it, too, and the Jamestown colonists were happy to grow all they could. Soon, the colonists were growing tobacco up and down the riverbanks, even in the streets of Jamestown!

King James warned against tobacco. He said smoking was "hateful to the nose, harmful to the brain, [and] dangerous to the lungs." But many Englishmen enjoyed smoking, and many colonists depended on growing and selling tobacco to make money. Over time, tobacco became the most important crop raised and sold by the settlers of Jamestown. Because tobacco was sold for high profits, it became known as Jamestown's "cash crop."

Ladies and Laws

One spring afternoon in 1619, the first shipload of women sailed into the Chesapeake Bay. Before then, few very women had sailed to Jamestown. For 120 pounds of tobacco, a man could pay a lady's travel expenses and make her his wife. This may not seem very romantic, but the arrival of female colonists meant big changes for Jamestown. Now the colonists could raise families in the New World.

In 1619, Jamestown took another huge step forward. The Englishmen gathered in the Jamestown Church to establish one government for all of Virginia. Male property owners from each of the colony's cities and plantations voted for two "burgesses" to represent their area. Although the Virginia Company's governor could veto their actions, these representatives were a way for the colonists to have a say in their own government.

Why is this important? At this time, Virginia was a colony, ruled by a far-away nation, England. But now, the colony could begin to make its own rules. Early on, Virginians had a democratic system of governing themselves.

The Arrival of the Africans

Early on, the British encouraged indentured servants to come work in America. Indentured servants worked for a landowner, but after a few years, they gained their freedom.

However, the white colonists decided that the Africans brought to Virginia should not be given their freedom, no matter how long they worked. By 1661, slavery was legal in Virginia. Ships came to the colonies carrying not just cocoa and linen but enslaved Africans. These Africans who stepped onto the shores of the Chesapeake Bay were likely doomed to a lifetime of servitude.

This drawing, from about 1730, shows a Virginia landowner puffing on his pipe with four slaves working hard in his tobacco fields. Tobacco was packed in large wooden barrels like these and shipped back to England for sale.

The Pilgrims at Plymouth

In September 1620, 102 settlers crowded aboard a small ship called the *Mayflower* in Plymouth, England, and set sail for the New World. They feared the vast ocean, but these men and women were eager to leave their troubles behind them in Europe. These travelers, called Pilgrims, had not had an easy life. A pilgrim is a person who goes on a journey, usually for religious reasons. The Pilgrims on the *Mayflower* had already made one hard journey, leaving their homes in England and sailing to the Netherlands in 1608. They had left because they did not agree with the practices of the Church of England. They thought its leaders had forgotten the simple faith that Jesus taught. They wanted to separate from the Church of England and worship in their own simpler way.

However, choosing to worship the way they wished was not a simple matter. As King James saw it, challenging the Church of England meant challenging the king himself. He would not put up with any "separatists"—people who wanted to separate from the Church of England. He ordered that they be found and punished. Some were thrown in jail, their homes destroyed and their businesses threatened.

During this time, the Netherlands was known for letting people worship as they wanted. This is why, with heavy hearts, the Pilgrims first fled to Holland. Yet the Netherlands still did not feel like home. The Pilgrims began to fear losing their English culture and language. They decided to leave Holland and start an even more difficult voyage, this time to North America. Other adventurers joined the voyage to America. The separatists called these adventurers "Strangers."

Under full sail, the *Mayflower* may have looked like the vessel in this painting.

The Mayflower Compact

Crossing the Atlantic Ocean was not easy. The winds howled. The seas swelled so high that one wave swept a sailor right off the deck. He grabbed a line from the topsail and swung himself back on board. Meanwhile, the Pilgrims huddled below, praying that God might deliver them from the fury of the sea.

While at sea, the Pilgrims needed to solve a problem that had come up. Some of the Strangers said they would not follow the Pilgrim leaders' rules. Because the group did not land in Virginia, their intended destination, some of the Strangers questioned whether they had the right to settle there. Some Strangers threatened to leave and settle on their own. As more problems arose, the Pilgrims believed they needed an agreement to preserve unity and avoid conflict.

On board the *Mayflower*, Pilgrims and "Strangers" sign the Mayflower Compact.

Before they left the *Mayflower*, Pilgrims and Strangers gathered around a massive wooden table in the captain's quarters. There, they signed their names to an agreement, which was called the Mayflower Compact. They chose to "combine [themselves] together into a civil body politick" (a group of people agreeing to work together) and to create "just and equal laws" for the colony. Every man signed the Mayflower Compact before stepping ashore. The Mayflower Compact shows that the colonists were concerned about the general good of everyone. They took the first step toward making their own laws and governing themselves.

After 66 days at sea, the *Mayflower* landed at Cape Cod, in today's Massachusetts, much farther north than their intended destination in Virginia. By the time they arrived in November, temperatures were dropping quickly and snow was in the air. The captain of the *Mayflower* declared this would be home for the Pilgrims. William Bradford, one of the Pilgrim leaders, wrote that "they fell upon their knees and blessed the God of Heaven, who had brought them over the vast and furious ocean . . . and again set their feet on the firm and stable earth."

Take a Look
Ask your child to look closely at the picture of Pilgrims arriving in Massachusetts. What details does he notice? What might the Pilgrims' expressions reveal about the journey they made?

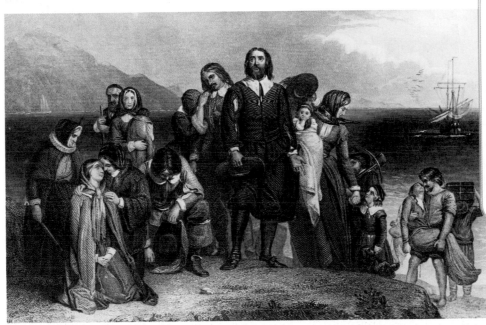

The Pilgrims had intended to go to Virginia, but the *Mayflower* sailed farther north, and they landed on the coast of what is now Massachusetts.

A "Wild and Savage" Land

Imagine stepping onto the shore of this strange new world, a land that William Bradford described as "wild and savage." Behind you, the ocean stretches out to the horizon. Before you, a thick and dark forest looms. Who knows what might be lurking behind those trees?

But there is no time to be afraid. Winter is close upon you. The damp smell of snow is in the air. Where will you build your home? What supplies will you gather first? How will you survive? *Will* you survive?

This uncertainty was the reality the Pilgrims faced in November 1620. Scouts from the *Mayflower* rowed out to search the rocky coast. They found some land, partly cleared by Native Americans and named Plymouth by John Smith years before. They had sailed from Plymouth, England, so it seemed fitting that they should make a new home in Plymouth, America. A stream fed the land, which sat on top of a small hill, making it easy to defend.

However, the Pilgrims had barely completed the first common house by January. During the winter, they struggled to build more homes, trudging back and forth to the *Mayflower* through frigid ocean water several times a day. Many caught colds that turned into pneumonia. They had few warm shelters and no hot meals to eat. Fewer than half the Pilgrims lived to see the spring. Still, the Pilgrims of Plymouth, like the settlers of Jamestown, survived—partly through courage and good leadership—but even more through the friendship of the Wampanoag tribe.

The Pilgrims and the Wampanoag

Imagine you are a Pilgrim child, one of the lucky ones who made it through the first winter. It's a windy March day, and leaves have not yet returned to the trees. Your stomach growls for food, but there is little to eat. Sometimes you see faces in the forest. When you look, they dart away. Who are they? What are they planning? Will they attack?

Then you hear a deep voice, "Welcome, Englishmen!" A man dressed in deerskins walks boldly into your camp. You can hardly believe your ears. A Native American speaking English!

Everyone gathers round. The man says his name is Samoset. He says he knows another who speaks English even better. Your governor gives him presents of food and tools, and Samoset promises to return.

Days later he comes back, bringing more members of the Wampanoag tribe. He introduces you to Tisquantum, who speaks English very well. Over time, Tisquantum teaches you and the other Pilgrims how to plant corn, pumpkins, and beans. He shows you the best places to fish. He guides you through the lands around Plymouth. He introduces your leaders to Massasoit, chief of the Wampanoag tribe, and helps translate between languages. Soon the Wampanoags and the Pilgrims sign a peace treaty of friendship that will last for many years.

Before Tisquantum helped the Pilgrims survive in their new land and live peacefully with the Native Americans, he had had to fight for his own survival. Like the Pilgrims, Tisquantum had to learn to survive in a new land where people had strange customs and ways of life. Let's read as one boy learns about Tisquantum's journey after he was kidnapped by European explorers and forced to fight his way back home.

Tisquantum's Fight

Lucas's eyes widened as he looked at the Thanksgiving feast spread out on the dining room table. Turkey, mashed potatoes, macaroni and cheese, and his favorite, yams, were all lined up down the center of the table. Lucas just had to have a taste of those yams. He looked to his left and then to his right. The coast was clear! Lucas carefully lifted the lid of the dish and slid his hand toward the golden goodness.

"Lucas!" his mother yelled. "Do not touch those yams—it's not time to eat yet!"

Lucas's dad interjected, "Lucas, come here. I want to tell you a story. Did you know that at the first Thanksgiving meal people from different families and cultures worked together to make a huge feast?"

Lucas sighed. "Yes, I know that. We learned all about it in social studies."

> ### Make a Connection
> Look back at the poem "First Thanksgiving of All" on page 16. Ask your child: According to the poem, what was the first Thanksgiving like? How does the poem's description compare to the first Thanksgiving as it is described in this chapter?

"But did you also know that Squanto, one of the heroes of the first Thanksgiving, lived right here in Cape Cod Bay, just like we do?"

Lucas sighed once more. "Yes, Dad."

"Ah, but did you know that Squanto's real name was Tisquantum, and he was a Native American who spoke English, survived a kidnapping, crossed the Atlantic four times, and had been to Spain and England?"

Lucas's eyes lit up at the sound of adventure. "No . . . What else do you know about him?" asked Lucas, now ready to hang on his father's every word.

"Tisquantum was a member of the Patuxet Native American group. Not much is known about Tisquantum's childhood and early years. But about seven years before the first Thanksgiving, when Tisquantum was in his early 30s, Tisquantum's life became a little more exciting," his father explained.

"Is this when he gets kidnapped?" Lucas interrupted excitedly.

"I'm getting there. You see, Tisquantum met Captain John Smith, a short man with a big, fiery red beard. Captain Smith had arrived at Cape Cod Bay with his crew. Tisquantum watched the fire-bearded man as he traded for furs with Patuxet leaders. Although Tisquantum and the other Patuxet people did not know how to speak the language of Captain Smith, he and his people found ways to communicate with them," Lucas's father continued.

"It must have been hard to talk to someone who speaks a different language," Lucas remarked.

"It was very hard! The men used hand gestures. After spending so much time trading, some Native Americans and Englishmen understood certain words from the other's language."

"I see," Lucas said with a nod. "But what happened to Tisquantum next?"

Lucas's father continued. "One day Captain Smith sailed away, leaving Thomas Hunt, one of his crew, in charge. Hunt seemed friendly and soon invited Tisquantum aboard his ship. Tisquantum was excited. He had never been on board one of the enormous European ships, with masts that could be seen on boats far off in the horizon. But what seemed like a friendly invitation was actually a trick. With guns drawn, Hunt and his crew locked Tisquantum in the hull, or body, of the ship."

"Oh, no!" Lucas exclaimed. "Well, you haven't gotten to the first Thanksgiving yet, so I'm sure Tisquantum will be fine, right?"

"Listen and you'll find out," Lucas's father said with a wink. "After being forced onto the ship, Tisquantum found himself in a pitch-black room. He blinked as his eyes struggled to adjust to the darkness. Although he could not see his surroundings, he knew he was at sea. The gentle rocking of the vessel and the soft splash of the waves hitting the ship's side told Tisquantum he was in the middle of the ocean. For six long weeks, Tisquantum was held captive on the ship. Over the course of the six weeks, Tisquantum began to lose track of time. Alone with his thoughts, he could only imagine what was waiting for him."

"What was waiting for him?" Lucas exclaimed.

"A whole new world was waiting for him! When the ship finally reached its final docking place, Tisquantum stepped off onto soil in a world he had never seen before. Hunt's ship had landed at Málaga, a coastal city in Spain. Tisquantum's first images of Europe were magnificent. He saw a grand city with stone buildings that touched the sky. Great wooden ships filled the harbor, and men poured out of them, going in every direction. Thousands of people in vast arrays of decorated fabrics walked the dusty streets. The sounds of the city came together in one loud hum, as if the city itself were speaking. Despite the beauty of the city, Tisquantum was instantly homesick for Cape Cod Bay."

What About You?
Remind your child of the farthest she has been from home. What was the trip like? Did she get homesick?

"I would have been homesick, too! I can't imagine living anywhere else but here. How did Tisquantum get back home?"

"It wasn't easy," Lucas's dad explained. "You see, Thomas Hunt planned to sell Tisquantum into slavery. Tisquantum did not want to become a slave, but there was nothing he could do to escape. One day, though, a group of Spanish monks took Tisquantum from Thomas Hunt and his crew. The monks were against the enslavement of Native Americans. They brought Tisquantum to their monastery and attempted to convert him to Christianity. Tisquantum wasn't interested. He was determined to get home. With barely a basic knowledge of their language and customs, Tisquantum was able to convince the monks to let him go."

"That's amazing! Mom and I speak the same language, and I can't even convince her not to give away my favorite yams," Lucas said with a chuckle.

"Keep listening to Tisquantum's story. I'm hoping it changes your attitude," Lucas's father said. Then he continued. "Tisquantum traveled north, using his growing talent for persuading people to help him. He soon found himself in London, England, the home of John Smith and Thomas Hunt. London was a wholly different city from Málaga. Even more people lived here, crammed into homes of brick and wood. Tisquantum felt like the city was strangling those who lived in it. He thought about how easy it would be to get lost on London's dark and narrow streets. Tisquantum would not allow himself to be trapped in London for long. Overwhelmed but still determined, he continued to look for a way home. His luck began to change when he met John Slaney, who took Tisquantum in and taught him English."

"So that's how he learned English," Lucas said. "Spending time with the Englishmen helped him learn the language."

"That's exactly right. And with the English he learned, Tisquantum convinced Slaney to secure a boat for him to North America, where Slaney had business connections. Tisquantum landed in Newfoundland, a cold and isolated place nearly 1,000 miles north of Cape Cod Bay. He was on the right continent, but nowhere near home. It was impossible for him to walk back. So Tisquantum had to get some help. He found a tiny fishing camp where he met an English merchant named Thomas Dermer. Dermer was impressed that Tisquantum spoke English and knew of his friend John Smith. By now, Tisquantum had plenty of experience dealing with Europeans. He spoke with Dermer about going to Massachusetts and showing him the best places to hunt and find resources. He helped Dermer trade and negotiate with Native Americans. The two soon left for England to find money to pay for an expedition near Tisquantum's home."

"Yes, I knew Tisquantum would make it back home safely!" Lucas said with a smile.

"He made it home, but he was not prepared for what he found. When he finally made it back to Cape Cod Bay, Tisquantum discovered that his village had been destroyed by disease. The home Tisquantum struggled for six years to return to was no more," his father said.

"You mean his family and friends were all gone?" Lucas asked sadly.

"Yes, they were. Tisquantum was distraught. He left Dermer and his crew and set off on his own. Near what was once his home, Tisquantum was seized by members of the Wampanoag confederation and sent to Massasoit, their great leader, as a captive. Unlike Tisquantum, Massasoit had witnessed the sickness and disease that killed off both Tisquantum's people and his own people. Massasoit struggled to keep the surviving people together and lead them against the Europeans who began living in sites where Native Americans used to live. He also had to protect his people against other Native American groups that had not been affected by the disease. Massasoit was not quick to trust the Europeans or other Native Americans, like Tisquantum," his father continued.

"How did Massasoit and Tisquantum begin working together?" Lucas inquired.

"Well, Tisquantum told Massasoit of his journey. Massasoit distrusted Tisquantum because of his association with the Europeans. What if Tisquantum decided to side with the Europeans? Tisquantum could give them the information they needed to defeat Massasoit's people. However, Massasoit knew that Tisquantum's English would come in handy for negotiations, and the two formed an uneasy partnership. With Tisquantum's people gone, he needed to ally himself with a new group to help him stay alive. Meanwhile, he was also hoping that he might form a new faction within the Wampanoag, essentially resurrecting his old tribe. Tisquantum's ability to speak both the Native American tongue and English gave him power. This threat pushed Massasoit to keep Tisquantum close."

"That was smart of Tisquantum," Lucas observed. "He needed Massasoit's help and found a way to make sure he got it!"

"Yes, he did. Massasoit and Tisquantum worked together, although neither man really trusted the other. Massasoit knew of people from England who had arrived at Patuxet, Tisquantum's old home, which they were calling Plymouth. These Pilgrims had struggled through the winter. They didn't know how to do tasks, like farming, that came easy to the Native Americans. But they did have interesting tools, such as knives and kettles, that Massasoit had never seen before. In the spring, Massasoit sent Tisquantum to speak with them. Massasoit hoped to ally himself with the Europeans to cut off an enemy tribe, the Narragansett. Tisquantum decided to befriend these Europeans. By allying himself with them, he planned to re-form the Patuxet tribe and distance himself from Massasoit. He used his experience in Europe and his knowledge of English to help the Pilgrims. He helped them grow huge crops of maize, or corn, and helped them hunt in their new surroundings. With Tisquantum's help, Plymouth turned from a small colony of survivors into a growing community. To give thanks for helping them survive, the Europeans shared a feast with the Native Americans. Over several days, they had several dinners, which became known as the first Thanksgiving!"

"That's the part of the story I know," said Lucas. "But now I understand why Tisquantum was so willing to help. Did he ever succeed in re-forming his tribe?"

"Unfortunately, no. This story does not have a happy ending for Tisquantum. Over time, the Wampanoag, just as the Patuxet had, dwindled in number due to disease and war. Tisquantum never re-formed his tribe," Lucas's father answered.

Massasoit and the Pilgrims meet to discuss how to live together peacefully.

Thanksgiving: Peace and Plenty

During the spring and summer of 1621, the Pilgrims built more homes near the ocean shore. Following Tisquantum's advice, they raised good crops. With William Bradford as their new governor, the Pilgrims decided to celebrate their success (and survival) with a harvest festival. They invited their Wampanoag friends to the celebration. Bradford sent fishermen and hunters to bring back food. Chief Massasoit and 90 of his men also hunted in the forest and brought deer.

For three days, the Wampanoag and Pilgrims feasted on goose, duck, turkey, venison, cod, bass, stewed pumpkin, corn bread, and wild onions, among other foods and drinks. The English fired guns, danced jigs, and sang psalms. The Wampanoag chanted hymns and danced in ways that made their stone necklaces bounce on their chests. They all struggled to communicate in broken Wampanoag and English. For three days in the fall of 1621, European and Native Americans gathered in peace and friendship. We still remember this gathering as the first Thanksgiving.

What do you see in this picture that reminds you of Thanksgiving at your house?

Massachusetts Bay: The Puritans

The Pilgrims soon had company on the shores of New England. Another group of English colonists, called the Puritans, began arriving in large numbers. The Puritans were deeply religious, well educated, and highly skilled at various crafts. They included tailors, cobblers, weavers, blacksmiths, lawyers, and teachers. Like the Pilgrims, they were dissatisfied with the practices of the Church of England. They wanted to "purify" their religion by bringing it closer to their sense of the Bible's teachings. While the Pilgrims wanted the freedom to worship in their own way, the Puritans wanted to change the Church of England.

Of course, changing the Church did not please the English kings. When King James died in 1625, his son became King Charles I, which was bad news for the Puritans. He threw them in jail, kept them from their jobs, and made life miserable for them.

The Puritan leaders decided to form a church in the New World. King Charles chartered the Massachusetts Bay Company, giving them the right to establish a colony in New England. He was happy to see the Puritans leave.

By the end of the summer in 1630, about 1,000 Puritans had arrived in New England. They were led by John Winthrop, a wealthy lawyer. Governor Winthrop told the Puritans that they must set an example for the world to see. "We must always consider that we shall be as a city upon a hill," he said. "The eyes of all people are upon us."

During the next 10 years, the Puritans did more than build a single "city upon a hill." With 20,000 more Puritans arriving in the Massachusetts Bay Colony between 1630 and 1643, they built *lots* of towns and cities. Salem came first, and then Boston, which was well placed on a bay and bordered by a river. Boston became the capital of the Massachusetts Bay Colony.

As the ambitious Puritans kept spreading, they established three new colonies: Connecticut, Rhode Island, and New Hampshire.

People of the Book

The Puritans cared most of all about their faith, which was based on a close and careful reading of the Bible. Most Puritans could read, and they were determined to keep it this way. One of the first laws the Massachusetts Bay Colony passed required parents to teach their children to read. This law was later copied in Connecticut, Rhode Island, and New Hampshire.

Then, the Massachusetts Bay Colony passed another important law. Every town with at least 50 families was to open a grammar school to teach reading, Latin, and Greek, "to instruct youth so far as they may be fitted for the university." A whole system of public schools—schools supported by the towns—sprang up in Massachusetts. The laws did not force students to attend, but the towns were required to provide the schools. This did not exist back in England. But here in New England, not just the children of wealthy parents but *any* child could receive an education. This was the primary goal of public education—and it began with the Massachusetts General School Law of 1647, a law the Puritans passed. The Puritans wanted to educate new ministers and lawmakers, too, so they founded Harvard College, still one of the most respected universities in the world.

Roger Williams and Rhode Island

The Puritans thought they were following the truth, and there could be only one truth. This belief ended up causing conflicts with people who had different beliefs.

One such person was Roger Williams, a Puritan minister. Williams had come to Massachusetts Bay in 1631, just a year after John Winthrop arrived with a large group of settlers. Williams was a thoughtful man, but in Massachusetts Bay his thoughts got him in trouble.

For one thing, Roger Williams said that the king of England had no right to grant the settlers of Massachusetts Bay a charter, because the land belonged to the Native Americans. Williams also said that a government had no right to decide the religion of its subjects, and that individuals should be free to decide their own religious beliefs.

These bold ideas worried Winthrop, the governor of Massachusetts Bay Colony. First, the Puritans warned Williams that he needed to change his beliefs. But when he didn't, they **banished** him from Massachusetts Bay. The Puritan leaders planned to send Williams back to England. However,

> **New Word**
> Talk about what the word **banished** means and identify other historical figures who were banished. "Banished" means "forced permanently out of a place."

Williams slipped out of Boston and traveled south, even though he was old and sick. He found shelter with the Narragansett tribe, who helped him make it through the winter.

Williams bought some of the land around the beautiful Narragansett Bay from the local tribe. He called the land Providence, which is another word for God. Providence became the capital of Rhode Island.

Williams was determined to start a colony based on the idea that government should not tell the people how to worship. He believed in the separation of church and state, which became one of the most important ideas upon which the United States was founded. "Separation of church and state" refers to the separation of religion and government. It means that governments should not tell people what to believe.

Williams also practiced religious toleration—accepting people of all religions, even atheists, who don't believe in God. While the Puritans and Pilgrims were rejecting other religious followers, including Quakers, Jews, and Catholics, Roger Williams welcomed them in Rhode Island.

When Roger Williams was banished from the Massachusetts Bay Colony, he traveled to the area we now call Rhode Island. The Narragansett made friends with him and helped him survive the winter.

Anne Hutchinson

Anne Hutchinson came to Massachusetts Bay with her family in 1634, though she was not an ordinary Puritan wife. She was brilliant, and she loved to teach. She held weekly meetings in her home, and more and more people, both men and women, came to hear her discuss the Bible and the teachings of the church.

"MY JUDGMENT IS NOT ALTERED, THOUGH MY EXPRESSION ALTERS," SHE DECLARED, IN RINGING TONES."

The stern Puritan ministers did not trust Anne Hutchinson.

Like Roger Williams, Hutchinson said bold and daring things that worried most Puritan leaders. For example, she said that God communicated with people directly, not through church officials. She also said that most of the ministers in Massachusetts Bay did not teach the Bible properly.

The Puritans could hardly believe their ears. Who was this woman, a mother of 14 children, who dared to tell the Puritan ministers what to think? Didn't she know that she should remain quiet and obedient, like a good Puritan wife?

In 1637, the Puritan leaders put Anne Hutchinson on trial. Governor Winthrop said she "troubled the peace of the commonwealth" with her ideas. Hutchinson told her judges, "Now if you do condemn me for speaking what in my conscience I know to be truth, I must commit myself unto the Lord." In the end, the Puritan court declared that she was "unfit for our society." As a result, they banished her from the colony and kicked her out of the church.

She and her family went to Rhode Island, which had become the colony for "dissenters"—people who did not agree with the official religion, whether the Church of England or the Puritans.

One People's Prosperity, Another's Peril

More and more people, most of them Puritans, left England for Massachusetts Bay. They spread out and settled in what are now the states of Connecticut and New Hampshire. They tended small farms. They chopped down trees to sell as lumber. They caught plenty of fish to sell. They also began a new industry, shipbuilding. The timber from New England forests supplied busy shipyards.

Talk and Think

New England bustled with busy ports and shipyards. But down south, Virginia and other colonies relied more on agriculture, growing crops such as tobacco, rice, and cotton. How do you think this affected the colonists' goals and lifestyles?

As the New Englanders built more towns and farms, they expanded into the land where Native Americans had hunted, fished, and farmed for centuries. Often small fights broke out between colonists and natives. Sometimes the Native Americans attacked the colonists first and burned their homes. The colonists struck back fiercely, attacking even the friendly Narragansett in Rhode Island.

However, the Native Americans suffered even more because of the diseases that came to the New World from Europe. The native people had never been exposed to European diseases, such as smallpox, chicken pox, and measles. Over time, the Native American population in New England decreased by 90 percent. Disease caused most of these deaths, but fighting and social disorder also contributed.

Maryland and Pennsylvania: Refuges for Other Religions

Soon other English colonies stretched between New England and Virginia. As in Massachusetts Bay, people seeking religious freedom founded both Pennsylvania and Maryland. First let's learn how Pennsylvania became a refuge, or safe place, for Quakers, who were being treated badly in England.

Their real name was the Society of Friends, but the English called them Quakers because the Friends appeared to shake or "quake" when they prayed. Quakers did not believe in churches or formal religious ceremonies. They thought war was morally wrong and refused to fight. They believed loyalty to anyone but God was wrong, so they refused to be loyal to the king.

Quakers believed God spoke to each individual and guided him or her through an "inner light" in the soul. They said that people did not need to listen to priests or ministers, or even study the Bible. Instead, they simply needed to sit quietly and learn to be guided by their inner light. In God's eyes, the Quakers said, all people are equal. As a result, they would not bow down to dukes, lords, or other members of the upper class in England.

Make a Connection

Quakers believed that all men and women are equal in God's eyes, including Native Americans and Africans. Quakers were among the first people in America to say that slavery was wrong. However, turn to page 227 to see why the slave trade continued.

William Penn was a wealthy, well-educated gentleman, and the son of a famous British naval hero. Penn had joined the Society of Friends when he was young. His father wanted him to stay in the Church of England, but Penn stayed true to his beliefs, even though he was thrown in jail for having them.

After his father died, William Penn went to see King Charles II. The king had borrowed money from William's father, and now Penn wanted to be paid back. For years, Penn had dreamed of starting a "holy experiment" by creating a Quaker colony in North America. He asked the king to pay him back with a large amount of land instead of money.

In 1677, the king gave Penn 45,000 square miles, an area larger than England itself. Penn wanted to name it Sylvania, which means "woods." The king suggested that William honor his father by calling it Pennsylvania, or "Penn's woods."

William Penn wasted no time. He printed brochures urging people to move to Pennsylvania, which welcomed not just Quakers but people of all religions, including Jews and Catholics. In 1680, there were only about 700 colonists in Pennsylvania. But by 1700, there were 18,000! People arrived from Germany, the Netherlands, Scotland, and other countries.

For the colony's capital, Penn chose a site on the Delaware River and named it

William Penn

Make a Connection

Much later, in 1776, when the colonies declared their independence from Great Britain, the southeastern part of Pennsylvania became Delaware—the first state in the United States.

Philadelphia, which means "city of brotherly love." Penn helped plan the city. He laid out the streets in an orderly crisscross pattern. Philadelphia quickly grew into a busy port town and one of the American colonies' most important cities.

A Refuge for Catholics

To understand why the colony of Maryland was founded, we should first consider religion in England. In the early 1600s, a wealthy nobleman, Sir George Calvert, shocked the English when he became Roman Catholic. At this time, almost all Englishmen belonged to the Church of England, which had separated from the Roman Catholic Church during the 1500s. Calvert had been forced to give up an important government job because of his religion. He thought his next step should be to start a colony in America that would welcome Catholics. Thankfully, King Charles I still liked him. In 1632, the king issued him a charter for a colony in America, stretching from the Potomac River to what is now Philadelphia.

A map of colonial Maryland from 1675

George Calvert died soon after the king granted him the charter. But his son Cecil [SESS-ul] Calvert carried on with his father's plans to start the new colony and sent his brother to be the first governor. They named the new colony Maryland after King Charles's wife, Queen Henrietta Maria (and also for Mary, the mother of Jesus).

In 1634, while Puritans were settling in Massachusetts Bay, about 250 colonists landed in Maryland. This time, the settlers had planned better and arrived in March, with plenty of time to plant crops and prepare for winter. They traded with friendly Native American tribes. They started growing tobacco. With its climate and many rivers, Maryland got off to a good start and continued growing.

Talk and Think

George Calvert held the title of Lord Baltimore. His son Cecil was the second Lord Baltimore. Now you know where Baltimore, Maryland's busy port city, got its name! What do you think the name of your hometown means? Do some research with your child to find out what it means.

New Netherland

By 1700, the British colonies in North America had grown into bustling, crowded places. Up and down the Atlantic seaboard, colonists of many different religions and backgrounds built their homes. Most of these colonists came from England. However, the area we call New York started out as New Netherland, which belonged to the Dutch.

Remember how the English explorer Henry Hudson, who sailed for the Dutch East India Company, had claimed this area for Holland? Try to find Holland (which is also called the Netherlands) on a map of Europe. The country is tiny, but during the 1600s, it was a powerful country with a strong navy and many colonies around the world.

The Dutch wanted to turn New Netherland into a fur-trading post. First, they needed more land, so in 1626, they bought a neighboring island from the local Manhate Indians. Legend says that the Dutch bought the island for a bunch of beads worth $24. You might think, "What a bargain," especially since this island is the one we call Manhattan, the heart of today's New York City.

Soon, windmills were going up everywhere. Dutch colonists built the port town of New Amsterdam on the tip of Manhattan Island. They planned to grow rich by shipping furs from this location. French, Germans, Swedes, and Finns came to settle in the colony, as did people from Brazil. Jews from Spain and Por-

A New Amsterdam street in the 1600s.

tugal also made their home in New Amsterdam. If you walked down the streets of New Amsterdam, you would have heard more than a dozen different languages—much as you can in New York City today!

Yet over time, the Dutch seemed more interested in maintaining their colonies in India and South America. They failed to set up an effective government in New Netherland. Everybody fought over money or argued about the laws. No one could make the colony work. The British decided to take advantage of the confusion. In 1664, English ships sailed into New Amsterdam, demanding that the Dutch surrender the colony to King Charles II. The king gave the land as a gift to his brother, the Duke of York, who changed its name to his own: New York. This area included most of New York and parts of New Jersey.

Charles's Carolina

Names of places often tell us who was important in history. Consider the names of the colonies south of Virginia that we call North and South Carolina. Where do you think the name "Carolina" came from? The answer is Carolus, Latin for "Charles," because Charles II was the king of England at the time.

King Charles granted a charter for one big colony between Virginia and

Florida, to be called Carolina. The colony had a fine harbor, which was named—I bet you can guess—Charles Town. In time, this name changed to Charleston, which grew to become one of the busiest ports in all the colonies.

With a charter that granted total religious freedom, Carolina attracted people from all over, including the northern colonies. During the 1680s, settlers moved into Carolina from the older colonies, which had high populations. Puritan New Englanders, land-hungry Virginians, English and French dissenters, Scots, and many colonists from the West Indies poured into Carolina.

Talk and Think
Ask your child to explain how the different economies of the northern and southern colonies set the stage for the Civil War.

Carolina had two big cash crops: rice and indigo (a fine blue dye). The large farms that grew these crops required lots of hard labor. At first, indentured servants—Europeans, Africans, and Native Americans—worked together on the Carolina farms. But farmers began to rely more on enslaved Africans, and soon there were more enslaved people than free people in the colony.

In the early 1700s, Carolina split into two colonies—North and South Carolina. Then the king of England took back the region farthest south for a new colony. He called it Georgia. Guess what the king's name was? If you guessed George, you're correct! It was King George II, to be exact.

Many enslaved African Americans worked in the fields in South Carolina and Georgia.

A Debtor's Tale

Imagine that the year is 1730. Your family lives in a small, dark room of a run-down building in a dirty section of London. Rats scurry beneath the rickety wooden table.

Your parents work hard every day, yet somehow they cannot afford to pay their bills. You and your little brother beg for food each day on a street corner. Then one day an English **constable** drags your father off to jail because he didn't pay his debts. He throws your father into debtors' prison, where he will stay for a long time. Now, without your father's income, how will your family ever survive?

Today we can see why debtors' prisons were a terrible idea. Back then, though, only a few people saw the problems with getting out of this prison. James Edward Oglethorpe wanted to give debtors a second chance. He went to King George II and said something to the effect of, "Don't send debtors to prison. Give them a chance to do something useful. Send them to a colony in the New World and let them work off their debts."

The king agreed. He liked the idea of sending more English people to the land that bordered Florida. Britain's main rival, Spain, owned Florida. King George II thought, "If I can get colonists to settle there, they will defend the land against the Spaniards."

So in 1733, James Oglethorpe set off for Georgia with about 115 colonists. As it turned out, most of them were *not* debtors. Oglethorpe found that most debtors preferred to remain in England, even in prison, rather than face the dangers of the New World.

Oglethorpe and his colonists settled between two rivers, in the area we now call Savannah, Georgia. The colonists in Georgia made friends with the Creek tribe, who hated the Spanish. Together, the colonists and the Creek drove the Spaniards back to Florida. However, they did not take over Florida from the Spanish, which is what the English wanted.

By 1743, James Oglethorpe had run up so much debt from his efforts that he had to go back to England to be put on trial! Would Oglethorpe himself be sent to debtors' prison? Fortunately, the jury let him go. But Oglethorpe was fed up. He returned the charter to King George II and told the king, ever so politely, to run the colony himself.

The Slave Trade

Today we can understand why slavery is wrong. No one should take away any person's freedom (except when a person has been convicted of a dangerous crime). No human can own another person the way you own a piece of furniture. But in the 1600s and 1700s, many people believed differently, and few people tried to prevent slavery.

Between the 1580s and early 1800s, European traders transported *10 million* enslaved people to European colonies in North and South America. More than 9 out of 10 of these slaves went to Central and South America, including Caribbean islands with big sugar plantations. About half a million slaves came to North America.

The growing demand for farmworkers in the colonies led to a horrible expansion of the business of buying and selling human beings. Europeans took goods such as guns and cloth to Africa and traded them for enslaved people. The slave-ship captains clamped chains onto the wrists and ankles of hundreds of Africans, cramming them into tightly packed quarters below deck. The Middle Passage—crossing the Atlantic Ocean from Africa to the Americas—became the nightmare of many Africans. Many died before they even reached America.

Those who did survive faced a life of hard work with little hope for freedom. They could not own property. They could not marry. They could be sold at any point. Families could be broken up, and the parents' children sold to a new master hundreds of miles away.

The southern colonies, such as Virginia and the Carolinas, came to rely more and more on enslaved Africans to work on the plantations. Most enslaved people worked as field hands, growing tobacco, rice, and indigo. Others worked as craftspeople and house servants.

> **Make a Connection**
> Turn to the story "The People Could Fly" on page 48 and discuss what this story says about the way enslaved people felt about their situation.

With an overseer watching, slaves worked to hoe the fields.

But slavery did not just exist in the southern colonies. It's true that during the 1800s, the South defended slavery, while the North opposed it. But back in the 1600s, people were enslaved in almost every colony. Most came from Africa, but some were Native Americans.

You might be thinking, "How horrible! Why didn't anybody stop them?" A few people tried, but they were a minority. The Quakers in Pennsylvania wanted slavery to end. But the sad truth is, when the United States was founded, not many people thought slavery was wrong.

Suggested Resources

World Geography
Helping Your Child with Maps and Globes, by Bruce Frazee and William Guardia (Good Year Books, 1994)
Living Near a River, by Alan Fowler (Children's Press, 2000)
Maps and Globes, by Jack Knowlton (HarperCollins, 1986)

World History

Ancient Rome, by Daniel Cohen (Doubleday Books for Young Readers, 1992)

Growing Up in Ancient Rome, by Mike Corbishley (Troll Communications, 1997)

What a Viking!, by Mick Manning and Brita Granstrom (R & S Books, 2000)

Who Were the Vikings?, by Jane Chishold and Struan Reid (E.D.C. Publishing, 2002)

American History

Children of the Earth and Sky: Five Stories About Native American Children, by Stephen Krensky (Scholastic Trade, 1992)

Children of the Wind and Water: Five Stories About Native American Children, by Stephen Krensky (Cartwheel Books, 1994)

Early Explorers in North America

Beyond the Sea of Ice: The Voyages of Henry Hudson, by Joan Elizabeth Goodman (Mikaya Press, 1999)

Explorers of the New World: Francisco Coronado and the Exploration of the American Southwest, by Hal Marcovitz (Chelsea House Publications, 1999)

Explorers of the New World: Hernando de Soto and the Exploration of Florida, by Jim Gallagher (Chelsea House Publications, 1999)

Explorers of the New World: Juan Ponce de León and the Search for the Fountain of Youth, by Dan Harmon (Chelsea House Publications, 2000)

English Colonies in North America

Colonial Life, by Brendan January (Children's Press, 2001)

If You Lived in Colonial Times, by Ann McGovern (Scholastic Paperbacks, 1992)

The New Americans: Colonial Times: 1620–1689, by Betsy Maestro (HarperCollins, 2004)

On the Mayflower, by Kate Waters (Scholastic Press, 1996)

III
Visual Arts

Introduction

For third graders, as in earlier years, the primary experience of art should come by *doing*: drawing, painting, cutting and pasting, working with clay and other materials. A few such activities are suggested here, but many more can be developed to complement your child's discovery of image and light, shape and color.

No book can offer the experience of actually viewing works of art in person by visiting museums and galleries. This chapter suggests how to introduce concepts and vocabulary to third graders, helping them talk about what they see, what the artist decided, and how it affects them. By looking closely at these works of art, both classic masterpieces and fine folk and ethnic artworks, you help enlarge your child's mental museum of our culture's finest works.

Caught in the Light

Think about waking up on a bright sunny day. As the sunlight pours through the windows of your room, it makes every detail stand out and every color seem brighter. You feel bright and alive inside, ready to face the day.

Now think about waking up on a dark and cloudy morning. Your room looks gray and blurred. Don't you wish you could pull the covers over your head and go back to sleep?

The Milkmaid, Johannes Vermeer, 1657–1658.

Light can affect the way you feel. It can lift your spirits and make you feel happy. Without light, you can feel sad and dreary. The way that artists use light in their paintings can affect your emotions as well.

Let's look at the painting called *The Milkmaid* by the Dutch artist Johannes Vermeer [YO-hon fair-MEER]. Vermeer has made this milkmaid's kitchen feel warm and bright and pleasant to be in. Sunlight pours through the window. It brightens the woman and all the objects in the room. It makes the metal lantern shine and highlights the rim of the pitcher.

Of course, there is no real sunlight in this painting. Vermeer has made you think that there is. By carefully studying how different surfaces reflect light, he painted what you would expect to see in a sunny room. The light seems to reflect off shiny objects. Even the white wall and the wood of the foot warmer on the floor seem to shine. He also made sure that some things in the painting were quite dark. The sharp contrast between dark and light makes the bright things look even brighter.

Look at the way Vermeer uses color. He knew that the colors we see depend on how much light is falling on them. He makes us think that sunlight is coming in through the window by making the white of the milkmaid's hat, the yellow of her dress, and the blue of her apron brightest on the side close to the window. The back of her skirt and the bottom of her apron are darker, because the light does not reach them. Compare the bright wall behind the milkmaid to the dark wall under the window.

Now let's look at the way another artist uses light. Look at the painting on the next page called *Ruby Green Singing* by the American artist James Chapin. This painting is full of light. But unlike Vermeer, Chapin decided not to show the source of the light. In *Ruby Green Singing*, where do you think the light is coming from? Is it sunlight? How are the dark and light colors in this painting different from the dark and light colors in *The Milkmaid*?

> **Talk and Think**
> What do you think the milkmaid is cooking? Do you see the bread? Bread pudding is made from bread and milk. One theory is that she is making bread pudding.

> **Make a Connection**
> Read about the way in which light travels in the science chapter. Explain to your child that light passes through transparent objects and is blocked by opaque objects. After reading that section, revisit Vermeer's painting *The Milkmaid*. Ask your child to point out transparent and opaque objects in the scene.

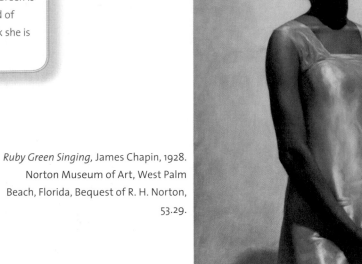

Ruby Green Singing, James Chapin, 1928. Norton Museum of Art, West Palm Beach, Florida, Bequest of R. H. Norton, 53.29.

Like the milkmaid in Vermeer's painting, Ruby Green is the only person in this painting. Her upturned face is framed by her dark hair and the shadows beneath her chin. Look at the flashes of light in Ruby Green's eyes and on her teeth. Why might Chapin have highlighted these features?

Out of the Shadows

Have you ever been surprised by a flash of lightning in a dark, stormy sky? The man standing in the center of the next painting looks as though the same thing just happened to him!

The Dutch artist Rembrandt [REM-brant] painted *Belshazzar's Feast*. The painting tells a story from the Bible. While King Belshazzar was giving a great feast, a hand suddenly appeared and wrote a message on the wall, predicting that the king would be overthrown. Belshazzar could not read the message, but seeing

Belshazzar's Feast, Rembrandt, c. 1635.

the hand appear out of nowhere astonished him. This painting captures his look of surprise.

Rembrandt was a master at showing sharp differences between light and shadow. You can clearly see the profile of King Belshazzar, but you have to strain to see the shapes in the dark shadows. You can see all the details of Belshazzar's robe but little of the clothes on the bearded man behind him. Rembrandt has used the contrast between dark and light to make the scene look more exciting.

Rembrandt applied dabs of white paint to indicate reflections from the light. There are glints of light on the metal surfaces, silky fabrics, and sparkling jewels. Can you find the strands of pearls, the crown, and the plate of grapes that Rembrandt has highlighted as well?

Do It Yourself

Light and shadow can affect facial expressions in dramatic ways. Have your child stand in front of a mirror in a well-lit room and make different expressions—fear, anger, surprise. Now darken the room and have your child repeat the faces while shining a flashlight on his face from the side, then from above, and then from below. Ask your child how the expressions look different with the flashlight rather than in full light.

Do It Yourself

Create a mosaic with your child using colored paper, glue, and cardboard. First, have your child draw a picture on the cardboard. Next, cut the colored paper into tiny pieces and glue them to the picture to create a mosaic.

A Wall Filled with Light

Let's take an imaginary trip to the beautiful city of Ravenna, Italy, to visit the church called San Vitale, which houses world-famous mosaics. A mosaic is made from thousands of tiny pieces of colored glass, jewels, or precious metals, fitted together like a puzzle to create an image.

Mosaics cover the walls of San Vitale. The mosaic you see here shows the empress Theodora and her court. In the world history section of this book, you can read about Theodora's husband, the emperor Justinian, who ruled the Byzantine Empire. This mosaic is a good example of Byzantine art.

This mosaic from Ravenna shows the empress Theodora and her court.

Many great works of art were created in the Byzantine Empire, which lasted from about 400 CE to 1400 CE. Because Christianity was so important during this period, much of this art was made for churches. This mosaic honors the empress Theodora because she and her husband built many new Christian churches.

The mosaic in San Vitale looks as if it is filled with light. Much of the background is made of gold, which catches and reflects the light coming through windows or from candles. Byzantine artists used gold to remind people of heaven and embellished mosaics with colorful glass and jewels. Imagine how it would feel to be in a room full of mosaics shimmering with all the colors of the rainbow!

Can you tell which figure is Theodora in the mosaic? She is the tallest figure, carrying a golden cup. What else makes her more noticeable than the others?

If you actually visited San Vitale, you would see that this mosaic is quite large.

Here is a close-up of Theodora's face so you can see the tiles that make up the mosaic.

The figures are almost life-size. Just think how many tiny squares it took to make Theodora!

Filling a Space

Circles, triangles, and squares are plane figures. Spheres, pyramids, and cubes are solid figures. A painter starts with a flat plane—a wall, piece of paper, or cloth—and paints shapes that are supposed to look solid. She begins in two dimensions—height and width—and creates something that looks like it has three dimensions: height, width, and depth. But how does a painter make something that looks round, thick, deep, or far away?

Try this experiment. Look out a window. Some of the things you see are farther away than others. Those things appear smaller and may be partially blocked from your view by other things that are closer to you. You can't see the trees behind your neighbor's house as clearly as you can see the tree in your own yard.

The trees that are far away are not as clear, and their colors are not as bright. They seem smaller, even though you know that they are as big as the nearby tree.

What you are seeing can be divided into three parts:

- The foreground (those things closest to you, like your tree)
- The background (those things farthest from you, like the trees in back of the house)
- The middle ground (those things between the foreground and the background, like the house)

Many paintings also have a foreground, background, and middle ground. For example, let's look at a farm scene called *The Gleaners*, painted by the French artist Jean-François Millet [mee-YAY]. The central figures in the painting are

The Gleaners, Jean-François Millet, 1857.

three women who are gleaning, or gathering what is left in a field after the harvest.

Millet makes you focus on the women by placing them in the foreground, where they are larger and more brightly colored than anything else in the painting. While their faces are not visible, you can see the detail of their clothes and the stalks they hold in their hands. In back of them, in the middle ground, you see a wagon, several large stacks of grain, and many people. There is hardly any detail in these shapes, and the colors are much paler. They seem little more than dabs of paint. The buildings and trees far in the background are even smaller. They seem out of focus, so pale they seem to fade away.

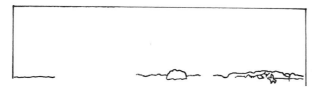

These buildings and trees and this person on a horse are in the background.

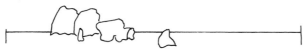

This wagon and these stacks of grain are in the middle ground.

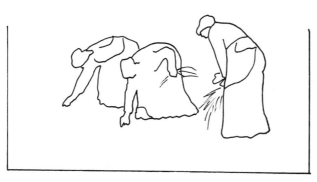

These figures are in the foreground.

Do It Yourself

Help your child practice drawing using what you've just read about foreground, middle ground, and background. It might help to fold the paper in thirds horizontally. The bottom section becomes the foreground, the middle section the middle ground, and the top section the background.

Take a Look

Look at the painting titled *Victorian Interior II* on page 251. Ask your child if this painting has a foreground, a middle ground, and a background, or if it is flat. Do the same for the paintings on pages 243 and 244.

Now let's look at a painting called *Peasant Wedding*, which gives us a view of a room filled with people. These are peasants, poor farm people like the women in *The Gleaners*.

Have you ever been to a wedding in a barn? When the artist Pieter Bruegel [BROY-gul] was painting in Northern Europe, peasant families would often hold weddings in barns.

Bruegel places people in the foreground, middle ground, and background to add depth to the painting and make the wedding look like a packed and lively event. What happens to the size of the faces and bodies of the people as you look down the table? Can you see the people waiting to enter the room? Did Bruegel paint them with the same amount of detail as the people in the front?

Bruegel used the brightest colors in the foreground. The colors in the background almost blend with the walls. The bride, seated in front of the dark green cloth, has pale skin. The hat hanging above her head makes her stand out. To what are the guests paying the most attention?

Peasant Wedding, Pieter Bruegel the Elder, 1567.

Speaking of Space

Now let's look at the painting called *The Interior of the Pantheon*. The Pantheon is a real building in Rome, Italy, which a Roman emperor built in the second century CE. It has a huge domed ceiling and an opening in the top called an oculus through which you can see the sky.

This painting, created by an Italian artist named Giovanni Panini [jo-VAH-nee pa-NEE-nee], shows the Pantheon in the 18th century, when Panini was alive. Imagine standing in the middle of this room and looking up. You would feel very small. Look how small the artist made the figures in this painting, to convey that sense of the space.

Panini has used lines, shapes, color, and shadow to make a two-dimensional painting look like a three-dimensional scene. The dome takes up most of the space of the painting—it towers high above the people inside. There are dozens of people inside, but the inside of the building still looks spacious and wide. The sunlight comes through the oculus and spreads into the vast indoor space. You can see far into the background where tiny specks of people are walking outside.

Make a Connection

Look at the pictures of Roman architecture on pages 145 and 147 of the geography and history chapter. Then have students study *The Interior of the Pantheon* on this page. Ask your child to describe the characteristics of Roman architecture.

Take a Look

Ask your child to look closely at the painting *The Interior of the Pantheon*. Point out ways the artist creates a sense of space, such as the size of the people, the darker shading near the top of the dome, and the circle of sunlight on the wall.

The Interior of the Pantheon, Giovanni Paolo Panini, c. 1734.

Design

What have we been looking at in these paintings? Light and shadow, bright colors and dark colors, shapes and lines, and a sense of space. All these different elements work together in every painting. We use the word "design" to refer to the way the artist made the elements of a piece of art work together. Let's look at some more artworks and think about their design.

First, let's look at *The Horse Fair.* The artist who painted it spent a year and a half attending horse sales, studying the animals, and making sketches. During the entire time, the artist wore a disguise—because she was a woman.

The Horse Fair, Rosa Bonheur, 1852–1855.

Her name was Rosa Bonheur [baw-NUR]. In the 1800s, when Bonheur lived, only men went to the horse market. But Bonheur wanted to go. She got permission from the head of police and dressed as a man, so no one told her to leave.

Let's look at the way she uses light in *The Horse Fair.* Where do you look first? Most people look first at the light-colored horses and the white shirts of the men near them. Do you see how Bonheur has made those horses and men seem to form a ring? As your eyes look at them, they move in a circle. You can almost feel all the motion in the painting.

Now, let's look at all the diagonal lines, made by the legs of the horses and the bodies of the men. Can you see the push and pull? The zigzag lines of some of the horses' legs make them seem alive and moving.

The Horse Fair is said to be the largest animal painting ever done, more than 16 feet long and 8 feet high—large enough to cover an entire wall! The painting makes such a strong impression not only because it is big but also because the artist's design includes so much movement and energy.

Using Lines to Design

When you decide to draw a picture, what do you do? You probably begin by drawing lines. Painters also design by using lines.

Let's look at how the artist uses lines in the next painting, called *The Child's Bath*, painted by the American artist Mary Cassatt [cah-SAHT] more than 100 years ago. In *The Child's Bath*, we see more than just a woman washing a child. We also sense the tenderness of mother and child. How does Cassatt show this?

The Child's Bath, Mary Cassall, 1893.

Look at the way the mother cradles her child on her lap. Look at how closely their heads are drawn together.

Cassatt uses lines to show the connection between the woman and her child. The lines of the mother's sleeve lead your eyes to the basin. Your eyes follow the curve of the basin, and then they move back up to see the body of the child. Then your eyes look again at the heads of the two figures. Your eyes have traveled in a circle, which is part of the artist's design in this painting.

Cassatt has used light in her painting, too. Look at the little

Take a Look
Ask your child to describe the colors in the painting *The Child's Bath*. Ask, "Why do you think the artist chose these colors?"

girl's legs. One side is darker than the other. Look at the glints of light in the hair of both mother and child. Whenever you notice lines and light in a painting, you are noticing the artist's design.

Lines, Shapes, and Colors Move

Now let's look at the design of a very useful object: a warm bedcover called a quilt.

Quilting has been an important part of American life and art for centuries. Quilts were inexpensive ways to help people survive cold weather. A quilt made from worn-out clothing and fabrics that had been sewn together could provide warmth for a family. However, quilting is also an art form that may be passed

Double Irish Chain Quilt, Margie Gorrect, c. 1850.

Make a Connection

Read about lines of symmetry on page 345 of the math chapter. After reading this section, ask students to identify at least two lines of symmetry in the Double Irish Chain Quilt or the Willow Oak Quilt.

down in families from generation to generation. The many distinct designs found on quilts tell the stories of the people who made them and the things that were important to them.

Quilting was mostly done by women and was often a group activity. Often all the women in town would turn their sewing work into a party, called a quilting bee. Quilting provided an opportunity for women in a community to come together and share ideas. Making art meant fun for everyone.

Let's look at a quilt made around 1850 by a woman named Margie Gorrect, who lived in Pennsylvania. The design in this quilt is called Double Irish Chain in Christmas Colors. This design is made by repeating a shape over and over in a regular pattern. The shapes inside the lines of red and green squares are symmetrical. A shape is symmetrical when you can fold it in half (maybe just in your imagination) and the halves match perfectly. What about the entire quilt? Is its design symmetrical?

The design of this quilt makes your eyes travel from square to square, along all the straight lines. Your eyes also travel because of the artist's choice of colors. Red and green are **complementary** colors. When complementary colors are placed side by side, they appear more vivid.

> **New Word**
> "Complementary" sounds like "complimentary," but it doesn't mean "to express a compliment or praise."
> **Complementary** means "to combine things in a way that emphasizes the qualities of each."

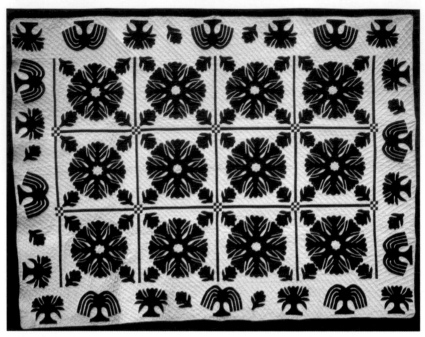

Willow Oak Quilt.

Now let's look at another quilt. Its pattern is called Willow Oak. We don't know who made it. We do know she cut many copies of the same shapes out of blue fabric and stitched them in a regular pattern onto a white piece of fabric. How many different shapes do you see?

To answer that question, you probably counted the blue shapes. But there are white shapes in this design, too. The blue shapes are the figures. The white shapes are the ground. An artist pays attention to both the figures and the ground in creating a design.

There's another element of design that adds beauty to these quilts, something you can't feel from a picture in a book. The quilt artist created a lovely texture. If you could run your hands over these quilts, you would feel the stitches. Even they form part of the quilt's design.

A Color Wheel

A color wheel shows the three primary colors (red, yellow, and blue) and, in between them, the colors (orange, green, and purple) made by mixing the primary colors. Complementary colors are found opposite one another on the color wheel. Can you name the three pairs of complementary colors on this color wheel?

Do It Yourself

Artists can create a wide range of colors by blending paints. Provide your child with paints representing the colors on the color wheel and ask him to combine different colors. What happens when he combines all three primary or secondary colors? What happens when he combines a little of one color with a lot of another color?

Drawing with Scissors

For years, the French artist Henri Matisse [on-REE ma-TEECE] painted bright, colorful pictures. When Matisse became too ill to stand at an easel, he started cutting out paper figures and gluing them onto a ground. Matisse said he was "drawing with scissors." He made collages, works of art made of pictures and papers pasted together in design.

One of Matisse's collages is called *Icarus*, after a Greek myth. Icarus's father,

Daedalus, made wings out of wax and feathers—one pair for himself and the other for Icarus. Before taking off, Daedalus warned Icarus not to fly too close to the sun, or his wings would melt. But Icarus did not listen to his father and flew higher and higher. The wax in his wings melted, and he fell into the sea.

Icare [Icarus], Henri Matisse, 1947, © 2015 Succession H. Matisse/Artists Rights Society (ARS), New York.

Which part of this story do you think Matisse's collage tells? The arms and shoulders of the figure are curved like wings, but he does not seem to be flying. It looks as though gravity is pulling his body down. His right leg hangs a bit below the blue background. What do you think Matisse meant by this? Do you think the blue is the sky or the sea?

Did you notice the bright yellow shapes? They could be feathers or stars. Their sharp straight lines contrast with the curves of the figure. They seem to be moving right off the page. And what about that tiny red oval? In his design, Matisse chose to show Icarus's heart instead of his face. Why do you think he did that?

A Very Formal Room

An African American artist named Horace Pippin painted *Victorian Interior II*. He taught himself and never went to art school. His paintings, like the quilts, belong to a category of art called folk art. Folk art is the art of everyday life, created by people who did not study art in school. Pippin liked to say, "My heart tells my mind what to draw."

Victorian Interior II, Horace Pippin, 1945.

This painting does not seem to have a lot of depth—it looks quite flat. Its design is not exactly symmetrical, but it does have balance. The shapes on one side are similar in size to the shapes on the other.

Pippin made many design decisions as he used lines and colors. What makes the rug look so lively and bright? Is it made of complementary colors? Are there more straight or curved lines in the room? How many circles and ovals? How many rectangles and squares? How many shapes are painted red? Notice how the delicate lines of the white lace doilies break up the heavy, solid furniture.

Make a Connection

Does your child remember the lesson from the American history section on the Quakers? Turn to page 220 so that your child can read the story of the Quakers. Then talk about what the painting *Peaceable Kingdom* expresses about Quaker ideas. Discuss with your child the Quakers' opposition to slavery.

Picturing an Idea

In the American history section of this book, you can read about the Quakers, who came to America looking for religious freedom. They settled in Pennsylvania and hoped to live in peace. Let's look at a painting by a Quaker artist named Edward Hicks. In this painting, he was trying to express a very important idea from the Bible. But before we talk about the idea, let's look carefully at the painting.

Peaceable Kingdom, Edward Hicks, c. 1833.

Do you see anything unusual? All those animals together in one place! What about the little children with the animals? And who are the people in the background?

This painting is called *Peaceable Kingdom*. The artist was probably remembering these lines from the Bible as he designed it: "The wolf shall dwell with the lamb, and the leopard shall lie down with the kid; and the calf and the young lion and the fatling [or young, fattened animal] together; and a little child shall lead them." These lines describe a perfect world of peace, which is what the Quakers hoped their new home in America would be. How does the painting express this idea of a peaceful world?

This painting is very three-dimensional. Hicks painted two scenes in one painting. The children and the animals are painted in the foreground. We can see each shape clearly because of the way Hicks placed dark shapes next to light ones.

The Native Americans and the Quakers are painted in the background, much smaller, to show that they are far away. None of them are looking out from the painting. They just look at each other, busy with their meeting. What do you think they are saying to each other? What do you think the foreground scene has to do with the background scene? Are they both about living in peace? Edward Hicks thought living in peace was so important that he created more than 50 paintings to convey that idea.

Can You Feel It?

What is your first reaction when you look at the painting on the next page by the Norwegian artist Edvard Munch [moonk]? Most people look first at the face of the figure in the foreground. The eye is also drawn to the strange, wavy lines and the colors in the background. Did you expect a red sky?

The artist called this painting *The Scream*. Munch explained that one day he was walking with some friends when suddenly all of nature seemed to cry out. He put his hands to his ears to close out the scream.

Munch belonged to a group of artists called the Expressionists. Expressionist artists tried to show their innermost feelings in their art. Munch had a lot of sadness in his life. Can you see it expressed in his work?

The Scream, 1893 Edward Munch/Erich Lessing/Art Resource, NY © 2014 The Munch Museum/The Munch-Ellingsen Group/Artists Rights Society (ARS), NY.

Do It Yourself

Ask your child to think of an emotion and quickly draw a picture of how that emotion feels. In what ways can a picture express feelings?

Look at the pale hands and skull-like head of the central figure. How would you describe his expression? Fear? Terror? Surprise? His body seems unable to bear the emotion. It seems wavy, as though it might collapse. Only the bridge seems straight and solid in the midst of all that is swirling around. We see these contrasts because of decisions the artist made in his design.

A Quilt That Tells a Story

Faith Ringgold, *Tar Beach*, 1988, acrylic on canvas with fabric borders,
74 × 69 inches. © Faith Ringold 1988.

Take a Look

Ask your child to compare *Tar Beach* to the quilts on pages 246 and 248. What is different about them?

Faith Ringgold, an African American artist, makes quilts that tell stories. This one, called *Tar Beach*, was made in 1988. It tells the story of a girl named Cassie Lightfoot, who lay on the tar-covered rooftop of her building (her "tar beach") and imagined herself flying over the city. Do you see Cassie lying on the rooftop? Do you see Cassie flying? If you read "The People Could Fly" on page 48 of this book, then you know another story in which flying refers to the feeling of being free.

This quilt may seem more complicated than the others in this chapter, but Ringgold used the same process of cutting pieces of cloth and stitching them together. She created a frame of fabric squares all around the quilt. There are other frames in the quilt's design as well. One is formed by the lines and colors that outline the rooftop. Another is formed by the colored fabric on which Cassie and her brother are lying. Ringgold also sewed in 10 fabric blocks, five at the top and five at the bottom, with words that tell Cassie's story. These blocks are stitched in between bright print fabric squares and rectangles. Faith Ringgold also wrote and illustrated a picture book called *Tar Beach* (Dragonfly Books, 1996), which tells the story of Cassie Lightfoot.

Over and Under with Wool and Thread

Here is an image of a beautiful rug that was woven by hand by Navajo Indians. It is called a Ganado [ga-NAW-do] rug, and it is named for a place in Arizona. Ganado rugs have a red background and a dark border around a design of diamonds in black, white, and gray.

We don't know the name of the woman who wove this rug. She probably raised sheep. She sheared the sheep, washed the wool, combed it, and then spun

Take a Look

Point out to your child the zigzag lines on the Ganado rug. Ask your child about the visual effects that these lines create. For example, "How do the zigzag colored lines make you feel? What do they remind you of?"

A Ganado rug.

it into thread. She probably gathered plants to make dyes to color the threads she used for weaving.

A rug like this is woven on a loom. A loom is a large wooden frame that holds lots of threads strung up and down in the same direction. The weaver laces more threads in and out of the threads on the loom, pulling them tight to make a piece

A Navajo woman weaving on a loom.

of cloth. The weaver makes sure the threads stay tight by pressing them down with a wide-toothed comb. She thinks about the design she is making and chooses the color of her next thread with that design in mind.

Just like a painting, this work of art has strong lines and colors that are important in its design. You can divide this rug in half two ways: down or across. The pattern is symmetrical either way. The weaver had to match the pattern from side to side and from top to bottom. She kept track of everything in her head—there were no written instructions for her to follow.

Have you ever woven anything? Maybe you have made a paper place mat by weaving strips of colored paper. Maybe you have made a pot holder by weaving colored loops on a frame. Many pieces of cloth are made by weaving. If you look closely at the clothes you are wearing, you might be able to see the threads that were woven together to make them.

What About You?

Ask your child, "How would you feel if paintings that took you hours to complete were destroyed the next day? Why do you think the Navajo spent so much time creating paintings that would be destroyed so quickly?"

Part of a Native American sandpainting.

A Painting Made Without Brushes or Paint

Have you ever played with sand on the beach, poking your finger in it to draw or letting handfuls of it dribble onto a flat surface? Can you imagine creating a beautiful work of art on the ground by using handfuls of sand? That is exactly how this painting was made. The artist took sand and let it flow between his thumb and forefinger to make a sandpainting. Every line and shape has been made with sand.

Are you surprised by the different colors? How many do you see? Sandpainting artists make colors by mixing ground-up stones with sand. Sometimes they add flower petals, charcoal, or flower pollen for color.

Some Navajo sandpaintings are as small as this book. Some are large, up to 20 feet across. What you see here is only part of a much larger sandpainting. Sandpaintings are more than just beautiful pictures to the Native Americans who make them. The paintings use symbols of nature and the gods. They often recall ancient stories. They are created as part of special ceremonies, and often they are created one day and destroyed the next.

See if you can find some of the special symbols in this sandpainting: cactus, feathers, rainbows. In the Navajo tradition, female holy people have square or rectangular heads, and male holy people have round heads. Which do you see?

Suggested Resources

Discovering Great Artists: Hands-On Art for Children in the Styles of the Great Masters, by Mary Ann Kohl and Kim Solga (Bright Ideas for Learning, 1997)

Henri Matisse: Drawing with Scissors, by Jane O'Connor (Grosset & Dunlap, 2002)

Horace Pippin, by Mike Venezia (Children's Press, 2008)

Johannes Vermeer, by Mike Venezia (Children's Press, 2002)

Magnificent Mosaics, by Jessica Mazurkiewicz (Dover Publications, 2009)

Mary Cassatt, by Mike Venezia (Children's Press, 1991)

Pieter Bruegel, by Mike Venezia (Children's Press, 1993)

Rembrandt, by Mike Venezia (Children's Press, 1988)

A Splash of Red: The Life and Art of Horace Pippin, by Jen Bryant (Knopf Books for Young Readers, 2013)

Tar Beach, by Faith Ringgold (Dragonfly Books, 1996)

IV
Music

Introduction

In music as in art, third graders will benefit from learning by doing. Singing, playing rhythm and musical instruments, counting to the beat, or dancing to rhythm sharpens a child's sense of how music works and what goes into its creation. In this chapter, we continue to teach musical notation so that as children grow they learn to read music for themselves and become more sensitive to the choices composers made.

This chapter introduces some vocabulary and concepts you can use to talk about music with your child. You can also help your third grader learn about composers' lives, the times in which they lived, and the stories that inspired their music. No talk or text, though, can substitute for a live performance. We encourage you to share good music with your children by attending concerts, tuning in to performances on radio, television, or the Internet, and playing good music at home.

Elements of Music

Have you ever whistled a tune, just making it up as you go? Or sat on the sidewalk and hummed just for fun? Maybe you sat down at a piano and played a few notes that you thought sounded nice together. If you have, then you did what a composer does. You created music.

What if you liked your musical creation so much that you wanted to share it with your friends? You could sing it for them and teach them to sing along. But what if you wanted to share it with a friend who had moved to another city? Sure, you could call and sing it, or you could record it and send it over the Internet. But you could also write the music down. That way your friend could read the music.

Just as you are learning how to write and read the words you

> **What About You?**
>
> Ask your child, "What kind of music do you like to listen to?" Discuss with your child what he likes about this kind of music. See how many elements of music—the notes, the beat, the instruments—he names.

say, musicians learn to write and read music. It's like learning a code. Different symbols tell you when to play a high note or low note or whether to play your instrument loudly or softly. There are also symbols that tell you what beat the music has. Let's learn some of those symbols.

Reading and Writing Musical Notes

A musical note represents each sound in a piece of music. Notes are written on a staff, the five lines running across a page of music. Here are the notes, on a staff, of a song you might know.

All Together

When played, the notes on the staff create a familiar tune—the first two lines of "Yankee Doodle." Hum the tune of the first two lines for your child. (If you're not familiar with the tune of the song, there are many versions available online.) Ask her to name the tune you are humming. Can she see how each note on the staff corresponds to a note in the song?

A note sits high or low on the staff, depending on its pitch. When you sing, you make some sounds that are low and some that are high, don't you? When you talk about how low or high you can sing, you are talking about the pitch of the notes you are singing.

Musical notes take their names from the first seven letters of the alphabet: A B C D E F G. When you get to G, you start all over again with A.

Try this. Instead of speaking those seven letters of the alphabet, sing them. Start low with A and go a little higher with each letter you sing. After you sing G, go a little higher and start with A again. That's the way letters name the notes in music.

Going backward is not so easy. Can you say the alphabet backward from G to A? Starting up high with G, go a little lower with each note. It's not much of a melody, but it's a start.

Now it's time to match the lines with the letters. On a musical staff, each note sits either on a line or on a space between lines, starting low and moving up.

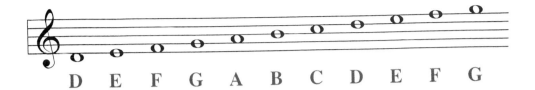

D E F G A B C D E F G

Here's one way to remember where the notes come on the staff. See the fancy swirling symbol on the left side of each staff? That is called a treble clef. It's a fun shape to draw. Try it.

When you draw a treble clef on the five lines of the staff, it always curls around the second line. The note that sits on that line is always G. In fact, sometimes the treble clef is called the G clef. If you remember that G is on the line where the clef swirls, you can figure out all the other notes around it.

What happens if the song you are composing has a note lower than E? It's simple. The next note down, D, sits just below the lowest line. The next note down, C, gets drawn with a short line through it.

Middle C

We call this note middle C. To find this note on the piano, you play the key that's right in the middle of the keyboard.

Reading and Writing Rhythm

Sometimes you sing a song slowly. Sometimes you sing it fast. The same song sounds different depending on the rhythm you give it. Rhythm is the way you keep time as you make music. To write down rhythm, musicians use another set of symbols.

Remember that piece of music you saw at the beginning of this chapter? Let's look at it again. See all those circles with tails? Each of them represents a note. Some circles are filled in, and others are empty. The way each note looks gives the musician instructions about the rhythm.

The notes with empty circles and tails are called half notes. They last longer than the notes with filled-in circles and tails, which are called quarter notes.

Every piece of music has a beat. You have to listen carefully to find it. Pick a song that you know how to sing and see if you can clap to the beat. The beat stays steady, like a ticking clock.

When you march around the room—one-two, one-two—you are following a steady beat. If you start to skip or run, you aren't following that beat anymore. No matter if it moves fast or slow, most music has a steady beat.

Let's try an example. Let's sing the first line of "Yankee Doodle," clapping out a steady beat. Clap for every beat, even if you don't sing for each time you clap.

Yan-	kee	Doo-	dle	went	to	town,
clap	clap	clap	clap	clap	clap	clap

A-	rid-	ing	on	his	po-		ny	
clap	clap	clap	clap	clap	clap	clap	clap	clap

Did you notice a time that you clapped without singing a new sound? It happened when you sang the two syllables of the word "pony," didn't it?

If we want to use musical notes to write the rhythm of this part of "Yankee Doodle," it would look like this:

Yan - kee   Doo - dle   went   to   town

A - rid - ing   on   his   po - ny

Let's put those notes on the treble clef where they belong.

Now you can sing the song and point to the notes as you sing them.

What if you want music to go faster? There is another note, called the eighth note, which lasts half the time of a quarter note. It looks something like a quarter note with a flag on the tail. Sometimes eighth notes get joined together when they're written.

Or maybe you want to hold a note even longer. Then you would write a whole note, which looks like an empty circle with no tail at all. A whole note lasts the same length of time as four quarter notes.

Keeping Time

What if we were going to put all the notes for all the verses of "Yankee Doodle" onto the treble clef? That would be a lot of notes, all in a row. To make it easier to read so many notes, musicians divide music into measures. They show each measure by drawing a line down through the staff. The line is called a bar line. They draw two thick lines, or a double bar line, to end a piece of music.

Let's use bar lines to divide the first part of "Yankee Doodle" into measures.

Every measure in a piece of music has the same number of beats. In "Yankee Doodle," every quarter note gets one beat. So how many beats per measure are in "Yankee Doodle"? How do you find out? Try clapping again as you sing. This time, notice how many times you clap between the bar lines. What's your answer? Four? That means there are four beats per measure in "Yankee Doodle."

There's another way to find the answer to that question. Musicians write down numbers called the time signature to tell about the rhythm of a piece of music.

The time signature is always made of two numbers. The top number tells how many beats are in each measure. The bottom number tells what kind of note equals one beat as you count the rhythm. Because "Yankee Doodle" has four beats per measure, and each of those beats equals a quarter note, the time signature for "Yankee Doodle" is 4/4. You read it "four-four," but you know it means "four beats per measure, and one beat equals a quarter note." Look at the very first piece of music you saw in this chapter, on page 264. See the time signature?

4/4 is just one time signature. There are many more. What would the time signature be if you saw 3/4 written on the staff? Three beats to the measure, and one beat equals a quarter note. Can you count out that rhythm? One-two-three, one-two-three. It feels like a swing. Sway up and back as you count: up-two-three, back-two-three, up-two-three, back-two-three.

Many songs have a 3/4 rhythm. Remember "My Bonnie Lies over the Ocean"?

Clap along and see if you feel the rhythm divide into three: "My BON-nie lies O-ver the O-cean, My BON-nie lies O-ver the SEA."

Rests

Music is made of silences as well as sounds. Musicians use symbols called rests to show when and for how long the singer or instrumentalist should be silent—and rest!

Talk and Think

Ask your child to think of other songs that have a 3/4 rhythm. Familiar examples might include "Rock-a-Bye Baby," "My Country, 'Tis of Thee," and "Amazing Grace."

Look at this musical notation and see how many things it tells you. The treble clef tells the pitch of every note on the staff's lines and spaces. The time signature says that each measure has three beats and that a quarter note equals one beat. The quarter and half notes tell you how long to hold the sounds. The bar lines divide the music in equal measures.

What's that squiggly sign at the end? That's a quarter rest, which lasts the same amount of time as a quarter note. It tells the musician to keep quiet and rest during that beat.

Rests have different rhythms, too, just as notes do. Here's a chart of the most common notes and rests, paired to show you which ones last the same number of beats.

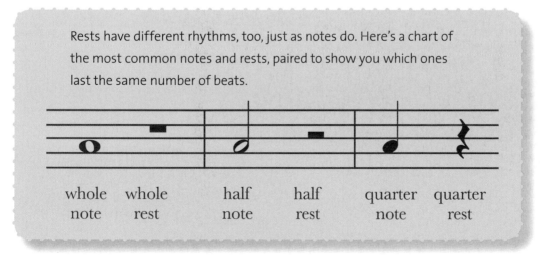

Loud and Soft

You could sing "Yankee Doodle" in a whisper or at the top of your lungs. Musicians have special ways to write down how loud the music should sound. They use words borrowed from Italian, the language spoken in Italy. When the music should be quiet, musicians say it should be "piano" [PYAH-no]. When the music should be loud, they say it should be "forte" [FOR-tay].

In Italian, you can add "-issimo" [EES-see-mo] to a word to emphasize its meaning. In music, "pianissimo" [pyah-NEES-see-mo] means "very soft," and "fortissimo" [for-TEES-see-mo] means "very loud." Sometimes a composer will write the whole word in the music, but abbreviations do just as well.

Do It Yourself

Pretend to be a composer and have your child hum or sing while you give instructions like "Forte!" or "Pianissimo!" Your child will learn how to understand the meaning of these words by adjusting the volume of her voice.

p = piano (quiet)	**f** = forte (loud)
pp = pianissimo (very quiet)	**ff** = fortissimo (very loud)

You have learned a lot from studying the first four bars of "Yankee Doodle." You have learned about notes and their pitch and rhythm, the treble clef, time signatures, rests, and measures. Turn back to the notes on page 264, and point to each note as you sing the words to "Yankee Doodle." Congratulations! Now you're reading music.

Let's Join the Orchestra

Let's pretend you're going to join an orchestra. Orchestras are made up of many different instruments. First you will have to choose which family of instrument you like the most: strings, brass, woodwinds, or percussion.

Bass drum

Kettle drum

Snare drum

Xylophone

Triangle

The percussion section sets the beat that the rest of the orchestra follows.

Percussion and Strings

Maybe you want to bang on a drum and help keep the beat. If this sounds like the role for you, join the percussion section! You can strike the gong, ring the bells, or pound on the timpani. You can even play a melody on a glockenspiel! All of these instruments are in the percussion family.

> **Make a Connection**
> Look at the bass drum, the double bass, and the bassoon. What do you notice about the size of these "bass" instruments? What can you guess about their sounds?

A celesta is similar to a piano. Both instruments are often included in the percussion family. When you press a key on a celesta's keyboard, you cause a hammer inside the celesta to strike a metal bar. In a piano, the hammers strike metal wires. Bars and wires of different sizes produce different notes. Viewed this way, playing a piano is not very different from playing a glockenspiel or a set of bells.

Maybe you would rather make the beautiful singing sound of a stringed instrument, like that of the violin, viola, cello, or big double bass. Usually musicians use bows to play stringed instruments, but sometimes they pluck the strings. What stringed instruments are played by plucking? Did you think of a guitar? A banjo?

Violin

Cello

Viola

Double bass

The string section creates the beautiful melodies of many orchestra pieces. Most orchestras contain many violins, so the violins are divided into two groups. The first violins play different notes from the second violins.

The Brass Family

Maybe you would rather toot on a horn. Then you should join the brass section of the orchestra. You have quite a few brass instruments to choose from, including the trumpet, trombone, French horn, and tuba.

Why do you think these are called "brass" instruments? It's because these differently shaped tubes are usually made of the metal brass. Each one is played by blowing into a cup-shaped mouthpiece at one end. The shape and design of the tube takes that burst of air from the horn player's mouth and turns it into a brilliant, often loud sound. Some horns have keys the musician can press, opening and closing valves to change the sound. Another horn has a tube that slides in and out to change the sound. Do you know which one that is? The trombone.

Trumpet

French horn

Trombone

Tuba

The brass section can add bright and exciting tones to an orchestra piece.

Here is Louis Armstrong, a famous jazz musician.

Long ago, horns weren't made with valves or fancy shapes. They were just long metal tubes with a mouthpiece at one end and a big opening at the other. The sound that each horn made depended on the length of the horn, so it took many horns to play a whole melody.

The French horn is shaped like a circle. When the player blows into the mouthpiece, the air goes around and around. French horn players change the shape of their mouths as they play in order to change the sound they are making. The Austrian composer Wolfgang Amadeus Mozart [VULF-gahng ah-mah-DAY-us MOAT-zart] wrote four different pieces in which the star instrument is the French horn. If you listen to Mozart's Horn Concertos, you will hear the sound of a French horn playing alone. Once in a great while the tuba plays the melody, but most of the time it keeps the rhythm in the background with an *oom-pa, oom-pa.*

Famous for Its Trumpets

The story of William Tell is told in the language and literature section of this book. The Italian composer Gioacchino Rossini [jwa-KEE-no ro-SEE-nee] liked the story so much, he wrote an opera about it. An opera is like a play in which the actors sing rather than speak. Usually an opera opens with an overture, played by the orchestra. The overture of Rossini's opera *William Tell* is a well-known piece of music. If you listen to a recording of it, you may find that you already know the tune. You will also hear how Rossini planned the music to include first one solo trumpet, then more, and more!

Make a Connection
Revisit the "William Tell" story on page 52. Ask your child to think about how the story could be turned into an opera. What might the music sound like?

The Woodwind Family

Do you like to whistle? Maybe you would like to join the woodwind section of our orchestra. You could play the flute or the piccolo, the clarinet or the oboe or the bassoon. They are all woodwinds.

Have you ever blown across the top of an empty glass bottle? Try it. You position your lips on the rim of the bottle, just so, and the "wind" from your mouth makes a breathy, hollow sound.

Now fill that same bottle one-third full with water. Blow across it again. What happens? Your bottle instrument changes pitch.

Musicians who play the flute hold their mouths the same way you did. They blow over a hole on the top of their instruments. Just as your breath vibrated through the bottle and made a pleasant sound, theirs does, too. Flute players also press keys with their fingers to change pitch as they play. A piccolo works the same way, but it is smaller than a flute. (In fact, the word "piccolo" means "little" in Italian.) A piccolo's sound is higher in pitch than a flute's.

The other woodwinds are played differently from the flute and the piccolo. They are called reed instruments, because the mouthpieces of these instruments contain a flat, flexible piece of wood (or other material), called a reed. The reed vibrates when you blow on it.

To understand how a reed works, you can make your own outdoors. Put a long, wide blade of grass flat between your thumbs and blow on it. If you do it just right, you'll get a buzz or a squawk. The sound comes when your breath makes the blade of grass vibrate. A reed in an instrument works like that blade of grass. The breath of the musician makes it vibrate, and that makes music.

A Dreamy Flute Song

Do you know what a faun is? It's a creature that comes from ancient Greek mythology, half man and half goat. The French composer Claude Debussy [clode deb-yoo-SEE] wrote a piece of music called *Prelude to the Afternoon of a Faun.* Maybe he was trying to write music that would carry us back to ancient times, when myths seemed real. Debussy made the flute an important instrument in his piece. He knew that the ancient Greeks played music on simple flutes.

Each of these woodwinds has a sound all its own. The oboe can sound sad. The bassoon can sound clownish. The clarinet may be the best known of the woodwinds. Clarinetists play in orchestras, bands, and jazz groups. Sometimes people call the clarinet a "licorice stick." Look at the picture—can you guess why?

You can get to know the sound of the clarinet by listening to *Rhapsody in Blue* by the American composer George Gershwin. The piece starts with a solo performance, one clarinet playing a swinging, swooping melody.

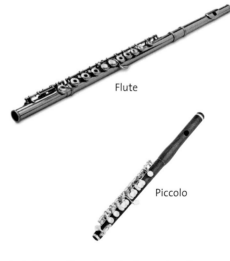

Flute

Piccolo

The woodwinds are often placed in the center of the orchestra, near the stringed instruments and piano.

Clarinet　　Oboe

Bassoon

All Together Now

Now that you've learned about the different families of instruments in the orchestra, which instrument will you play? Perhaps you would rather create the music than play the compositions of someone else. In that case, you should try being a composer!

Composers and Their Music

One way to learn about music is to learn about different great composers like Rimsky-Korsakov, Tchaikovsky, Sousa, and Copland. Knowing about the lives of great composers can help you hear new things in their music.

Musical Connections

Do you remember, earlier in this book, the two stories from *A Thousand and One Nights* (pages 28–37)? They were said to have been told by Scheherazade, the beautiful queen of Persia who made up stories, night after night, to save her life.

> **Make a Connection**
> Revisit the stories of Scheherazade on pages 28 to 37. Play the music as you read with your child and talk about how the sounds connect to events and characters in the stories.

A Russian composer named Nikolai Rimsky-Korsakov [NEE-ko-lie RIM-skee-KOR-sa-koff] was so enchanted by these stories that he wrote a suite (or a collection) of pieces of music called *Scheherazade*.

Rimsky-Korsakov's *Scheherazade* suite has four movements. ("Movement" is a word used to name a part within a larger piece of music.) In each movement, we hear the voice of the storyteller as a melody played by a solo violin. Whenever we hear that theme, we think of Scheherazade spinning one of her fantastic tales.

As a young man, Rimsky-Korsakov served in the Russian navy and went to sea. He probably used those memories to compose the first movement of his suite, called "The Sea and Sinbad's Ship." At the very beginning, we hear a forceful theme that suggests the sultan demanding another tale. The solo violin answers, as if the clever queen has begun to speak. Next, we hear a rocking and swelling rhythm, played by the strings, like waves lapping against a ship. The music goes on and on, just like the sea, as Sinbad's ship sails over it.

Tchaikovsky: Music That Brings Strong Feeling

Peter Ilyich Tchaikovsky [IHL-yich chy-KOFF-skee] was born in Russia in 1840. Tchaikovsky was a sensitive child who shared a deep connection with his mother. He was obsessed with music. After an evening of listening to a musical performance, he had trouble going to sleep. "This music! This music!" he told his parents. "It's here in my head and won't let me sleep!"

Peter Ilyich Tchaikovsky (1840–1893).

Playing and writing music came naturally to Tchaikovsky, but his parents sent him to school to become a government clerk. While he was at school, his mother died. Tchaikovsky was devastated. Later in life, he was able to channel his emotions into his music. He worked as a government clerk for only a short time before his love for music pushed him to return to school to become a composer.

Tchaikovsky grew to be a man of strong fears and emotions. Some say that when he conducted an orchestra, he kept his eyes shut tight, afraid to see either the musicians or the audience. But maybe he closed his eyes to hear the music better. Try it and see if it works for you.

Tchaikovsky's music has the ability to bring out strong emotions in those who listen to it. Sometimes it sounds bright and happy. Sometimes it sounds dark and sad. Tchaikovsky also found ways to make his music exciting. One of his most famous pieces, the *1812 Overture*, conveys the feeling of winning a war. Tchaikovsky called the piece "very loud and noisy." During some performances, a musician in the percussion section shoots off a real cannon!

Tchaikovsky composed many pieces of music for orchestras. He also composed three ballets, which are stories told through dance performed to orchestra music. You may already know Tchaikovsky's third ballet, called *The Nutcracker*. His second ballet

What About You?

Play the *1812 Overture* for your child (there are many versions available on the Internet). Ask him to think about where he might have heard it before. It's often used for fireworks shows!

tells the story of Sleeping Beauty. He wrote his first ballet, *Swan Lake*, about another fairy tale. It's a story with magic, an evil wizard, and true love, but not everyone lives happily ever after. Here is the story. Maybe you can listen to a recording of Tchaikovsky's ballet music, too.

The Story of *Swan Lake*

On the night before the grand ball in Prince Siegfried's palace, the prince's mother told her son he must choose a wife. But Siegfried preferred to go hunting. He grabbed his crossbow and set off into the forest. A flock of wild swans flew overhead.

As darkness fell, Siegfried came upon a mysterious lake. A line of swans glided silently toward him. He raised his crossbow to shoot.

The nearest swan rose from the water and transformed herself into a beautiful young woman.

"I am Odette, princess of the swans," she said. "An evil magician cast a spell on us. We are human from midnight to dawn, but by day we are swans, always under the power of the evil Von Rothbart."

Siegfried asked if there was a way to break the spell, and Odette answered, "Only when someone falls in love with me and promises to stay faithful forever."

Siegfried knew he could make that promise. As their eyes met in a moment of true love, the air grew cold and an owl swooped down with a shriek.

"Von Rothbart!" cried Odette, and she became a swan again.

The next night, at the palace ball, all Siegfried could think about was the swan princess. Suddenly two new guests arrived, a tall man in a swirling black cape and a beautiful young woman in a flowing black dress.

Siegfried stared. Could it be? The swan princess? What he didn't know was that Von Rothbart had cast a spell on his own daughter, Odile, to make her look just like Odette.

Just before midnight, Siegfried announced that he had found the girl he wished to marry. The caped man stepped forward.

"Do you truly love her?" he demanded.

"I do," said Siegfried.

A crash of thunder shook the castle. A bolt of lightning ripped the sky. Instantly Odile changed into an ugly hag. Only then did Siegfried see the white swan, beating its wings at the window. What a mistake he had made!

He ran out into the storm. "Odette!" he cried. He ran to the lake and found the swan maidens huddled together on the shore, weeping. Standing apart, on a high rocky ledge, was his beloved Odette.

Here is a performance of the *Swan Lake* ballet. Prince Siegfried dances with Odette in the center, surrounded by her companion swans.

"Forgive me," cried Siegfried. "I was tricked by Von Rothbart. It's you that I love." They embraced, long and silently.

"My dear prince," said Odette, "I cannot be yours, but I will not be Von Rothbart's. Remember, I will love you for all time." Then she slipped from his arms and leaped into the dark water.

Without a pause, Siegfried leaped in after her. There was a splash, then the waters closed quietly over them both.

A shrill cry pierced the night, like the scream of an owl dying. Von Rothbart's evil was destroyed by the love between Odette and Siegfried.

John Philip Sousa: The March King

When John Philip Sousa [SOO-zuh] was 13 years old, in 1867, he declared to his parents that he was going to join a circus band. His father said, "You can play in a band, but not with the circus," and signed his son up to play with the U.S. Marine Band. Sousa played trumpet and trombone and studied the violin as well. He was 18 years old when he composed his first piece of music.

How is a band different from an orchestra? Both are groups of musicians, playing music together. In a typical band, you'll hear instruments from the percussion, brass, and wind families. What's missing? The strings. In a typical orchestra, you'll hear percussion, brass, wind, and stringed instruments. In fact, many orchestras have more strings than any other kind of instrument.

When Sousa was 25, he became the leader of the Marine Band. He grew a beard to make himself look older and more dignified. Later he formed his own band, called the Sousa Band, which toured the United States and Europe. People especially enjoyed the marches that Sousa composed. Many bands, to this day, march to the music of John Philip Sousa.

Sousa's most famous march is called "The Stars and Stripes Forever." The

John Philip Sousa (left) prepares to lead a marching band.

composer was on a ship crossing the Atlantic Ocean from Europe. He began pacing back and forth. "Suddenly," said Sousa, "I began to sense the rhythmic beat of a band playing within my brain." In his mind, Sousa heard every note of the melody, every thump of the drum, every tweet of the piccolo. "When we reached shore, I set down the measures that my brain-band had been playing for me, and not a note of it has ever been changed."

Americans over the years have come to know "The Stars and Stripes Forever" as one of our great patriotic marches, a piece of music that is all about the United States of America. Just listen to it—you can't keep from clapping and marching along.

Aaron Copland: Making American Music

Aaron Copland [COPE-land], born in 1900, grew up in Brooklyn, New York. He called his childhood neighborhood "drab," which means it was brown and gray, without bright colors. He didn't start playing piano until he was 12 years old, but when he started, he learned quickly. By the time he was a young man, he knew that music would be his life.

At that time, many young Americans interested in music went to study in Europe. So Copland went to France. Exciting things were happening in the music world in Paris. In 1913, the Russian composer Igor Stravinsky debuted his ballet called *The Rite of Spring*. The ballet used experimental rhythms and melodies that people had never heard before. It was so sensational that people rioted in the theater! In the years that followed, Paris became the center of modern classical music.

Copland came home full of new ideas, but he wanted to write music that was truly American. Even though he was writing pieces of music for the orchestra, he used sounds and rhythms from folk music, jazz, and blues. Some people didn't like his new ideas. One newspaper reporter wrote that his music sounded like a jazz hall next to a chicken yard!

Copland decided that he should try to write music that more people liked. He wrote an orchestra piece full of tunes from Mexican folk songs. He wrote music for two ballets about the Wild West, *Billy the Kid* and *Rodeo*. No one had ever based serious music on folk music, but Copland showed it could be done.

When you listen to the music of Aaron Copland, it's fun to try to recognize the folk songs woven into the orchestra music. In his ballet *Appalachian Spring*, Aaron Copland uses the folk song "Simple Gifts" as a main melody. You'll find the words to that song in the next section of this chapter.

Aaron Copland (right) discusses a song with Hungarian-born composer Antal Doráti.

Some Songs for Third Graders

Here are the words for some favorite children's songs. You may already know the music, but if you don't, you will find many of these either in books or recordings of collected children's music. See page 293 for a few that we recommend.

Alouette

(French Canadian folk song)

"Alouette" means "lark" in French.

In French:	In English translation:
Alouette, gentille Alouette,	Alouette, sweet Alouette,
Alouette, je te plumerai.	Alouette, I will pluck your feathers.
Je te plumerai la tête,	I will pluck the feathers on your head,
Je te plumerai la tête,	I will pluck the feathers on your head,
À la tête, à la tête,	On your head, on your head.
Alouette, Alouette,	Alouette, Alouette,
Alouette, gentille Alouette,	Alouette, sweet Alouette,
Alouette, je te plumerai.	Alouette, I will pluck your feathers.

Hey-Ho, Nobody Home

(English round)

> Hey-ho, nobody home,
> Meat nor drink nor money have I none.
> Yet I will be merry.

Li'l Liza Jane

(American folk song)

> I've got a gal in Arkansas, li'l Liza Jane,
> She sleeps in the kitchen with her feet in the hall, li'l Liza Jane.
>
> *Chorus:*
> Oh, Eliza, li'l Liza Jane,
> Oh, Eliza, li'l Liza Jane.
>
> I've got a gal and you've got none, li'l Liza Jane,
> I've got a gal that calls me "hon," li'l Liza Jane.
>
> House and a lol in Baltimore, li'l Liza Jane,
> Lots of children running out of the door, li'l Liza Jane.

All Together

A round is a song that different people can sing in sequence. One person starts, followed by another person, followed by another, until everyone is singing different parts at the same time. With your child, sing "Hey-Ho, Nobody Home" as a round. If possible, get one or two more people to join in!

Take a Look

Look at a map of the United States. Challenge your child to find all of the locations mentioned in "Li'l Liza Jane" and the songs on the coming pages.

Down in the Valley

(American folk song)

Down in the valley, valley so low,
Hang your head over, hear the wind blow.
Hear the wind blow, love, hear the wind blow,
Hang your head over, hear the wind blow.

Roses love sunshine, violets love dew,
Angels in heaven know I love you.
Know I love you, dear, know I love you.
Angels in heaven know I love you.

Write me a letter, send it by mail,
Send it in care of Birmingham jail.
Birmingham jail, love, Birmingham jail.
Send it in care of Birmingham jail.

Polly Wolly Doodle

(American folk song)

Oh, I went down south for to see my Sal,
Sing polly wolly doodle all the day,
My Sal she is a spunky gal,
Sing polly wolly doodle all the day.

Chorus:
Fare thee well, fare thee well, fare thee well my fairy fay,
For I'm going to Louisiana for to see my Susianna,
Singing polly wolly doodle all the day.

Simple Gifts

(Shaker song)

'Tis a gift to be simple, 'tis a gift to be free,
'Tis a gift to come down to where we ought to be,
And when we find ourselves in the place just right,
'Twill be in the valley of love and delight.
When true simplicity is gained,
To bow and to bend we won't be ashamed.
To turn, turn will be our delight
'Til by turning, turning we come 'round right.

> ### What About You?
> Ask your child, "Why do you think some of these songs use made-up nonsense words in their lyrics?"

This Little Light

(African American spiritual)

This little light of mine, I'm gonna let it shine.
This little light of mine, I'm gonna let it shine.
This little light of mine, I'm gonna let it shine,
Let it shine, let it shine, let it shine!

He's Got the Whole World in His Hands

(African American spiritual)

He's got the whole world in His hands,
He's got the whole world in His hands,
He's got the whole world in His hands,
He's got the whole world in His hands.

He's got you and me, brother, in His hands,
He's got you and me, sister, in His hands,
He's got you and me, brother, in His hands,
He's got the whole world in His hands.

My Bonnie

(Scottish folk song)

My bonnie lies over the ocean.
My bonnie lies over the sea.
My bonnie lies over the ocean.
Oh, bring back my bonnie to me.

Bring back, bring back,
Oh, bring back my bonnie to me, to me.
Bring back, bring back,
Oh, bring back my bonnie to me.

The Sidewalks of New York

(by Charles B. Lawlor and James W. Blake, 1894)

East side, west side, all around the town.

The tots play ring a rosie, London Bridge is falling down.

Boys and girls together,

Me and Mamie Rorke.

We trip the light fantastic

On the sidewalks of New York.

The Man on the Flying Trapeze

(words by George Leybourne, music by Alfred Lee, 1868)

New Word

Does your child know the word **purloined**? It is the past-tense form of the verb "purloin," which means "to steal."

He flies through the air with the greatest of ease,

The daring young man on the flying trapeze.

His movements are graceful, all girls he does please,

and my love he has **purloined** away.

In the Good Old Summertime

(by George Evans, 1902)

In the good old summertime,
In the good old summertime,
Strolling through the shady lanes,
With your baby mine.
You hold her hand and she holds yours,
And that's a very good sign
That she's your tootsy-wootsy in
The good old summertime.

Bicycle Built for Two

(by Harry Dacre, 1892)

Daisy, Daisy, give me your answer, do.
I'm half crazy all for the love of you.
It won't be a stylish marriage,
I can't afford a carriage.
But you'll look sweet
On the seat
Of a bicycle built for two.

You're a Grand Old Flag

(by George M. Cohan, 1906)

New Word
Does your child know the word **emblem**? The noun "emblem" is another word for symbol.

You're a grand old flag, you're a high-flying flag,
And forever in peace may you wave.
You're the **emblem** of the land I love,
The home of the free and the brave.
Every heart beats true under red, white, and blue
Where there's never a boast or brag.
Should auld acquaintance be forgot,
Keep your eye on the grand old flag.

America

(old English tune; words by Samuel Francis Smith)

My country, 'tis of thee,
Sweet land of liberty,
Of thee I sing.
Land where my fathers died,
Land of the Pilgrims' pride,
From every mountainside,
Let freedom ring.

Suggested Resources

Aaron Copland, by Mike Venezia (Children's Press, 1995)

The Best of Tchaikovsky: Classical Kids (Classical Kids, 2004)

Do Re Mi: If You Can Read Music, Thank Guido D'Arezzo, by Susan Roth (HMH Books for Young Readers, 2007)

John Philip Sousa, by Mike Venezia (Children's Press, 1999)

My First Classical Music Book, by Genevieve Helsby (Naxos Book, 2009)

101 Rhythm Instrument Activities for Young Children, by Abigail Flesch Connors (Gryphon House, 2004)

Peter Tchaikovsky, by Mike Venezia (Children's Press, 1995)

The Story of the Orchestra: Listen While You Learn About the Instruments, the Music and the Composers Who Wrote the Music, by Robert Levine (Black Dog & Leventhal Publishers, 2000)

Swan Lake, by Lisbeth Zwerger (North-South Books, 2002)

Those Amazing Musical Instruments: Your Guide to the Orchestra Through Sounds and Stories, by Genevieve Helsby (Naxos Books, 2007)

V
Mathematics

Introduction

Success in learning math comes through practice, practice, practice: steady practice, thoughtful practice, and practice with a variety of problems. Encourage your child to approach problems from different angles. Psychologists who have studied how math is learned explain that ability gained through practice is *not* different from mathematical understanding. Indeed, practice is the prerequisite for more advanced problem solving. While practice is the key to success in learning math, be careful that this practice does not become mindless and repetitive.

However, some well-meaning people still fear that practice in mathematics—memorizing arithmetic facts or doing timed worksheets, for example—constitutes joyless, soul-killing drudgery for children. Nothing could be further from the truth. It is not practice but anxiety that kills the joy in mathematics. One effective way to practice with your child is to have her talk out loud while doing problems, explaining computational steps along the way. Your child's mental process becomes visible to you, and you can correct misunderstandings as they happen.

The best math programs incorporate the principle of incremental review: once a concept or skill is introduced, the child practices it again and again through exercises of gradually increasing difficulty. One result of this approach is that a child's arithmetic skills become automatic. Only when children achieve automatic command of basic facts—when they can tell you instantly what 9 plus 8 equals, for example—are their minds prepared to tackle more challenging problems. Math learning programs that offer both incremental review and varied opportunities for problem solving get the best results.

This chapter presents a brief outline of the math skills and concepts that should be part of a good third-grade education. We emphasize, however, that this outline does not constitute a complete math program, because it does not include as many practice problems as a child ought to do while learning this material. To learn math thoroughly at the third-grade level, children need to be shown these concepts and then encouraged to practice, practice, practice.

Multiplication—Part 1

Multiplication Words

In the equation $2 \times 5 = 10$, 2 and 5 are factors, and 10 is the product. You can multiply factors in any order without changing the product.

$$2 \times 5 = 10 \qquad 5 \times 2 = 10$$

Multiplying Vertically

Equations can be written both horizontally and vertically. For example, consider the two problems below:

$$4 \times 5 = 20 \quad \text{can also be written} \quad \begin{array}{r} 5 \\ \times 4 \\ \hline 20 \end{array}$$

You read both as "four times five equals twenty." Notice that when you read a vertical multiplication problem, you begin with the number next to the multiplication sign and read up.

Showing Multiplication

You can make a "picture" of a multiplication problem using graph paper. For example, you can show 3×5 by a rectangle with 3 rows and 5 columns.

Make a Connection
Look at the Willow Oak quilt on page 248. Ask your child to create an equation to quickly figure out how many squares it has.

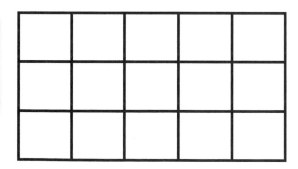

If you count the squares by the rows, you have:

$$5 + 5 + 5, \text{ which is } 3 \times 5$$

If you count the squares by the columns, you have:

$$3 + 3 + 3 + 3 + 3, \text{ which is } 5 \times 3$$

Either way, there are 15 squares in all.
You can also show 3×5 by a rectangle with 5 rows and 3 columns.

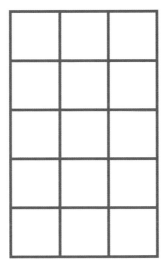

Do It Yourself

Now have some fun making at least three other multiplication facts into graph paper pictures like 3×5. Try 3×4 or 4×5. What about 5×5?

Multiplication is a quick way of doing repeated addition. It's good to practice writing multiplication as repeated addition, and repeated addition as multiplication. For example, 4×5 can also be written $5 + 5 + 5 + 5$. And $3 + 3 + 3 + 3 + 3 + 3$ can also be written 6×3.

The Multiplication Table

As a second grader, you learned the multiplication tables up to 5. Here are the rest of the multiplication tables.

6 as a factor	*7 as a factor*	*8 as a factor*	*9 as a factor*
$0 \times 6 = 0$	$0 \times 7 = 0$	$0 \times 8 = 0$	$0 \times 9 = 0$
$1 \times 6 = 6$	$1 \times 7 = 7$	$1 \times 8 = 8$	$1 \times 9 = 9$
$2 \times 6 = 12$	$2 \times 7 = 14$	$2 \times 8 = 16$	$2 \times 9 = 18$
$3 \times 6 = 18$	$3 \times 7 = 21$	$3 \times 8 = 24$	$3 \times 9 = 27$
$4 \times 6 = 24$	$4 \times 7 = 28$	$4 \times 8 = 32$	$4 \times 9 = 36$
$5 \times 6 = 30$	$5 \times 7 = 35$	$5 \times 8 = 40$	$5 \times 9 = 45$
$6 \times 6 = 36$	$6 \times 7 = 42$	$6 \times 8 = 48$	$6 \times 9 = 54$
$7 \times 6 = 42$	$7 \times 7 = 49$	$7 \times 8 = 56$	$7 \times 9 = 63$
$8 \times 6 = 48$	$8 \times 7 = 56$	$8 \times 8 = 64$	$8 \times 9 = 72$
$9 \times 6 = 54$	$9 \times 7 = 63$	$9 \times 8 = 72$	$9 \times 9 = 81$

Only the 16 multiplication facts that are red are actually new. The others you already know. For example, if you know $5 \times 9 = 45$, then you know $9 \times 5 = 45$. Learn these facts so you can say them easily. Also be able to give any product quickly, without making any mistakes.

Remember that you can skip-count to get to the next fact in a table.

$8 \times 6 = 48$, so 9×6 is 6 more, or 54.
$7 \times 7 = 49$, so 8×7 is 7 more, or 56.

When you know all the multiplication facts well, practice filling in a table, like the one on the next page, with all of them. We've filled in a few to show you how it is done.

×	0	1	2	3	4	5	6	7	8	9
0										
1										
2										
3						15				
4										
5								35		
6								42		
7										
8										
9										

Square Numbers and Square Roots

How many squares are there in each of these grids?

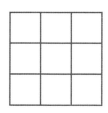 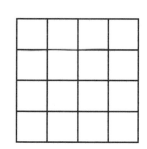 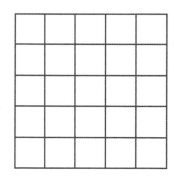

To find out, you can add the number of squares in each row.

$$3 + 3 + 3 = 9 \quad 4 + 4 + 4 + 4 = 16 \quad 5 + 5 + 5 + 5 + 5 = 25$$

Or you can multiply the number of rows by the number of columns.

$$3 \times 3 = 9 \qquad 4 \times 4 = 16 \qquad 5 \times 5 = 25$$

The numbers 9, 16, and 25 are called square numbers. A square number is the product of any number multiplied by itself. The number 3 is the square root of 9, because 3 multiplied by itself equals 9. The number 4 is the square root of 16, because 4 multiplied by itself equals 16.

You can do square root problems in the other direction, too. What is the square root of 25? In other words, what number multiplied by itself equals 25? (The answer can be found in the grids on the previous page.)

The sign for square root looks like this: $\sqrt{}$. For example, $\sqrt{9} = 3$ and $\sqrt{16} = 4$.
Find the square numbers:

$$7 \times 7 = \rule{2cm}{0.4pt} \qquad 9 \times 9 = \rule{2cm}{0.4pt} \qquad 10 \times 10 = \rule{2cm}{0.4pt}$$

Find the square roots:

$$\sqrt{64} = \rule{2cm}{0.4pt} \qquad \sqrt{36} = \rule{2cm}{0.4pt} \qquad \sqrt{100} = \rule{2cm}{0.4pt}$$

Extra and interesting: If you fill in the square numbers on the practice table on page 301, what sort of line will the square numbers make on the table?

Parentheses, Multiplying Three Numbers

The symbols ( ) are parentheses. In math, you do what is inside the parentheses *first*.

You add $(2 + 3) + 5$ like this: You add $2 + (3 + 5)$ like this:

$$(2 + 3) + 5 = \qquad\qquad 2 + (3 + 5) =$$
$$5 \quad + 5 = 10 \qquad\qquad 2 + \quad 8 \quad = 10$$

Notice that whether you put $2 + 3$ in the parentheses or $3 + 5$ in the parentheses, the sum is the same. No matter how you group the numbers you are adding, the sum stays the same.

You can also multiply three or more numbers using parentheses.

Multiply $(3 \times 2) \times 4$ like this: Multiply $3 \times (2 \times 4)$ like this:

$(3 \times 2) \times 4 =$ $3 \times (2 \times 4) =$

$6 \phantom{{}} \times 4 = 24$ $3 \times 8 \phantom{{})} = 24$

Notice that the product is the same both times. No matter how you group factors, the product is the same.

Division—Part 1

Operations

Addition, subtraction, and multiplication are called operations. They are three of the four operations of arithmetic. The fourth operation is called division.

You already know that subtraction is the inverse of addition. We also say that addition and subtraction are inverse operations. The inverse operation of multiplication is division. Let's see how division works.

An Example of Division

Peter has 18 pencils. He wants to divide them into groups of 3. How many groups will he have?

$$18 \div 3 = 6$$

This is a division problem, because you need to divide the 18 pencils into groups of 3 to solve it. How many groups of 3 are there in 18? There are 6 threes in 18. So Peter will have 6 groups of pencils. We write this division problem $18 \div 3 = 6$. We read it "18 divided by 3 equals 6." The sign $\div$ means "divided by" and shows that you are dividing.

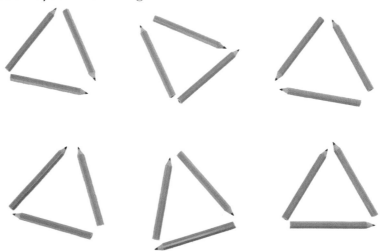

Solving Division Problems

Division and multiplication are called inverse operations. Sometimes the easiest way to solve a division problem is to think of a multiplication problem. Here is an example. What is 30 ÷ 6? You want to know how many 6s there are in 30. **Think:** What times 6 equals 30? **5 × 6 = 30**. So, 30 ÷ 6 = **5**. In the picture below, the 30 pennies are divided into 5 groups, with 6 pennies in each group.

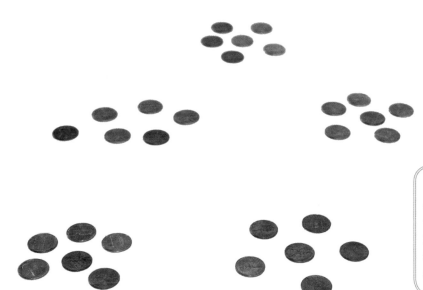

Do It Yourself
Ask your child to demonstrate the equation 30 ÷ 6 using a group of small, identical objects, such as pennies.

$$5 \times 6 = 30$$
$$30 \div 6 = 5$$

Here is another example. What is 54 ÷ 9? You want to know how many 9s there are in 54. **Think:** What times 9 equals 54? **6 × 9 = 54**. So, 54 ÷ 9 = **6**.

Division Words

All Together

Write out a few division problems to share with your child. Point out the different parts of each problem and have your child call out the names aloud.

The answer to a division problem is called the quotient. The number you are dividing is called the dividend. The number you are dividing by is called the divisor.

Learn to use these words to describe the numbers in a division problem. For example, in $12 \div 4 = 3$, 12 is the dividend, 4 is the divisor, and 3 is the quotient.

There are two ways to write division. You can write it like this:

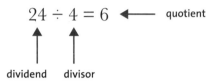

or like this:

$$\text{divisor} \longrightarrow 4\overline{)24} \quad \substack{6 \longleftarrow \text{quotient} \\ \longleftarrow \text{dividend}}$$

Notice that the answer, the 6, goes over the ones place. Learn to write division in both ways. For example:

$8 \div 2 = 4$ is the same as $2\overline{)8}^{\,4}$

$8\overline{)56}^{\,7}$ is the same as $56 \div 8 = 7$

Division Facts

Learn the basic division facts. These facts will help you solve any division problem. You can use the multiplication facts you already know to find the quotient of each division fact. We'll talk more about this later. Here are the division facts with 2, 3, 4, and 5 as divisors.

2 as a divisor	*3 as a divisor*	*4 as a divisor*	*5 as a divisor*
$0 \div 2 = 0$	$0 \div 3 = 0$	$0 \div 4 = 0$	$0 \div 5 = 0$
$2 \div 2 = 1$	$3 \div 3 = 1$	$4 \div 4 = 1$	$5 \div 5 = 1$
$4 \div 2 = 2$	$6 \div 3 = 2$	$8 \div 4 = 2$	$10 \div 5 = 2$
$6 \div 2 = 3$	$9 \div 3 = 3$	$12 \div 4 = 3$	$15 \div 5 = 3$
$8 \div 2 = 4$	$12 \div 3 = 4$	$16 \div 4 = 4$	$20 \div 5 = 4$
$10 \div 2 = 5$	$15 \div 3 = 5$	$20 \div 4 = 5$	$25 \div 5 = 5$
$12 \div 2 = 6$	$18 \div 3 = 6$	$24 \div 4 = 6$	$30 \div 5 = 6$
$14 \div 2 = 7$	$21 \div 3 = 7$	$28 \div 4 = 7$	$35 \div 5 = 7$
$16 \div 2 = 8$	$24 \div 3 = 8$	$32 \div 4 = 8$	$40 \div 5 = 8$
$18 \div 2 = 9$	$27 \div 3 = 9$	$36 \div 4 = 9$	$45 \div 5 = 9$

Learn to find the quotient of each division fact quickly, without making any mistakes. Here are the division facts with 6, 7, 8, and 9 as divisors.

6 as a divisor	*7 as a divisor*	*8 as a divisor*	*9 as a divisor*
$0 \div 6 = 0$	$0 \div 7 = 0$	$0 \div 8 = 0$	$0 \div 9 = 0$
$6 \div 6 = 1$	$7 \div 7 = 1$	$8 \div 8 = 1$	$9 \div 9 = 1$
$12 \div 6 = 2$	$14 \div 7 = 2$	$16 \div 8 = 2$	$18 \div 9 = 2$
$18 \div 6 = 3$	$21 \div 7 = 3$	$24 \div 8 = 3$	$27 \div 9 = 3$
$24 \div 6 = 4$	$28 \div 7 = 4$	$32 \div 8 = 4$	$36 \div 9 = 4$
$30 \div 6 = 5$	$35 \div 7 = 5$	$40 \div 8 = 5$	$45 \div 9 = 5$
$36 \div 6 = 6$	$42 \div 7 = 6$	$48 \div 8 = 6$	$54 \div 9 = 6$
$42 \div 6 = 7$	$49 \div 7 = 7$	$56 \div 8 = 7$	$63 \div 9 = 7$
$48 \div 6 = 8$	$56 \div 7 = 8$	$64 \div 8 = 8$	$72 \div 9 = 8$
$54 \div 6 = 9$	$63 \div 7 = 9$	$72 \div 8 = 9$	$81 \div 9 = 9$

Division Rules for 0 and 1

Here are some rules for dividing with 0 and 1.

Rules for 0

1. 0 divided by any number (except 0) equals 0.

   $0 \div 8 = 0 \qquad 0 \div 5 = 0$

2. You cannot divide by 0.

   $5 \div 0$ is an impossible problem.

Rules for 1

1. Any number (except 0) divided by itself equals 1.

   $8 \div 8 = 1 \qquad 6 \div 6 = 1$

2. Any number divided by 1 equals that number.

   $5 \div 1 = 5 \qquad 7 \div 1 = 7$

These rules can help you learn the division facts. For example, the last rule makes it easy to learn all the division facts that have 1 as a divisor: $0 \div 1 = 0$; $1 \div 1 = 1$; $2 \div 1 = 2$; $3 \div 1 = 3$; $4 \div 1 = 4$; $5 \div 1 = 5$; and so on.

Division Word Problems

Here are two kinds of division problems. Learn to solve both kinds.

1. Margaret has 35 red peppers. She wants to put 5 on each plate. How many plates does she need?

You want to know how many groups of 5 there are in 35. You write 35 ÷ 5 = 7. She needs 7 plates. (What other way can you write 35 ÷ 5?)

2. Mrs. Fletcher has 27 flowers. She wants to divide them equally into 3 cups. How many flowers should she put into each cup?

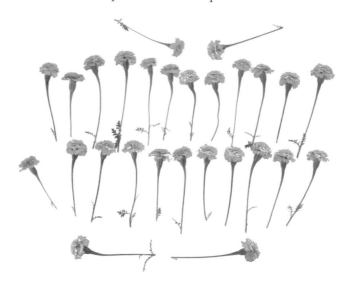

You want to know how many will be in each group if you divide 27 into 3 groups. You write $27 \div 3 = 9$. She should put 9 flowers into each cup.

Sometimes you want to know how many groups there are. Sometimes you want to know how many are in each group. You solve both kinds of problems in the same way.

Picturing Multiplication and Division Facts

As you've just read, multiplication and division are inverse operations. For example, the inverse of multiplying by 9 is dividing by 9. The inverse of $7 \times 9 = 63$ is $63 \div 9 = 7$. Here is a picture of how this works.

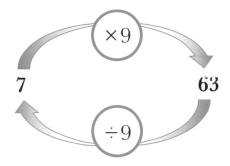

Here is another example. The inverse of $48 \div 6 = 8$ is $8 \times 6 = 48$.

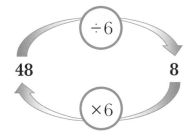

Learn to draw pictures like these to show inverse multiplication and division facts. When you can do this, you can find inverse multiplication and division facts.

Picturing Multiplication and Division Facts with Blank Spaces

Learn to fill in the blanks in pictures like these:

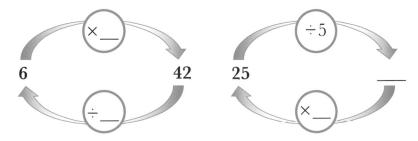

You should also be able to do the same thing with equations that have blank spaces.

$$\rule{3cm}{0.4pt} \times 5 = 40$$

Think: What times 5 equals 40? 8. So, $8 \times 5 = 40$.

Try these:

1. $\rule{1.5cm}{0.4pt} \times 8 = 56$ 3. $63 \div \rule{1.5cm}{0.4pt} = 9$ 5. $3 \times \rule{1.5cm}{0.4pt} = 24$
2. $\rule{1.5cm}{0.4pt} \div 8 = 9$ 4. $4 \times \rule{1.5cm}{0.4pt} = 28$ 6. $12 \div \rule{1.5cm}{0.4pt} = 2$

Division and Fractions

When something is divided into 3 equal parts, each part is one-third, written as a fraction: $\frac{1}{3}$.

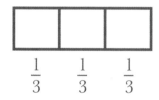

$$\frac{1}{3} \qquad \frac{1}{3} \qquad \frac{1}{3}$$

If you want to find $\frac{1}{3}$ of 24, you divide it into 3 equal parts. To divide 24 into 3 equal parts, you divide by 3.

$$24 \div 3 = 8$$

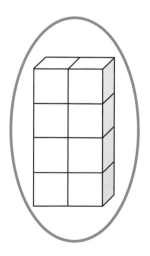 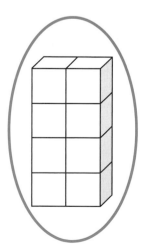 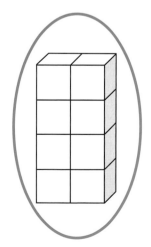

In the same way, if you want to find one-fourth (or $\frac{1}{4}$) of 36, you divide 36 by 4. $36 \div 4 = 9$, so $\frac{1}{4}$ of 36 equals 9.

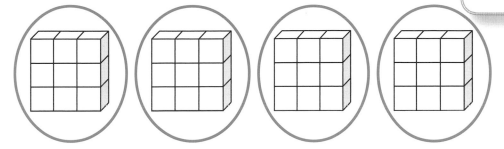

Using the division facts, learn to find the fractions $\frac{1}{2}$, $\frac{1}{3}$, $\frac{1}{4}$, $\frac{1}{5}$, $\frac{1}{6}$, $\frac{1}{7}$, $\frac{1}{8}$, and $\frac{1}{9}$ of different numbers.

Numbers Through Hundred Thousands

Thousands

PARENTS: Point to the multidigit numbers without reading them out loud to see how your child pronounces them first.

We have been learning how to build and recognize numbers. You can count to 100. Now let's count by hundreds, like this: 100, 200, 300, 400, 500, 600, 700, 800, 900. What comes next? 1,000. Remember that 10 hundreds are the same as 1,000.

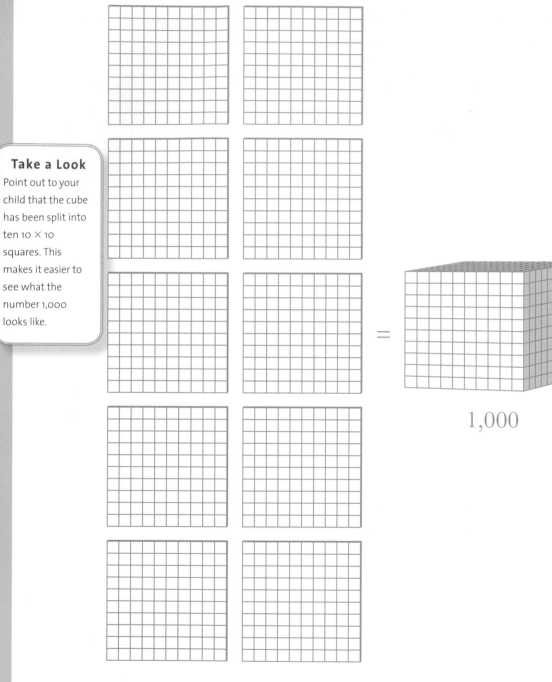

Take a Look

Point out to your child that the cube has been split into ten 10 × 10 squares. This makes it easier to see what the number 1,000 looks like.

=

1,000

Ten hundreds

The number 1,000 has four digits. The place of a digit in a number affects its value. Let's look at the place values in the four-digit number 2,453.

thousands	,	hundreds	tens	ones
2	,	4	5	3

The 2 in the thousands place is 2,000.

The 4 in the hundreds place is 400.

The 5 in the tens place is 50.

The 3 in the ones place is 3.

You read 2,453 as "two thousand, four hundred fifty-three."

Make a place value chart and practice putting four-digit numbers in it. 1,965 would look like this:

thousands	,	hundreds	tens	ones
1	,	9	6	5

Reading and Writing Four-Digit Numbers

In digits, the thousands are written 1,000, 2000, 3,000, 4,000, 5,000, 6,000, 7,000, 8,000, 9,000. In words, the thousands are written one thousand, two thousand, three thousand, four thousand, five thousand, six thousand, seven thousand, eight thousand, nine thousand.

Learn to read any four-digit number, beginning with the thousands place. For example, 8,329 is read "eight thousand, three hundred twenty-nine." How would you read 5,791? How would you read 2,015?

Learn to write any four-digit number in digits or in words. For example, in digits, two thousand, seven hundred thirty-three is written 2,733. In words, 6,364 is written "six thousand, three hundred sixty-four." Notice that you always put a comma between the thousands place and the hundreds place. This comma makes it easier to read large numbers.

Do It Yourself

Create a table modeled after the one at the top of this page. Ask your child to think of a few other numbers and have him insert them into the table.

If we were to fill in the place value chart with some numbers we have learned so far, it would look like this:

thousands	,	hundreds	tens	ones
				1
			1	0
		1	0	0
1	,	0	0	0

The place value chart can show numbers so big we couldn't fit the whole chart on the page. For now, let's learn these two new place values.

Ten Thousands and Hundred Thousands

The next two place values we will learn are the ten thousands place and the hundred thousands place.

hundred thousands	ten thousands	thousands	,	hundreds	tens	ones
2	6	7	,	3	5	3

The 2 in the hundred thousands place is   200,000.

The 6 in the ten thousands place is   60,000.

The 7 in the thousands place is   7,000.

The 3 in the hundreds place is   300.

The 5 in the tens place is   50.

The 3 in the ones place is   3.

You read 267,353 as "two hundred sixty-seven thousand, three hundred fifty-three."

Learn to read and write five- and six-digit numbers. For example, you read 864,374 as "eight hundred sixty-four thousand, three hundred seventy-four."

You write six hundred thousand, eighty-four in digits as 600,084. You write 450,057 in words as "four hundred fifty thousand, fifty-seven."

Get the picture? Now write down a few numbers above 100,000 and say them out loud.

Expanded Form

We say that 287 is in standard form, but the expanded form of 287 is $200 + 80 + 7$. Learn to write numbers with places in the thousands in expanded form.

4,325 in expanded form is $4,000 + 300 + 20 + 5$.
50,802 in expanded form is $50,000 + 800 + 2$.
72,981 in expanded form is $70,000 + 2,000 + 900 + 80 + 1$.

Practice writing many large numbers like these in expanded form. Also practice writing numbers that are in expanded form in standard form. In standard form, $700,000 + 5,000 + 600 + 7$ is 705,607.

Counting with Thousands

You count from a thousand to the next thousand by counting all 999 numbers in between. From 1,000 to 2,000, the numbers are 1,001, 1,002, 1,003, . . . 1,999, 2,000. (The three dots [. . .] mean "and so on.")

It takes too long to count from any one thousand to the next. Practice counting in short stretches. Count from 4,994 until you reach the next thousand: 4,994, 4,995, 4,996, 4,997, 4,998, 4,999, 5,000. Or count backward from 56,003 like this: 56,003, 56,002, 56,001, 56,000. Can you count forward from 7,989 to the next thousand and backward from 23,010 to the nearest thousand?

Counting forward is the same as adding 1 each time. Learn to add 1 to numbers quickly in your head, like this:

$3,999 + 1 = 4,000 \quad 62,099 + 1 = 62,100 \quad 124,999 + 1 = 125,000$

Counting backward is the same as subtracting 1 each time. Learn to subtract 1 from numbers quickly in your head, like this:

$3,000 - 1 = 2,999 \quad 94,260 - 1 = 94,259 \quad 300,000 - 1 = 299,999$

Also practice writing the numbers that come before and after a number. Here are the numbers that come before and after 76,609.

Before
76,608 ⟵

76,609 ⟶

After
76,610

Skip-Counting with Thousands

Do It Yourself

Pick numbers in the thousands to practice skip-counting by fives and tens and by either evens or odds. Practice going both forward and backward from that number.

Learn to continue a line of numbers either forward or backward, counting by tens, fives, evens, or odds. Here are some examples.

counting by tens: forward — 7,210, 7,220, 7,230, 7,240
                        backward — 7,210, 7,200, 7,190, 7,180

counting by odds: forward — 23,995, 23,997, 23,999, 24,001
                        backward — 23,995, 23,993, 23,991, 23,989

counting by fives: forward — 8,005, 8,010, 8,015, 8,020
                        backward — 8,005, 8,000, 7,995, 7,990

Rounding Numbers

Sometimes it is easier to say *about* how much something is instead of *exactly* how much it is. For instance, you might say that the night sky looks as if it contains "about 100,000 stars," not "128,347 stars." This is called rounding numbers. You round a number to show about how large it is. You can round a number to the nearest ten, hundred, thousand, or hundred thousand.

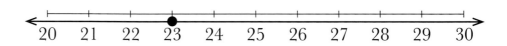

To round a number to the nearest ten, you make it into the ten that is closer. Take the number 23, for example. The number 23 is between 20 and 30. It is closer to 20 than it is to 30. So, 23 rounded to the nearest ten is 20.

The number 27 is also between 20 and 30, but it is closer to 30. So, 27 rounded to the nearest ten is 30.

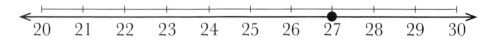

There is a rule you need to learn about rounding. When a number is exactly between two numbers, you round *up* to the greater number. For example, take 25, which is exactly between 20 and 30. You round 25 up to 30.

You round to the nearest hundred or thousand in the same way. Round 362 to the nearest hundred. 362 is between 300 and 400. It is closer to 400, so 362 rounded to the nearest hundred is 400. Round 8,257 to the nearest thousand. 8,257 is between 8,000 and 9,000. It is closer to 8,000. So 8,257 rounded to the nearest thousand is 8,000.

You do not always round numbers to the highest place value. 7,048 rounded to the nearest ten is 7,050. 6,152 rounded to the nearest hundred is 6,200.

Comparing and Ordering Thousands

When you compare two numbers to see which is greater, always compare the digits in the largest place value first. That means you start from the left. Then compare the number in the next-largest place value, and so on. As soon as you find that a number is greater in a place value, the entire number must be greater. Of course, any number that has thousands is greater than any number that just has hundreds. For example, 1,002 > 998. In the same way, 100,002 > 99,998.

Let's look at an example that will help you see how to figure out whether <, >, or = belongs between two large numbers. Our numbers are 4,827 and 4,900. If you think of them arranged by place values, you can set them up like this:

thousands	,	hundreds	tens	ones
4	,	8	2	7
4	,	9	0	0

The hundreds are different.

The thousands are the same.

First, compare the thousands place. 4,000 = 4,000. The thousands are the same. So far the numbers seem equal. Then compare the hundreds place. 800 < 900. So 4,827 < 4,900.

Now compare 53,505 and 53,089.

ten thousands	thousands	,	hundreds	tens	ones
5	3	,	5	0	5
5	3	,	0	8	9

Remember that you can order numbers from least to greatest. To order 4,567; 5,892; 3,853; 5,889 from least to greatest, you would write 3,853; 4,567; 5,889; 5,892.

You can also order numbers from greatest to least. These six numbers are ordered from greatest to least: 58,694; 58,599; 46,822; 46,083; 1,003; 99.

Order these numbers from least to greatest: 65; 96; 4,560; 4,575; 4,556; 45,765; 79,243; 67,221. Now find numbers all over your house, at least six of them, and order them from greatest to least. (Hint: Appliance serial numbers are fun. So are grocery store product code numbers.)

Working with Numbers

Equations and Inequalities

Remember that a number statement that uses an equals sign is called an equation. $5 + 4 = 9$ and $221 = 221$ are both equations.

A number statement that uses the sign > or < is called an inequality. An inequality shows in what way numbers are *not* equal. $4{,}827 < 4{,}900$ and $1{,}002 > 997$ are both inequalities, saying that 4,827 is less than 4,900 and that 1,002 is greater than 997.

Ordinal Numbers Through One-Hundredth

Ordinal numbers give the place of something in an order. For example, June is the *sixth* month of the year. "Sixth" is an ordinal number.

You may already know some ordinal numbers, like "first" and "tenth" and "thirty-first." The ordinal numbers continue in the same way to one-hundredth: thirty-first, thirty-second, thirty-third, thirty-fourth, thirty-fifth, thirty-sixth, thirty-seventh, thirty-eighth, thirty-ninth, fortieth, forty-first, . . . , ninety-ninth, one-hundredth.

You don't always have to write ordinal numbers out; sometimes they can be abbreviated. Here's a chart that gives you a few examples of the ways to abbreviate them.

Ordinal Number	Abbreviation	Ordinal Number	Abbreviation
first	1st	thirty-first	31st
second	2nd	thirty-second	32nd
third	3rd	thirty-third	33rd
fourth	4th	thirty-fourth	34th

All the ordinals that end in "-th" are abbreviated in the same way as fourth and thirty-fourth. For example, sixty-fifth is 65th. Eighty-ninth is 89th.

Using Number Lines

A *number line* shows numbers in order. A number line has arrows because the numbers on the line keep going on forever.

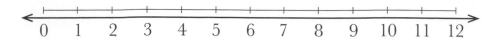

A number line can show the larger numbers you've been learning about.

And a number line can show negative numbers. Negative numbers are the numbers to the left of zero on a number line.

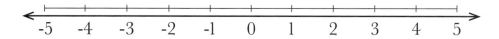

Positive numbers are the numbers to the right of zero on the number line. Zero is neither positive nor negative. You can write positive numbers with or without a + sign: +2 = 2 (positive two equals two). You *must* write a negative sign with a negative number: –2 = negative 2.

Addition and Subtraction

. . . .

Column Addition

Learn to add four or more numbers in a column. Here is an example. Begin by adding the ones column down.

Add the ones.
Regroup if necessary.

Add the tens.

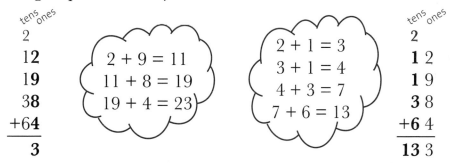

To do column addition, you often need to add combinations like $11 + 8 = 19$ or $19 + 4 = 23$ in your head. You also often have to regroup more than 1 ten. 23 ones is the same as 2 tens and 3 ones.

When you do a math problem, you should always check your work. To check column addition, you add up from the bottom. Here's a check of the problem we just did.

Add the ones.

Add the tens.

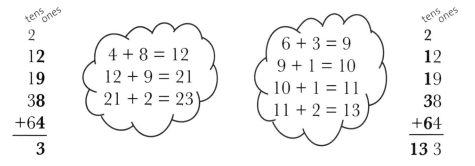

Mental Addition

Remember that you can use parentheses to group addends in different ways without changing the sum.

$$(8 + 2) + 3 = 13 \qquad 8 + (2 + 3) = 13$$

You can also add numbers in a different order without changing the sum.

$$2 + 3 = 5 \qquad 3 + 2 = 5$$

So when you are adding many numbers together, you can group them, and then add them, in the easiest way. To find the sum of $8 + 6 + 2 + 9 + 4$ easily, group the pairs of numbers that add to 10, like this:

$$8 + 6 + 2 + 9 + 4 = (8 + 2) + (6 + 4) + 9$$
$$= 10 + 10 + 9$$
$$= 29$$

When you are adding two-digit numbers in your head, look for two numbers that make an even 10. To add $28 + 35 + 12$ easily, group the numbers like this:

$$28 + 35 + 12 = (28 + 12) + 35$$
$$= 40 + 35$$
$$= 75$$

More Mental Addition Techniques

Here is another method to help you add numbers in your head. When you are adding a number that ends in 9, you can make it an even 10, and then subtract 1 from the final sum. For example, to add 37 and 29, you can think $29 = 30 - 1$.

Think: $37 + 29 = 37 + 30 - 1 = 67 - 1 = 66$

You can make an addend an even hundred and then subtract in the same way. To add 253 and 198, you can think $198 = 200 - 2$.

Think: $253 + 198 = 253 + 200 - 2 = 453 - 2 = 451$

When you are adding in your head, it is often easier to add a number in two parts. To find the sum of 84 and 28, you can think: $84 + 16$ makes an even hundred. So, make 28 into $16 + 12$.

Think: $84 + 28 = 84 + 16 + 12 = 100 + 12 = 112$

Here is another example.

Think: $365 + 411 = 365 + 400 + 11 = 765 + 11 = 776$

Practice doing many mental addition problems, using these methods whenever they will help you.

Estimating Sums and Differences

To "estimate" means to come quickly to an answer that is close to right. When you do not need to know an answer exactly, you can estimate to find out quickly what the approximate answer is. You can estimate the sums of two-digit numbers by rounding each number to the nearest ten and then adding. Here is an example.

$$
\begin{array}{ccc}
 & \text{rounds to} & \\
29 & \longrightarrow & 30 \\
+45 & \longrightarrow & +50 \\
\hline
 & & 80
\end{array}
$$

$29 + 45$ is about 80.

You can estimate the differences of two-digit numbers in the same way.

$$
\begin{array}{ccc}
 & \text{rounds to} & \\
87 & \longrightarrow & 90 \\
-41 & \longrightarrow & -40 \\
\hline
 & & 50
\end{array}
$$

$87 - 41$ is about 50.

You can estimate the sums and differences of three-digit numbers by rounding to the nearest hundred, and then adding or subtracting.

$$\begin{array}{r} \text{rounds to} \\ 559 \quad \longrightarrow \quad 600 \\ +318 \quad \longrightarrow \quad +300 \\ \hline 900 \end{array}$$

$$\begin{array}{r} \text{rounds to} \\ 419 \quad \longrightarrow \quad 400 \\ -187 \quad \longrightarrow \quad -200 \\ \hline 200 \end{array}$$

Practice adding and subtracting by estimating. Because you can add and subtract very quickly when you estimate, you can also use estimation as a quick way to check an answer. But estimation can only tell you if your answer is *about* right; it is not a sure way to check.

More than One Operation

Sometimes you have to do more than one operation in a problem. For example, sometimes you have to both add and multiply. When there is more than one operation, always do the operation inside the parentheses first. Here is an example.

$$7 \times (12 - 8) = 7 \times 4 = 28$$

Practice doing many problems with different kinds of operations. Here are some more examples.

1. $(10 + 2) - (6 + 2) =$
   $\quad 12 \quad - \quad 8 \quad = 4$

2. $(43 - 38) \times (5 + 3) =$
   $\quad 5 \quad \times \quad 8 \quad = 40$

3. $(9 \times 4) + (6 \times 5) =$
   $\quad 36 \quad + \quad 30 \quad = 66$

4. $(36 \div 6) \div (4 - 1) =$
   $\quad 6 \quad \div \quad 3 \quad = 2$

Practice writing >, <, or = in problems like these, which use more than one operation.

$$8 \times 6 < 82 - 31 \qquad 63 \div 9 > 3 \times 2 \qquad 21 + 11 = 4 \times 8$$

Remember that $8 \times 6 < 82 - 31$ and $63 \div 9 > 3 \times 2$ are inequalities. $21 + 11 = 4 \times 8$ is an equation.

Mental Subtraction

Here is a method to help you subtract numbers in your head. When you are subtracting a number that ends in 9, you can subtract an even 10 instead, and then add 1.

For example, to take 19 away from 54, you can think: subtracting 19 is the same as subtracting 20 and then adding 1.

Think: $54 - 19 = 54 - 20 + 1 = 34 + 1 = 35$

You can make a number you are subtracting an even hundred in the same way. For example, to subtract 198 from 426, you can think: subtracting 198 is the same as subtracting 200 and then adding 2.

Think: $426 - 198 = 426 - 200 + 2 = 226 + 2 = 228$

When you are subtracting in your head, it is often easier to subtract a number by first taking away part of the number, and then taking away the rest. For example, to subtract 23 from 48, you can first subtract 20, and then subtract 3 more.

Think: $48 - 23 = (48 - 20) - 3 = 28 - 3 = 25$

To solve $125 - 29 = $ _____, you can think: $125 - 25$ makes an even hundred. So, think of taking away 29 as first taking away 25, then taking away 4 more.

Think: $125 - 29 = (125 - 25) - 4 = 100 - 4 = 96$

Practice doing many mental subtraction problems, using these methods whenever they will help you.

Sums and Differences of Four-Digit Numbers

Adding with Thousands

Sometimes when you add, you need to regroup hundreds as thousands. When you add vertically, always work from right to left. Let's find the sum of 2,635 and 3,728. To find this sum, add the ones, then the tens, then the hundreds, and then the thousands.

$$
\begin{array}{r}
2{,}635 \\
+\,3{,}728 \\
\hline
\end{array}
\qquad\qquad
\begin{array}{r}
1\,\,1 \\
2{,}635 \\
+\,3{,}728 \\
\hline
6{,}363
\end{array}
$$

In the same way you have learned to regroup ones as tens, regroup when necessary as you move to the left. In this problem, you do not need to regroup tens as hundreds, but you do need to regroup hundreds as thousands. Six hundreds plus 7 hundreds equals 13 hundreds. You regroup 13 hundreds as 1 thousand, 3 hundreds. Then you add the thousands. The sum equals 6,363.

$$
\begin{array}{r}
5{,}627 \\
7{,}482 \\
38 \\
+\quad 975 \\
\hline
\end{array}
\qquad\qquad
\begin{array}{r}
1\,2{,}2\,2 \\
5{,}627 \\
7{,}482 \\
38 \\
+\quad 975 \\
\hline
14{,}122
\end{array}
$$

Practice finding sums with three or more addends, as well as with two addends. Sometimes when you are adding four-digit numbers, you need to regroup thousands as ten thousands. You write 14 thousands as 1 ten thousand, 4 thousands.

You often have to add numbers together that have a different number of digits. Given a problem like 3,584 + 723 + 19 + 250, practice writing the numbers in columns and then adding them. Make sure to keep the numbers in the correct place value column.

$$
\begin{array}{r}
\text{thousands} \; \text{hundreds} \; \text{tens} \; \text{ones} \\
1,1\,1 \\
3,5\,8\,4 \\
7\,2\,3 \\
1\,9 \\
+ \quad 2\,5\,0 \\
\hline
4,5\,7\,6
\end{array}
$$

In general, practice doing addition in columns until it is easy for you and you are very good at regrouping. With three addends, add up to check. With only two addends, rewrite the addends in a different order, and then add up. Also practice estimating, to see if the sum is about right.

To estimate the sum of four-digit numbers, round to the nearest thousand.

rounds to

$$
\begin{array}{ccc}
5{,}334 & \longrightarrow & 5{,}000 \\
+2{,}926 & \longrightarrow & +3{,}000 \\
\hline
& & 8{,}000
\end{array}
$$

5,334 + 2,926 is about 5,000 + 3,000, which equals 8,000. So you know that the sum of 5,334 and 2,926 should be *about* 8,000. When you actually add the two numbers, what do you get? Is it near 8,000?

Subtraction: Regrouping More than Once

Sometimes when you subtract, you need to regroup more than once. When you subtract vertically, work from right to left.

Because you cannot take 9 from 4, regroup.

$$
\begin{array}{r}
524 \\
-389 \\
\hline
\end{array}
$$

Subtract the ones.

$$
\begin{array}{r}
1\;14 \\
5\cancel{2}\cancel{4} \\
-389 \\
\hline
5
\end{array}
$$

Because you cannot take 8 tens from 1 ten, regroup again.

$$
\begin{array}{r}
11 \\
4\;\cancel{1}\;14 \\
\cancel{5}\cancel{2}\cancel{4} \\
-389 \\
\hline
35
\end{array}
$$

Subtract the tens. Subtract the hundreds.

$$
\begin{array}{r}
11 \\
4\;1\;14 \\
\cancel{5}\cancel{2}\cancel{4} \\
-389 \\
\hline
135
\end{array}
$$

The difference is 135.

Make up subtraction problems in which you have to regroup more than once and practice them many times.

Subtracting Across Zeros

Sometimes when you need to regroup, there is a zero in the next place. Then you need to regroup in a different way. Here is an example. Find the difference of 304 and 187.

$$
\begin{array}{r}
\text{hundreds tens ones}\\
3\,0\,4\\
-\,1\,8\,7\\
\hline
\end{array}
$$

Subtract the ones. Because you cannot take 7 from 4, you need to regroup. But there are no tens to regroup. Change 3 hundreds to 2 hundreds and 10 tens. The 1 in front of the 0 in the tens column indicates a ten in that column. Now change the 10 tens to 9 tens and 10 ones.

$$
\begin{array}{r}
\quad 9\\
2\;1\cancel{0}\;14\\
\cancel{3}\cancel{0}\cancel{4}\\
-\,1\,8\,7\\
\hline
1\,1\,7
\end{array}
\qquad
\begin{array}{r}
2\;\;9\;14\\
\cancel{3}\cancel{0}\cancel{4}\\
-\,1\,8\,7\\
\hline
1\,1\,7
\end{array}
$$

You can also think: change 30 tens to 29 tens and 10 ones, adding those to the 4 in the ones place.

Let's see how this process works when you have to subtract across several zeros. When subtracting four-digit numbers, first subtract the ones, then the tens, then the hundreds, and then the thousands.

$$
\begin{array}{r}
4{,}0\,0\,0\\
-\,2{,}8\,9\,6\\
\hline
\end{array}
$$

Think: You need an extra ten for the ones place. Change 400 tens to 399 tens and add the extra ten to the ones place. Then subtract the ones, the tens, the hundreds, and the thousands, column by column.

$$
\begin{array}{r}
3\;\;9\;9\;10\\
\cancel{4}{,}\cancel{0}\cancel{0}\cancel{0}\\
-\,2{,}8\,9\,6\\
\hline
\end{array}
\qquad
\begin{array}{r}
3\;\;9\;9\;10\\
\cancel{4}{,}\cancel{0}\cancel{0}\cancel{0}\\
-\,2{,}8\,9\,6\\
\hline
1{,}1\,0\,4
\end{array}
$$

Four-Digit Subtraction

Practice subtracting with four-digit numbers until you can do it easily, especially across zeros. Practice writing a subtraction problem in columns and then subtracting. Here is an example. Find the difference of 3,037 and 1,682.

$$
\begin{array}{r} 3,037 \\ -1,682 \\ \hline \end{array}
\qquad
\begin{array}{r} 3,037 \\ -1,682 \\ \hline 5 \end{array}
\qquad
\begin{array}{r} {}^{2\ \ 9\ 13} \\ 3,0\cancel{3}7 \\ -1,682 \\ \hline 55 \end{array}
\qquad
\begin{array}{r} {}^{2\ \ 9\ 13} \\ 3,\cancel{0}\cancel{3}7 \\ -1,682 \\ \hline 355 \end{array}
\qquad
\begin{array}{r} {}^{2\ \ 9\ 13} \\ \cancel{3},\cancel{0}\cancel{3}7 \\ -1,682 \\ \hline 1,355 \end{array}
$$

Remember to check each subtraction problem by addition, like this:

$$
\begin{array}{r} {}^{2\ \ 9\ 13} \\ 3,037 \\ -1,682 \\ \hline 1,355 \end{array}
\qquad\qquad
\begin{array}{r} 1,355 \\ +1,682 \\ \hline \end{array}
\qquad\qquad
\begin{array}{r} {}^{1\ \ 1} \\ 1,355 \\ +1,682 \\ \hline 3,037 \end{array}
$$

You can also check to see if the difference of four-digit numbers is about right by estimating. Round each number to the nearest thousand and then subtract.

$$
\begin{array}{ccc}
 & \text{rounds to} & \\
3,037 & \longrightarrow & 3,000 \\
-1,682 & \longrightarrow & -2,000 \\
\hline
 & & 1,000
\end{array}
$$

3,037 − 1,682 is about 1,000. What would 1,355 round to? 1,000.

Adding and Subtracting Amounts of Money

You add and subtract amounts of money the same way you add and subtract other numbers. Here are two examples.

		7 17			2 1
1.	$85.87	$85.8̶7̶	2.	$51.68	$51.68
	−13.48	−13.48		2.80	2.80
		$72.39		0.56	0.56
				+12.84	+12.84
					$67.88

Do not forget to write the dollar sign and the decimal point between dollars and cents in your answer.

Mental Addition and Subtraction

You can add and subtract thousands the same way you add and subtract ones.

$$7 + 2 = 9 \qquad\qquad 60 - 20 = 40$$
$$7{,}000 + 2{,}000 = 9{,}000 \qquad 60{,}000 - 20{,}000 = 40{,}000$$

Learn to add and subtract thousands mentally in problems like these.

$$6{,}000 \ + \underline{\hspace{1.5cm}} = 9{,}000$$
$$54{,}000 \ - 24{,}000 = \underline{\hspace{2cm}}$$
$$350{,}000 + \underline{\hspace{1.5cm}} = 450{,}000$$

Also practice adding the amount it takes to make the next thousand. This will help you learn place value.

$$9{,}990 \ + \underline{\hspace{3cm}} = 10{,}000$$
$$39{,}900 + \underline{\hspace{3cm}} = 40{,}000$$
$$59{,}980 + \underline{\hspace{3cm}} = 60{,}000$$

Time, Money, and Graphs

Time to the Minute

Learn to tell time to the minute quickly. Remember that the minute hand moves from one number to the next in 5 minutes. On many clocks there is a short mark for each minute in between. In 1 minute, the minute hand moves from one of these short marks to the next.

It is 9:20.

It is 9:21.

In the picture, the minute hand is on the third mark between 1:45 and 1:50.

It is 1:48.

Practice writing time in minutes before and after an hour. To find how many minutes it is before the next hour, subtract how many minutes it is after the hour from 60. 2:38 is 22 minutes before 3:00.

$$\begin{array}{r} 5\ 10 \\ \not{6}\not{0} \\ -\ 3\ 8 \\ \hline 2\ 2 \end{array}$$

Elapsed Time in Minutes

Learn to find how much time has elapsed in minutes. From 10:15 to 10:45 is 30 minutes, because 45 − 15 = 30.

To find how many minutes it is from 2:35 to 3:18, you do the problem in two steps. First, find how many minutes it is from 2:35 to 3:00: 25 minutes, because 60 − 35 = 25. Then add 18 more minutes for the time from 3:00 to 3:18. So, 25 minutes + 18 minutes = 43 minutes. From 2:35 to 3:18 is 43 minutes.

Do It Yourself

Try this: Ask your child to create a schedule for his perfect day. Make sure he keeps track of time!

A.M. and P.M.

You already know there are 24 hours in a day. Do you remember that in each day there are 12 a.m. hours and 12 p.m. hours? The a.m. hours are between 12 midnight and 12 noon. The p.m. hours are between 12 noon and 12 midnight.

Do you get up and get dressed at 7:30 a.m. or 7:30 p.m.?

Do you eat dinner closer to 6 a.m. or 6 p.m.?

Do you go to bed closer to 9 a.m. or 9 p.m.?

The abbreviations "a.m." and "p.m." stand for the Latin phrases *ante meridiem* and *post meridiem,* which mean "before noon" and "after noon."

Make a Connection

After looking at the calendar and observing the name of the month and the names of the days of the week, turn back to page 142 (Roman history) to remind your child where the name December came from. Then turn to page 64 (Norse mythology) and remind your child of the Norse origins of the words we use for the days of the week.

Working with the Calendar

Let's learn how to find a date that comes weeks before or after another date. Here's how.

Remember that a week has 7 days. One week before December 12 is December 5, because $12 - 7 = 5$. What is 2 weeks after December 12? There are 14 days in 2 weeks, because $2 \times 7 = 14$. Because $12 + 14 = 26$, we know that 2 weeks after December 12 is December 26.

Learn to find the date weeks before and after another date.

DECEMBER

SUNDAY	MONDAY	TUESDAY	WEDNESDAY	THURSDAY	FRIDAY	SATURDAY
		1	2	3	4	5
6	7	8	9	10	11	12
13	14	15	16	17	18	19
20	21	22	23	24	25	26
27	28	29	30	31		

You can also find out on which day of the week a date comes. Look at the calendar on the next page to work out these examples. If May 10 is a Saturday, May 17, a week later, will also be a Saturday. What day of the week will be 10 days after Wednesday? In 7 days, it will be Wednesday again. Thursday is the 8th day, Friday the 9th, and Saturday the 10th. So, 10 days after Wednesday will be a Saturday.

			MAY			
SUNDAY	MONDAY	TUESDAY	WEDNESDAY	THURSDAY	FRIDAY	SATURDAY
				1	2	3
4	5	6	7	8	9	10
11	12	13	14	15	16	17
18	19	20	21	22	23	24
25	26	27	28	29	30	31

Writing Dates

You can write dates using words and numbers or using only numbers.

October 31, 2014

Use 10 for → 10/31/14 ← Use 14 for
the 10th month. the year 2014.

Use 31 for the 31st day of the month.

Now write your birthday using words and numbers and using only numbers.

Money

Time to count some money. First, learn these new bills.

A five-dollar bill

$5.00

500¢

A ten-dollar bill

$10.00

1,000¢

A twenty-dollar bill

$20.00

2,000¢

Learn to write amounts of money in dollars and in cents. $8.45 is 845¢ and 1,127¢ is $11.27.

Learn how to make change. Here's a problem to practice.

Alice buys a granola bar for 54¢. She gives the clerk a $1 bill. The clerk makes change by counting forward from the cost of the granola bar. She starts at 54¢. She adds 1 penny = 55¢, plus a dime = 65¢, plus another dime = 75¢, plus a quarter = $1. So the clerk gives Alice a penny, two dimes, and a quarter.

Alice can check her change with subtraction. $1 minus 54¢ is 100¢ − 54¢ = 46¢. So, Alice will get 46¢ in change. A penny, two dimes, and a quarter add up to 46¢.

You make change by counting forward from the cost of what was bought to the amount paid for it. You should use a few coins or bills of least value and work toward the coins or bills of greatest value. For example, a customer gives Roberta $20 for a book that costs $11.43. What change should Roberta give? Two pennies come to $11.45. A nickel comes to $11.50. Two quarters come to $12. Three $1 bills make $15. A $5 bill makes $20.

Practice making change using as few bills and coins as possible. You can make up your own examples, but here's one to get you started. How much change does Ron get from a hundred-dollar bill if his groceries cost $73.18?

Reading and Writing Graphs

A graph is a way of showing information in a diagram. Learn to read line graphs and bar graphs. Here is a bar graph.

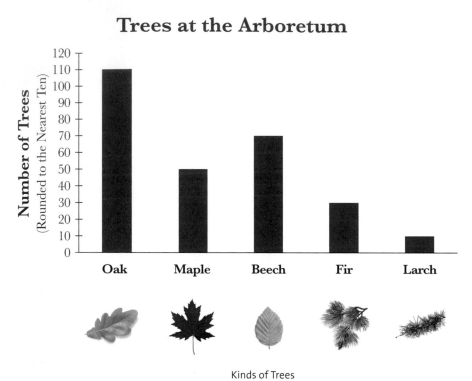

Trees at the Arboretum

Kinds of Trees

This bar graph shows how many of each kind of tree there are at the arboretum, rounded to the nearest ten. Each bar, or rectangle, on the graph shows about how many trees of a certain kind there are. For example, there are about 70 beeches. About how many more oaks than maples are there? Sixty more oaks, because $110 - 50 = 60$.

Here is a line graph.

Daily High Temperatures for the Week of February 7–13

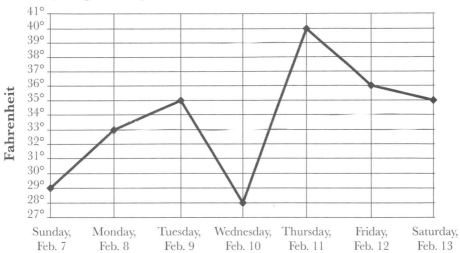

This line graph shows the daily high temperatures for the week of February 7 to 13. Each point shows the high temperature on that day. The line segments connect the points to show how the high temperature changed from day to day. The change in high temperature from Wednesday to Thursday was 12°F. How much warmer was the high temperature on Friday than on Sunday? 7°F, because 36 − 29 = 7.

You can make a graph, too. Here is a bar graph we made when we tossed a penny in the air 20 times and recorded how it fell each time. First we recorded how each toss fell. Nine tosses came up heads, and 11 tosses came up tails.

Then we wrote the same information on a graph. For the number of heads that came up, we made one bar. For the number of tails that came up, we made a second bar.

Now you try it. Toss a penny into the air 20 or even 30 times, and record how many times it comes up heads or tails. Then make your own graph.

Talk and Think

Ask your child what kind of graph she would use to show:

• The number of fish a fisherman caught per day this week

• The amount of money a person made per year over 10 years

• How many votes different candidates in an election for class president received

	1	2	3	4	5	6	7	8	9	10	11	12	13	14	15
Heads															
Tails															

Geometry

Polygons

Remember these kinds of lines?

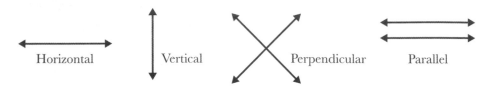

Horizontal   Vertical   Perpendicular   Parallel

Remember the difference between closed figures and open figures?

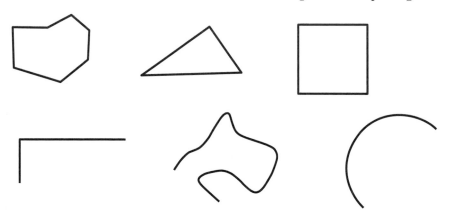

A closed figure can be formed entirely with line segments. Here is line segment TS or ST. A line segment gets its name from the letters assigned to its end points.

S   T

Do It Yourself

Ask your child to draw the first shapes that come to mind. Then ask her to identify them as open figures or closed figures.

A closed figure that is formed by line segments is called a polygon. Triangles, rectangles, and squares are polygons; circles are not polygons.

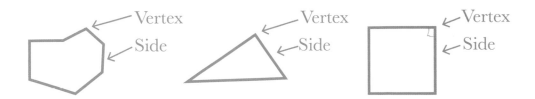

In a polygon, each side is a line segment. The point where two line segments meet is called a vertex. (The plural of "vertex" is "vertices" or "vertexes.")

Like all points, vertices are named by letters. You name a polygon by starting at one vertex and naming all the other vertices in order. Here are two examples.

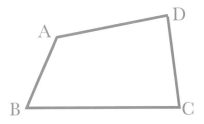

Starting at point B, you could name this figure polygon BADC; you could also name it by naming the vertices in the other direction: polygon BCDA. Or you could start with any of the other points and name the vertices in order in either direction. Altogether, there are eight possible names for this polygon. Can you write all of them?

> **Do It Yourself**
> Have fun with polygons. Draw a polygon with a certain number of sides— let's say five. Now draw another polygon with five sides that looks very different. See how many polygons you can make with five sides. Now do the same thing with a 10-sided polygon.

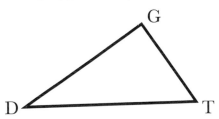

Here are the six possible names for the triangle above: triangle DGT, triangle DTG, triangle TGD, triangle TDG, triangle GTD, triangle GDT.

Angles

Whenever two sides of a polygon meet, they form an angle. Here's an example of an angle.

Angle

This polygon has four sides, four vertices, and four angles.

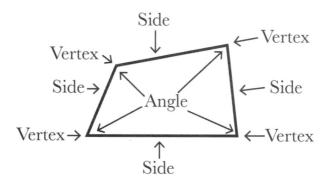

A right angle is an angle that forms a square corner.

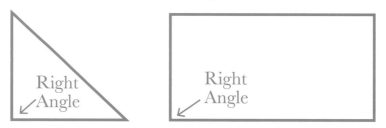

Squares and rectangles have four right angles.

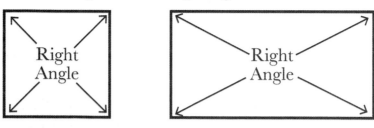

Congruent and Symmetric Figures

Two figures that are exactly the same shape and size are said to be *congruent*. Sometimes you have to turn one figure around to see if it is congruent with another. These two triangles are congruent.

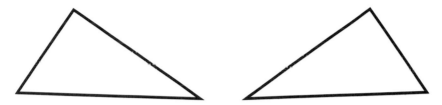

These two triangles are not congruent. They have the same shape but not the same size.

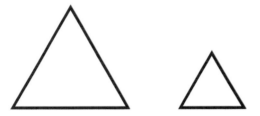

When a figure can be folded in half and both halves match, the figure is said to be *symmetrical*. The fold line is called the *line of symmetry*. Sometimes figures have more than one line of symmetry. For example, a square has four lines of symmetry.

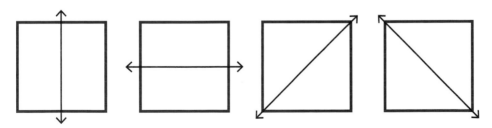

A circle has more lines of symmetry than you can count. Think how many different folds you can make down the center of a circle. Every time you do it, the two halves match.

Do It Yourself

Try this: Cut shapes out of paper with your child and fold them in half to create lines of symmetry.

You can fold figures to see if they are symmetric. If they are symmetric, you can see how many lines of symmetry they have.

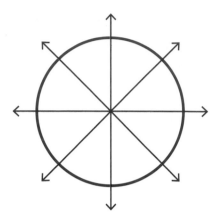

Make a Geometry Mobile

Make four or five symmetrical shapes out of construction paper. What sorts of symmetrical figures would you like to see floating in the air? All triangles, or an assortment of hearts, circles, and cones? Use a hole puncher or poke a hole in each. Then cut string or thread into 12-centimeter lengths and tie the threads through the holes in your figures. You can use twigs or craft sticks to hang the figures. The hard part is finding the right lengths for each string to make the pieces balance each other in a pattern you like.

Perimeter

Perimeter is the distance around a figure. To find the perimeter of a figure, add the lengths of its sides together.

Practice measuring the sides of polygons to the nearest inch or centimeter, and then add the lengths together to find the perimeter of the polygon in inches or centimeters. Here is an example in centimeters.

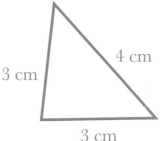

3 cm + 4 cm + 3 cm = 10 cm. The perimeter of the triangle is 10 centimeters.

Area

The area of a figure is the number of square units that cover its surface. A square unit has sides that are each 1 unit long. For example, this is a square centimeter:

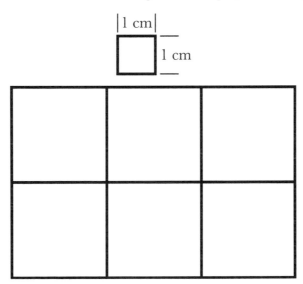

This rectangle has an area of 6 square inches. You write 6 square inches as 6 in.^{2}.

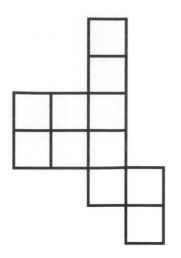

This polygon has an area of 11 square centimeters. You write 11 square centimeters as 11 cm².

Learn to find the area of a figure by counting square units. Make sure always to write your answer in square units, such as in.² or cm².

Solids

Three-dimensional objects are often called solids.

Some solids have curved surfaces, and some solids have flat surfaces. A flat surface on a solid is called a face. The line segment where two faces meet is called an edge. Edges come together at a vertex.

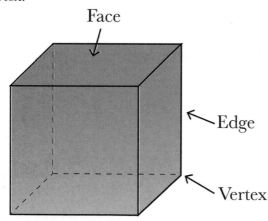

Learn to count the number of faces, edges, and vertices on solids. The point of a cone is also called a vertex.

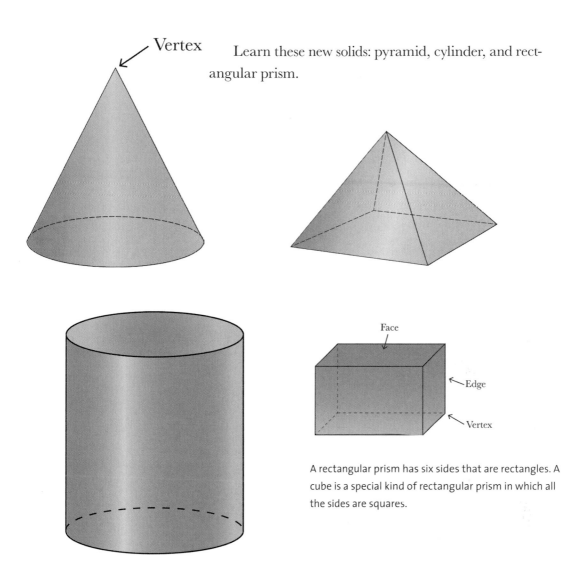

Vertex

Learn these new solids: pyramid, cylinder, and rectangular prism.

Face

Edge

Vertex

A rectangular prism has six sides that are rectangles. A cube is a special kind of rectangular prism in which all the sides are squares.

A cylinder has curved surfaces and flat surfaces.

Measurement

The U.S. Customary System and the Metric System

In the United States, we use two systems of measurement: the U.S. customary system and the metric system. You may already be familiar with both systems from your work in science.

Here are some of the units used to measure length, weight, and volume in each system. Volume means how much something can hold. The abbreviation for each unit is in parentheses.

U.S. Customary System

Length	Weight	Volume
mile (mi.)	pound (lb.)	gallon (gal.)
yard (yd.)	ounce (oz.)	quart (qt.)
foot (ft.)		pint (pt.)
inch (in.)		cup (c.)

Metric System

Length	Weight	Volume
kilometer (km)	kilogram (kg)	liter (L)
meter (m)	gram (g)	
centimeter (cm)		

Learn to change a measurement from one unit in a system to another. Here are some equations to show you how to change units in the U.S. customary system.

$$1 \text{ ft.} = 12 \text{ in.} \quad 1 \text{ lb.} = 16 \text{ oz.} \quad 1 \text{ gal.} = 4 \text{ qt.}$$
$$1 \text{ yd.} = 3 \text{ ft.} \quad 1 \text{ qt.} = 2 \text{ pt.} \quad 1 \text{ pt.} = 2 \text{ c.}$$

Here are three examples of changes between units in a system.

1. Because 1 ft. = 12 in., to find out how many inches are in 3 feet, you can add 12 inches and 12 inches and 12 inches. 12 + 12 + 12 = 36, so 3 ft. = 36 in.
2. You can find out how many quarts are in 6 gallons of milk by multiplying.

1 gal. = 4 qt.
6 × 4 = 24
6 gal. = 24 qt.

3. How many pints are in 8 cups? You can divide by 2, because 2 c. = 1 pt.

$$8 \div 2 = 4$$
$$8 \text{ c.} = 4 \text{ pt.}$$

In the metric system, it is even easier to change units because it is just like working with place value. Here are some equations for changing units in the metric system.

1 cm = 10 mm   1 kg = 1,000 g
1 m = 100 cm
1 km = 1,000 m

Each meter is 100 centimeters. So, 5 meters are 500 centimeters, because 5 × 100 = 500. Each kilometer is 1,000 meters. So, 6 kilometers are 6,000 meters, because 6 × 1,000 = 6,000. In the same way, 9 kg = 9,000 g.

Measurement Word Problems

Learn how to solve problems that involve units of measurement. For example, Mrs. Johnson has a kilogram of flour. She uses 500 grams to make 2 loaves of bread. She uses another 250 grams to make some brownies. How many grams of flour does she use, and how many does she have left?

$$500 \text{ g} + 250 \text{ g} = 750 \text{ g}$$

So, Mrs. Johnson uses 750 grams of flour. She started with 1 kilogram of flour: 1 kg = 1,000 g.

So, Mrs. Johnson has 250 grams of flour left.

$$
\begin{array}{r}
{\scriptstyle 0\ 9\ 10} \\
\cancel{1},\cancel{0}\cancel{0}0\text{g} \\
-\ \ \ 750\text{g} \\
\hline
250\text{g}
\end{array}
$$

Practice problems like these, in which you first have to add and then subtract. Be careful in measurement problems to remember which units you are working with. Always write the units you are working with in your answer.

Measure and Draw Line Segments

You've learned what a line segment is. Now you can learn to measure the lengths of line segments in metric and U.S. customary units.

To measure the line segment **AB** to the nearest inch or the nearest centimeter:

1. Line up one end of the segment with the 0 mark on your ruler.
2. Look at the other end of the segment. Find the closest inch mark or centimeter mark.

 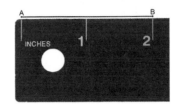

You can also measure line segments to the nearest half inch (1/2 in.) or quarter inch (1/4 in.) by using the smaller lines between the inch markers.

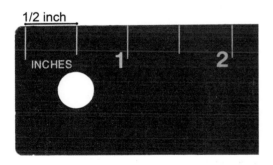 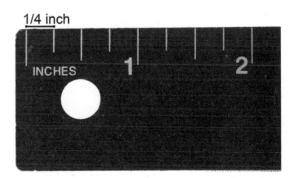

Here are some line segments. Measure each to the quarter inch and to the nearest centimeter.

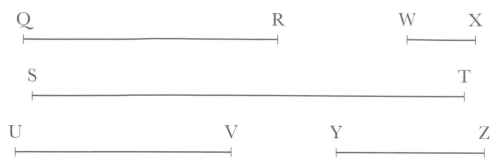

Now draw line segments of the following lengths.

4 1/2 in.	5 1/2 cm	20 cm	5 mm
10 cm	3 3/4 in.	11 1/2 in.	5 in.

Estimating Linear Measurements

When you are familiar with measuring inches, feet, centimeters, and meters, you can begin to estimate linear measurements. See the word "line" in "linear"? That's because linear measurements mean measuring on a straight line.

Would you use feet or inches to measure this turtle? Why would inches or centimeters work better for measuring the turtle than feet, yards, or meters? Estimate how many inches long this image of a turtle is. Estimate how many centimeters it is.

What about the chair you're sitting in? What measurement would work best to tell how tall it is?

Estimate the height of your chair back. Then measure your chair and compare your answers.

Estimate and then measure five real objects of different sizes. Why did you choose each measurement you used?

Do It Yourself

Keep measuring! Have your child continue to look for objects to measure around the house. With enough practice, he may be able to estimate an object's measurements without using a ruler.

Measuring Weight

When you measure how heavy something is, you are measuring weight. Have you ever learned how to use a balance scale for measuring weight? Look at the balance scales in these pictures. When one side of the balance is lower than the other, which object weighs more?

Look at the balances again. Which is heavier: the cherries or the tomatoes?

Measuring Ounces, Pounds, Grams, and Kilograms

If you have a scale to use, you can practice measuring weight. Some scales measure in ounces; some measure in pounds. Some measure in grams and kilograms. What does your scale show?

Find five objects that feel as if they weigh different amounts. Weigh your objects and write a list of them with their weights, from lightest to heaviest.

Measuring Volume

There is a system of measurement used just for liquids (like milk, juice, water, or paint). In the U.S. customary system, we use ounces, cups, pints, quarts, and gallons. In the metric system, we use liters and milliliters. A liter is a little more than a quart.

Use this table to help you answer the following questions.

UNITS OF MEASUREMENT FOR LIQUIDS

U.S. Customary Units

8 ounces = 1 cup

16 ounces = 1 pint

2 pints = 1 quart

4 quarts = 1 gallon

Metric Units

1,000 milliliters = 1 liter

1. If you pour 1 gallon of milk into quart bottles, how many quart bottles will you fill?
2. Two pints equal 1 quart. How many ounces are in a quart?
3. How many milliliters are in 3 liters?

Extra: About how many liters are in a gallon?

Measuring Temperature

Do you remember the graph, earlier in this section of the book, on page 341, that showed the daily high temperatures during a week in February? To describe the temperature, we used units called degrees, and we used a little circle to stand for that unit. The highest temperature we plotted on that graph was 40°, and the lowest temperature was 28°.

When talking about temperatures, it is best to tell whether you are using the U.S. customary system or the metric system. The U.S. customary system measures temperature in degrees Fahrenheit. The metric system measures temperature in degrees Celsius. You use the initials of those words, "F" and "C", to show which scale of measurement you are using.

What kind of weather is it when the thermometer looks like this? Can you read the temperature in degrees Celsius? In degrees Fahrenheit? Is it very hot, very cold, or just right?

The thermometer on page 357 shows temperatures using both scales of measurement. Let's use it to tell the temperature at which water freezes, in both Celsius and Fahrenheit.

A thermometer that measures temperature in degrees Celsius will read 0°C (zero degrees Celsius) when the temperature is just cold enough for water to freeze. At this same temperature, the freezing point of water, on a thermometer that measures temperature in degrees Fahrenheit will read 32°F (thirty-two degrees Fahrenheit).

Sometimes you have to use negative numbers to talk about cold temperatures. On a fall day, a Celsius thermometer might read 10°C in the middle of the afternoon, but in the middle of the night, the temperature might go down to –2°C. This temperature can be described as "negative two degrees Celsius," but people also say "two degrees below zero Celsius."

Multiplication—Part 2

Multiplying Tens, Hundreds, and Thousands

It is easy to multiply tens, hundreds, and thousands. Use the multiplication facts you already know.

3×2 **tens** $= 6$ **tens** 4×7 **hundreds** $= 28$ **hundreds**

3×20 $= 60$ 4×700 $= 2{,}800$

$$\begin{array}{r} 20 \\ \times 3 \\ \hline 60 \end{array} \qquad \begin{array}{r} 700 \\ \times\ 4 \\ \hline 2{,}800 \end{array}$$

3×6 **thousands** $= 18$ **thousands**

$3 \times 6{,}000$ $= 18{,}000$

$$\begin{array}{r} 6{,}000 \\ \times\ \ 3 \\ \hline 18{,}000 \end{array}$$

Practice solving problems like these quickly. Remember that you are multiplying tens, hundreds, or thousands. Be sure to keep the right number of zeros in the product!

A Way to Multiply

One way to multiply 3 by 16 is to break 16 into smaller numbers. Graph paper can help show how this works. On graph paper, draw a rectangle with 3 rows and 16 columns.

$$3 \times 16$$

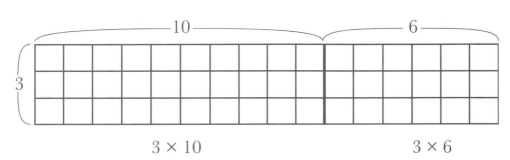

$$3 \times 10 \qquad 3 \times 6$$

You can see from the picture that 3×16 is the same as $(3 \times 10) + (3 \times 6)$. So, you can multiply 3×16 like this:

$$3 \times 16 = (3 \times 10) + (3 \times 6) = 30 + 18 = 48$$

You can also write this multiplication problem vertically, like this:

$$\begin{array}{r} 16 \\ \times\ 3 \\ \hline \end{array}$$

When you multiply vertically, you start with the ones and move to the left to the greater values.

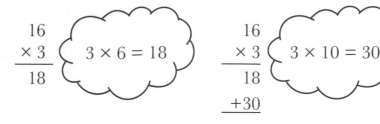

Multiply the ones.

16
× 3
18

$3 \times 6 = 18$

Multiply the tens.

16
× 3
18
+30

$3 \times 10 = 30$

16
× 3
18
+30
48

Notice how you write in the 0 to show that 3×10 is 3 tens, not 3 ones.

You can multiply 6×28 in the same way. First draw the problem on graph paper in rows and columns. Then write it vertically and multiply. Notice that first you multiply 6 by the ones, and then you multiply 6 by the tens.

28
× 6
48
+120
168

$6 \times 8 = 48$
$6 \times 20 = 120$

Practice multiplying this way, making a separate product for the ones and the tens, and then adding.

The Short Way to Multiply

Now learn the short way to write multiplication. In this method, you write the products on the same line. Let's use 23×3 as an example.

First we write it vertically.

23
× 3

Next we multiply 3 by the ones in 23.

$$
\begin{array}{r}
23 \\
\times\ 3 \\
\hline
\mathbf{9}
\end{array}
$$

Next, we multiply 3 by the tens in 23 and write the product on the same line.

$$
\begin{array}{r}
23 \\
\times\ 3 \\
\hline
69
\end{array}
$$

Often when you multiply this way, you need to regroup. See what happens when you multiply 6 by 28 this way.

Multiply 6 by 8 ones. Regroup 48 as 4 tens 8 ones. Carry the 4 to the top of the tens place.

$$
\begin{array}{r}
4 \\
28 \\
\times\ 6 \\
\hline
8
\end{array}
\qquad
\begin{array}{r}
4 \\
28 \\
\times\ 6 \\
\hline
168
\end{array}
$$

Multiply 6 by 2 tens, and then add the 4 tens: $(6 \times 2) + 4 = 12 + 4 = 16$.

Multiplying Three-Digit and Four-Digit Numbers

You can multiply a three-digit number by a one-digit number by writing separate products for the ones, tens, and hundreds. Then you can add the separate products.

$$
\begin{array}{r}
284 \\
\times\ 7 \\
\hline
28 \\
560 \\
+1{,}400 \\
\hline
1{,}988
\end{array}
$$

$7 \times 4 = 28$
$7 \times 80 = 560$
$7 \times 200 = 1{,}400$

The product of 7×284 is $1{,}988$.

Practice multiplying three-digit numbers this way. Then learn to multiply a three-digit number the quick way, writing the products on one line.

$$
\begin{array}{r}
2 \\
284 \\
\times\quad 7 \\
\hline
8
\end{array}
$$

Multiply 7 by the ones. Regroup 28.
Multiply 7 by the tens. Add the 2 tens. Regroup 58 tens.

$$
\begin{array}{r}
5\,2 \\
284 \\
\times\quad 7 \\
\hline
\mathbf{8}8
\end{array}
$$

Multiply 7 by the hundreds. Add the 5 hundreds.

$$
\begin{array}{r}
5\,2 \\
284 \\
\times\quad 7 \\
\hline
\mathbf{1,9}88
\end{array}
$$

Here is an example where one of the digits in the number you are multiplying is 0. Remember that the product of any number and 0 is 0.

$$
\begin{array}{r}
4 \\
507 \\
\times\quad 6 \\
\hline
3,042
\end{array}
$$

In this example, 6 × 0 tens = 0. You add 0 and the 4 tens you carried to the tens place.

Learn to multiply a four-digit number. You multiply from right to left. First you multiply the ones, then the tens, then the hundreds, then the thousands. Often you have to regroup. Here is an example.

$$\begin{array}{r} 5 \quad 3 \\ 1{,}704 \\ \times \quad\quad 8 \\ \hline 13{,}632 \end{array}$$

The process of regrouping multiplying in the next place and then adding takes time to learn, and you need to practice it a lot. Practice multiplying one-digit numbers by two-digit, three-digit, and four-digit numbers. You can make up your own numbers to multiply. Be sure to practice with numbers that have zeros in them.

Checking Multiplication

One good way to check multiplication is to estimate in order to see if the product is about right.

When you are multiplying a two-digit number, find the two tens that the number is between. You found that $8 \times 26 = 208$. To check this product, think: 26 is between 20 and 30. So, 8×26 should be between 8×20 and 8×30. $8 \times 20 = 160$. $8 \times 30 = 240$. 208 is between 160 and 240.

You can write this check like this:

$$8 \times 20 < 8 \times 26 < 8 \times 30$$
$$160 \quad < \quad 208 \quad < \quad 240 \quad \checkmark$$

A number statement like $8 \times 20 < 8 \times 26 < 8 \times 30$ is called a double inequality because there are two inequality signs.

When you are multiplying a three-digit number, check the product by finding the two hundreds that the number is between.

To check $6 \times 507 = 3{,}042$, you can think: 507 is between 500 and 600.

$$6 \times 500 < 6 \times 507 < 6 \times 600$$
$$3{,}000 < \quad 3{,}042 \quad < 3{,}600 \quad \checkmark$$

When you are multiplying a four-digit number, find the two thousands that it is between to check. Does $8 \times 1{,}704 = 13{,}632$?

$$8 \times 1,000 < 8 \times 1,704 < 8 \times 2,000$$
$$8,000 \quad < \quad 13,632 \quad < \quad 16,000 \checkmark$$

Check each multiplication problem by estimating in this way.

Another Way to Write Expanded Form

Remember that the expanded form of 7,836 is 7,000 + 800 + 30 + 6. Now that you know how to multiply tens, hundreds, and thousands, you can write the expanded form of a number in another way.

$$7,000 = 7 \times 1,000$$
$$800 = 8 \times 100$$
$$30 = 3 \times 10$$

So, you can write 7,000 + 800 + 30 + 6 like this:

$$(7 \times 1,000) + (8 \times 100) + (3 \times 10) + 6$$

Practice writing numbers in this new expanded form. For example, write 3,604 as (3 × 1,000) + (6 × 100) + 4. Write 9,078 as (9 × 1,000) + (7 × 10) + 8.

Solving Word Problems Using Multiplication

Solve these word problems using multiplication:

1. At the beach, Andrea found 8 shells. Jeff found 5 times as many shells. How many shells did Jeff find?
2. Megan's truck gets 21 miles per gallon of gasoline. How far can she drive on 9 gallons?

Division—Part 2

Remainders

Mrs. Hughes wants to divide 33 sheets of construction paper among 7 students so that each student has the same number of sheets. If she gave each student 4 sheets, she would use 28 sheets ($4 \times 7 = 28$). If she gave each student 5 sheets, she would use 35 sheets ($5 \times 7 = 35$). She only has 33 sheets: she has enough to give 4 sheets to each student, but not enough to give 5 sheets. Because $33 - 28 = 5$, there will be 5 sheets left over if she gives 4 to each student. Here is how you write this division problem.

Mrs. Hughes wants to divide 33 sheets of construction paper among her 7 students.

$$7\overline{)33}$$

What is 33 divided by 7? Seven doesn't go into 33 evenly. The closest we can come is $7 \times 4 = 28$. So we write 4 in the ones place for the quotient. Then we put 28 below the 33 (or the dividend) and subtract it to show how many we have left over: 5. Our remainder is 5. So we write R5 next to the quotient 4, like this:

$$
\begin{array}{r}
4 \text{ R5} \longleftarrow \text{ quotient (with remainder)} \\
\text{divisor} \longrightarrow 7\overline{)33} \longleftarrow \text{ dividend} \\
-28 \longleftarrow \text{ product of } 7 \times 4 \\
\hline
5 \longleftarrow \text{ remainder}
\end{array}
$$

Notice how you multiply the divisor and the quotient, and then subtract this product from the dividend to find the remainder.

When you do a division problem like this, make the quotient as big as you can. If the problem is 23 divided by 5, what would your quotient be: 3 or 4? It would be 4, because $3 \times 5 = 15$ and $23 - 15$ gives you 8 left over. Because you can still subtract 5 from 8, you know that your quotient can be greater. $4 \times 5 = 20$ leaves you 3 left over. Because you can't take 5 away from 3, you know you've found the largest possible quotient.

When you find the quotient, multiply the divisor by the quotient, and then subtract this product. The result is the remainder. You can always check your work by making sure that the remainder is less than the divisor. If the remainder is not less, you need to try again, with a larger quotient. Here is an example.

$$
\begin{array}{r} 5 \ \text{R}9 \\ 8\overline{)49} \\ -40 \\ \hline 9 \end{array}
$$

Subtract 8×5

$9 < 8?$

NO

$$
\begin{array}{r} 6 \ \text{R}1 \\ 8\overline{)49} \\ -48 \\ \hline 1 \end{array}
$$

Subtract 8×6

$1 < 8?$

YES

Practice doing problems like $41 \div 6$ or $58 \div 7$, finding the quotients and the remainders. Remember that $6\overline{)41}$ and $41 \div 6$ are the same problem.

Dividing Tens, Hundreds, and Thousands

Sometimes you can divide tens, hundreds, and thousands easily, using the division facts.

$9 \div 3 = 3$
and
$90 \div 3 = 30$

$35 \div 7 = 5$
and
$3,500 \div 7 = 500$

$18 \div 6 = 3$
and
$18,000 \div 6 = 3,000$

Notice how the quotient has the same number of zeros as the dividend? Practice doing problems like these in your head.

Two-Digit Quotients

Sometimes when you divide a two-digit number, the quotient has two digits. Divide 64 by 2. Remember, in division you start with the highest place value in the dividend and move right. So, in $2\overline{)64}$, we first divide the tens.

$$2\overline{)64}$$

$$\begin{array}{r} 3 \\ 2\overline{)64} \\ -6 \\ \hline 0 \end{array}$$

Subtract 2 × 3

0 < 2

Make sure the remainder is less than the divisor.

Then bring down the 4 ones in 64. Divide the ones.

$$\begin{array}{r} 32 \\ 2\overline{)64} \\ -6 \\ \hline 04 \\ -4 \\ \hline 0 \end{array}$$

Subtract 2 × 2

0 < 4

Make sure the remainder is less than the divisor.

You can tell that 64 ÷ 2 will have a two-digit quotient because you can divide the 6 by 2. In the same way, 84 ÷ 5 has a two-digit quotient because you can divide the 8 by 5. 47 ÷ 8 has a one-digit quotient because you cannot divide 4 by 8. You need to divide 47 by 8 instead.

Here is a problem with a two-digit quotient and a remainder.

First divide the tens.

$$\begin{array}{r} 1 \\ 5\overline{)84} \\ -5 \\ \hline 3 \end{array}$$

Subtract 5 × 1

Check   3 < 5

Then divide the ones.

$$\begin{array}{r} 16 \\ 5\overline{)84} \\ -5 \\ \hline 34 \\ -30 \\ \hline 4 \end{array}$$

Subtract 5 × 6

Check   4 < 5

Checking Division

You can check division by multiplying and then adding the remainder, if there is one. Remember that multiplying by a number is the inverse of dividing by that number.

To check division:

$$2\overline{)64} \quad \begin{array}{r} 32 \\ -6 \\ \hline 04 \\ -4 \\ \hline 0 \end{array}$$

Multiply:

$$\begin{array}{r} \times 32 \\ \times\; 2 \\ \hline 64 \end{array} \checkmark \quad \begin{array}{l} \text{quotient} \\ \text{divisor} \end{array}$$

There is no remainder to add.

To check division:

$$5\overline{)84} \quad \begin{array}{r} 16\ \text{R}4 \\ -5 \\ \hline 34 \\ -30 \\ \hline 4 \end{array}$$

Multiply:

$$\begin{array}{r} 16 \\ \times\; 5 \\ \hline 80 \\ +\; 4 \\ \hline 84 \end{array} \checkmark \quad \begin{array}{l} \text{quotient} \\ \text{divisor} \\ \\ \text{add} \\ \text{remainder} \end{array}$$

When you check, you should end up with the number into which you first divided. Remember that this number is called the dividend. Check every division problem by multiplying, then adding the remainder, to get the dividend.

Dividing Three-Digit Numbers

Learn how to divide three-digit numbers by one-digit numbers.

First divide the hundreds.

$$3\overline{)758} \quad \begin{array}{r} 2 \\ -6 \\ \hline 1 \end{array}$$

Subtract 3 × 2

1 < 3

Next divide the tens.

$$3\overline{)758} \quad \begin{array}{r} 25 \\ -6 \\ \hline 15 \\ -15 \\ \hline 0 \end{array}$$

Subtract 3 × 5

0 < 3

Then divide the ones.

$$\begin{array}{r} 252 \ \ \text{R2} \\ 3\overline{)758} \\ -6 \ \ \ \\ \hline 15 \ \ \\ -15 \ \ \\ \hline 08 \\ -6 \\ \hline 2 \end{array}$$

Subtract 3 × 2
1 < 3

Check. Multiply and add.

$$\begin{array}{r} 252 \quad \text{quotient} \\ \times \quad 3 \quad \text{divisor} \\ \hline 756 \quad \text{add} \\ + \quad 2 \quad \text{remainder} \\ \hline 758 \quad \checkmark \end{array}$$

Sometimes there are not enough hundreds to begin by dividing hundreds. Then you need to think of the hundreds as tens and divide the tens.

In the following example, divide the tens, because you cannot divide 6 hundreds by 8.

Think of 6 hundreds 2 tens as 62 tens.

Divide the tens.

$$\begin{array}{r} 7 \\ 8\overline{)627} \\ -56 \\ \hline 6 \end{array}$$

Subtract 8 × 7
6 < 8

Divide the ones.

$$\begin{array}{r} 78 \ \ \text{R3} \\ 8\overline{)627} \\ -56 \ \ \\ \hline 67 \\ -64 \\ \hline 3 \end{array}$$

Subtract 8 × 7
3 < 8

Learning long division takes lots of careful practice. Each time you divide and subtract, make sure the remainder is less than the divisor. When you are all done, multiply the dividend by the quotient and add the remainder to check.

This Roman soldier is XXVIII years old.

Roman Numerals

The numerals we use most often—the digits 0, 1, 2, 3, 4, 5, 6, 7, 8, 9—are called Arabic numerals because they came from people who spoke Arabic. The ancient Romans used different symbols as their numerals. Even today you may come across Roman numerals on clocks and in books.

Here are some of the symbols that the Romans used.

I is 1.
V is 5.
X is 10.

Those are all symbols you need in order to write the numbers from 1 to 20. Here are the rules.

1. When a Roman numeral that is the same value or smaller comes after another numeral, you add the values together.

II = 1 + 1 = 2
XX = 10 + 10 = 20
XI = 10 + 1 = 11

Try to answer these:

III = _____ + _____ + _____ = _____
XX = _____ + _____ = _____
VIII = _____ + _____ + _____ + _____ = _____

2. When a Roman numeral of smaller value comes right before another, you subtract the smaller one from the larger.

$$IV = 1 \text{ subtracted from } 5 \text{ or } 5 - 1 = 4$$
$$IX = 1 \text{ subtracted from } 10 \text{ or } 10 - 1 = 9$$

Here's a problem for you. What's this number?

$$XXIX$$

It's 10 + 10 + (10 − 1), or 29.

The Romans had symbols for 50 (L), 100 (C), 500 (D), and 1,000 (M). Those were the only number symbols they used, and they could write thousands of numbers with them!

Look in the movies to find Roman numerals! Sometimes the year that a film was made is expressed not as "1945" or "1969" but in the Roman numerals for the year. So, "1983" is MXMLXXXIII. Look on a DVD case or in the credits of a movie to see if you can find a date written like that.

Fractions

Numerator and Denominator

A fraction represents a portion of a whole. It can be a part of one thing or a part of a group of things. The bottom number of a fraction, called the *denominator*, tells how many equal parts the whole was divided into. The top number of a fraction, called the *numerator*, tells how many of the equal parts you are talking about. For example, if you have an apple and you slice it in half, you have made 2 equal portions. Each portion represents $\frac{1}{2}$, or 1 out of the 2 equal parts of the apple.

In the fraction $\frac{4}{8}$, 4 is the numerator and 8 is the denominator. In the fraction $\frac{9}{10}$, what is the numerator? What is the denominator?

numerator	2 red spools of thread
denominator	3 spools of thread

$\frac{2}{3}$ of the spools of thread are red.

Recognizing Fractions from 1/2 to 1/10

Look over this list of fractions. You should learn to recognize these fractions just the way you recognize the numbers 1 to 10.

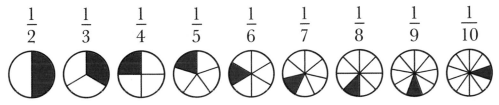

$$\frac{1}{2} \quad \frac{1}{3} \quad \frac{1}{4} \quad \frac{1}{5} \quad \frac{1}{6} \quad \frac{1}{7} \quad \frac{1}{8} \quad \frac{1}{9} \quad \frac{1}{10}$$

Equivalent Fractions

Sometimes fractions with different numerators and denominators name the same amount. Fractions that name the same amount are called equivalent fractions.

> **Do It Yourself**
>
> Take a piece of paper and cut it into quarters. Then put it back together and show it to your child. Take away pieces of the paper and ask your child what fraction of the piece of paper is left.

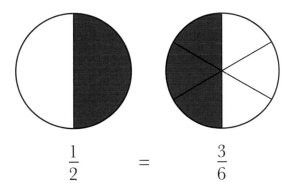

$$\frac{1}{2} \quad = \quad \frac{3}{6}$$

$\frac{1}{2}$ and $\frac{3}{6}$ are equivalent fractions: they name the same fraction of the circle.

Learn to recognize equivalent fractions. For example, from the picture you should know that $\frac{2}{4} = \frac{4}{8}$.

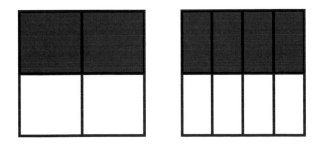

Comparing Fractions

Learn to compare fractions that have the same denominator by using the signs >, <, and =.

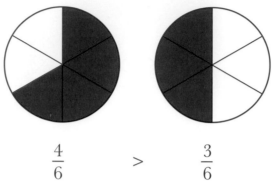

$$\frac{4}{6} \quad > \quad \frac{3}{6}$$

$\frac{4}{6}$ is greater than $\frac{3}{6}$. In $\frac{4}{6}$, there are 6 equal parts, and you are talking about 4. In $\frac{3}{6}$, there are 6 equal parts, and you are talking about only 3.

Rule: When two fractions have the same denominator, the one with the greater numerator is the greater fraction.

Without using a picture, you should know that $\frac{5}{9} > \frac{3}{9}$; $\frac{2}{7} < \frac{3}{7}$; $\frac{1}{6} = \frac{1}{6}$.

Mixed Numbers and Whole Numbers

The numbers $0, 1, 2, 3, 4, \ldots$ are called the whole numbers. By calling them "whole numbers," we mean that they are not fractions and that they name a whole.

A number like $1\frac{1}{2}$ is called a mixed number. It has a part that is a whole number and a part that is a fraction. You read $1\frac{1}{2}$ as "one and one-half." When you read a mixed number, you always put an "and" between its whole-number part and its fractional part. Here are some more mixed numbers: $2\frac{1}{4}$, $6\frac{1}{8}$, $5\frac{7}{9}$, $3\frac{3}{4}$.

On a number line, $1\frac{1}{2}$ is between 1 and 2. It is 1 *plus* $\frac{1}{2}$ more. In the same way, $5\frac{1}{4}$ is between 5 and 6. It is 5 plus $\frac{1}{4}$ more. $5\frac{1}{4}$ is more than 5, but less than 6.

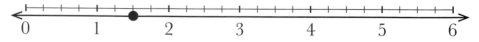

You often use mixed numbers when you measure in inches. Practice measuring to the nearest half inch or quarter inch using a ruler divided into quarter inches. For example, draw a line segment $5\frac{3}{4}$ inches long.

Decimals: Tenths

You can write the fraction $\frac{1}{10}$ as the decimal 0.1. You read both the same way. You say "one-tenth."

The period to the left of the 1 is called a decimal point. The decimal point shows that the value of the digits to its right is anywhere between 0 and 1, like a fraction. A decimal is any number that uses places to the right of the decimal point to show a fraction.

The first place to the right of the decimal point is the tenths place.

ones		tenths
1	.	7

You can write the mixed number $1\frac{7}{10}$ as the decimal 1.7. You read both the same way: "one and seven-tenths."

Decimals and Hundredths

The second place to the right of the decimal point is the hundredths place. The fraction $\frac{1}{100}$ can also be written 0.01.

ones		tenths	hundredths
0	.	0	1

You read both the same way: "one-hundredth."

The mixed number $2\frac{47}{100}$ can also be written as a decimal.

$2\frac{47}{100}$	ones		tenths	hundredths
	2	.	4	7

You read both as "two and forty-seven hundredths."

Notice that when there are both tenths and hundredths in a decimal, you read the tenths and hundredths together in terms of the hundredths. Also, remember to put an "and" between the whole-number part and the fractional part of a decimal, just as in mixed numbers.

Decimals and Fractions of 100

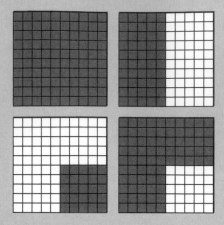

Each of these squares contains 100 smaller squares. The shaded areas can be represented by decimal numbers. The square at the top left, with all 100 squares shaded, is represented by 100 hundredths, or 1.00. The square at the top right, with 50 squares shaded, is represented by 50 hundredths, or 0.50. What proportion of the square at the top right is shaded? Half of it. It shows you clearly that $0.50 = \frac{50}{100} = \frac{1}{2}$.

What can we say about the square at the bottom left? Of its 100 squares, how many are shaded? 25. The decimal number representing that proportion is 0.25. Those smaller squares make up one-fourth of the full square, showing that $0.25 = \frac{25}{100} = \frac{1}{4}$.

What about the square at the bottom right? How many smaller squares are shaded? 75. What proportion of the total is shaded? $\frac{3}{4}$. This shows that $0.75 = \frac{75}{100} = \frac{3}{4}$.

Multiplying and Dividing Amounts of Money

Now that you've learned about decimals, you can multiply and divide amounts of money the same way you multiply and divide other numbers. Here are two examples.

$$\begin{array}{r} 3\ 2 \\ \$9.97 \\ \times 0.04 \\ \hline \$39.88 \end{array}$$

$$\begin{array}{r} \$3.31 \\ 5\overline{)\$16.55} \\ -15 \\ \hline 15 \\ -15 \\ \hline 05 \\ -5 \\ \hline 0 \end{array}$$

Remember to write the dollar sign and the cents point in your answer.

Word Problems

In word problems, the important step is deciding what mathematical problem you need to solve. Once you can write the problem in numbers, then you can solve it.

You have already done problems that ask you to add, subtract, multiply, or divide. Sometimes you have to do two different operations in the same problem. These are called two-step problems.

A Two-Step Word Problem

Lisa has saved up $28.50. For a party, she buys 8 party favors. Each favor costs her $2.39. How much money does she have left after buying the favors?

First you have to multiply to find out how much the party favors cost her in all.

You multiply amounts of money the same way you multiply other numbers. Include the cents point and the dollar sign in the product when you are done.

$$\begin{array}{r} \overset{3\ 7}{\$2.39} \\ \times\ \ \ \ 8 \\ \hline \$19.12 \end{array}$$

Then you have to subtract to find out how much money she has left.

$$\begin{array}{r} \overset{1\ 18\ \ 4\ 10}{\$\cancel{2}\cancel{9}.\cancel{5}\cancel{0}} \quad \text{— the money she began with} \\ -19.12 \quad \text{— the cost of the favors} \\ \hline \$\ \ 9.38 \quad \text{— the money she has left} \end{array}$$

An Estimation Problem

Sometimes you do not need to know an exact answer for a word problem. You can estimate. Here is an example.

Kim has $20. She wants to buy a purse for $13.49 and a bracelet for $8.98. Does she have enough money?

Estimate:

$8.98 is about $9.00 $\begin{array}{r} \$\ \ 9.00 \\ +13.00 \\ \hline \$22.00 \end{array}$

$13.49 is about $13.00

The purse and the bracelet together cost about $22. So, Kim does not have quite enough money.

If your answer is close when you estimate, you need to figure the problem out exactly. For example, if the cost of the purse and the bracelet came to about $19 or $20, you would have to add up exactly how much they cost to answer the problem.

A Problem Where You Need to Guess

Black goldfish cost 85¢, and orange goldfish cost 99¢. Lewis buys some black goldfish and some orange goldfish, 5 in all. He pays $4.53. How many of each kind of fish does he buy?

You must make a guess to start. Guess that he buys 2 black goldfish. Then he must buy 3 orange goldfish. How much will these cost?

$$(2 \times 85¢) + (3 \times 99¢) = 170¢ + 297¢ = 467¢ \text{ or } \$4.67$$

$4.67 is too much. Try another guess. Lewis buys 3 black goldfish and 2 orange goldfish.

$$(3 \times 85¢) + (2 \times 99¢) = 255¢ + 198¢ = 453¢ \text{ or } \$4.53$$

The second guess is correct. He buys 3 black goldfish and 2 orange goldfish.

Suggested Resources

The Complete Book of Time and Money (American Education Publishing, 2009)

Divide and Ride (MathStart 3), by Stuart J. Murphy and George Ulrich (HarperCollins, 1997)

Family Math, by Jean Kerr Stenmark, Virginia Thompson, and Ruth Cossey (Lawrence Hall of Science, 1986)

Funny and Fabulous Fraction Stories: 30 Reproducible Math Tales and Problems to Reinforce Important Fraction Skills, by Dan Greenberg and Jared Lee (Scholastic Teaching Resources, 1999)

Geometry and Measurement, Grade 3 (Kumon Publishing North America, 2009)

Grade 3 Multiplication (Kumon Math Workbooks) (Kumon Publishing North America, 2008)

Lemonade for Sale (MathStart 3), by Stuart J. Murphy and Tricia Tusa (HarperCollins, 1997)

The Sir Cumference series, by Cindy Neuschwander and Wayne Geehan (Charlesbridge)

Spectrum Math, Grade 3, by Thomas Richards (Columbus/Frank Schaffer Publications, 2006)

Third Grade Super Math Success (Sylvan Learning Publishing, 2006)

VI
Science

Introduction

Children gain knowledge about the world by linking their own observations and experiences with information they learn from other sources. They should be encouraged to view the world scientifically: to ask questions about nature; to seek answers through observation and study; and to collect, count, measure, and make both quantitative and qualitative observations.

As children amass information, their hypotheses may be based on intuition more than on solid knowledge. Balancing a child's personal observations with well-expressed scientific fundamentals will guide her understanding in the right direction. Book learning also provides knowledge not likely to be gained by simple observations, such as the nature of the planets and the universe or the structure of a cell.

The topics that follow are consistent with those offered to children in countries that have had outstanding results from teaching science in the elementary grades. Also included are biographies of people who have contributed to our advancement in science, from the Renaissance astronomer Nicolaus Copernicus to the modern astronaut Mae Jemison. A list of further resources can help you take your child's investigations of science even further.

Classifying Animals

What Do They Have in Common?

An owl isn't much like a goldfish, and you would never mistake an elephant for a butterfly! Even though these creatures are very different, they all have something in common. They are living creatures that move and breathe and have babies. They are all animals.

An owl is a kind of bird. What other birds can you name? Eagle, robin, blue jay, flamingo, duck—there are so many different kinds of birds. They come in different sizes and different colors. Some are tiny, like hummingbirds, which can weigh less than a handful of paper clips. Others are large, like ostriches, which can stand nine feet tall and weigh more than 300 pounds. Some birds are dull brown, some are black and white, and some are brightly colored. But whatever their sizes or colors, they all have feathers and wings, and they all lay eggs. That is what makes them all birds.

Now, name a kind of insect. You have many to choose from: ants, honeybees, ladybugs, flies, crickets. Do you remember what insects have in common? All insects have six legs, three main body sections, and a tough **exoskeleton**. No matter whether they are black or green, or whether they have dots or stripes, or whether they have wings or no wings, as long as they have six legs, three body sections, and an exoskeleton, they are insects.

Whenever you group things that have a lot in common, you are classifying. When we classify things, it helps us understand and talk about them. Many living things can be classified as animals: horses, dogs, cats, monkeys, robins, flies, whales, jellyfish, worms, and even you! But what about pine trees or rosebushes or blades of grass? They're not animals. They are plants.

When scientists want to classify the living things in the world, they begin by dividing living things into several very big groups. Two of these big groups are animals and plants. (You'll learn about the other big groups in a later grade.)

> **New Word**
> An **exoskeleton** is the rigid outer covering that protects certain animals such as insects, spiders, and crustaceans. Ask your child to name some animals with exoskeletons and search together for photographs of them.

Vertebrates and Invertebrates
. . . .

Does It Have a Backbone?

When we classify things, we often need to take a big group, such as animals, and break it into smaller groups. Scientists classify animals into two smaller groups by examining their skeletons. Reach your hand around behind you and run your fingers up and down the center of your back. That long, bumpy ridge you feel is

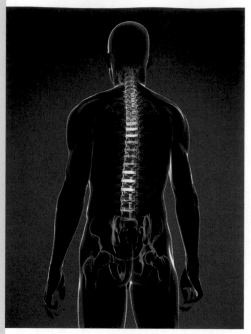
The spinal vertebrae are colored red in this illustration.

your backbone, which is also called your spine. It is made of a stack of small bones, each one called a vertebra [VUR-tuh-bra]. That is why animals with backbones are called vertebrates [VUR-tuh-bruts].

You have a backbone. So does a horse, a dog, a cat, a fish, a bird, and a frog. Many animals have backbones, but many do not. An animal that does not have a backbone is called an invertebrate, a word that means "no backbone." Can you think of an animal with no backbone? How about a little creature that droops like a noodle and slithers through the dirt? That's right, an earthworm does not have a backbone. Neither does a moth, an oyster, or a spider. They are all invertebrates. In fact, more than 90 percent of Earth's animals are invertebrates.

Now you know how scientists divide animals into two big groups: invertebrates (which have no backbone) and vertebrates (which do have a backbone).

Classifying the Vertebrates

Now let's see how scientists divide the vertebrates into five smaller groups, called *classes*. The five classes of vertebrates are:

fish   amphibians   reptiles   birds   mammals

Let's learn about what makes a fish a fish, what makes a bird a bird, and so on. As you learn about the different features of each class, try to name some animals in that class.

Cold-Blooded and Warm-Blooded

Fish, amphibians, and reptiles are cold-blooded. Birds and mammals are warm-blooded. What do we mean by cold-blooded and warm-blooded?

Some animals get the warmth they need from the air or water around them. When it's hot outside, their body temperatures rise. When it's cold, their body temperatures drop. These animals are called cold-blooded. Cold-blooded animals do not have blood that is always cold. Rather, the term means their body temperatures go up or down depending on the temperature around them.

Snakes are cold-blooded animals, which means that their body temperature changes according to the temperature around them.

Other animals stay nearly the same temperature no matter whether the air around them is hot or cold. These animals are called warm-blooded. Mammals and birds are warm-blooded. If they need to produce more heat in cold environments, they may shiver. If they need to cool down in hot environments, they may pant or sweat. Cold-blooded animals cannot control their body temperatures in these ways.

Are you cold-blooded or warm-blooded? On winter days you might shiver with cold, and on summer days you might feel like you're about to melt, but your body temperature normally stays right around 98.6° Fahrenheit. So that makes you warm-blooded.

Fish

- Fish are cold-blooded.
- Fish live in water.
- Fish use gills to take oxygen from the water.
- Most fish are covered with scales.
- Most fish hatch from eggs, which a female fish lays outside her body.
- Goldfish, trout, and sharks are different kinds of fish.

The gills on each side of this shark allow it to get oxygen from the water.

Amphibians

- Amphibians are cold-blooded.
- Amphibians live part of their lives in water and part on land. (The word "amphibian" means "living in two places.")
- When they are young, amphibians have gills to take oxygen from the water. When they grow up, most amphibians develop lungs that allow them to take oxygen from the air.
- Amphibians usually have moist skin with no scales.
- Frogs, toads, and salamanders are amphibians.

Frogs are amphibians. Baby frogs, or tadpoles, hatch from eggs and live underwater. Frogs live on land when they grow up. See how the tadpoles grow into frogs?

Reptiles

- Reptiles are cold-blooded.
- Reptiles have dry, thick, scaly skin.
- Reptiles breathe with lungs.
- Reptiles hatch from eggs.
- Snakes, lizards, and turtles are reptiles.

This box turtle is a reptile.

Make a Connection

Have your child read Lewis Carroll's poem "The Crocodile" (page 11). Based on Carroll's descriptions and the bulleted lists on these pages, ask your child to classify the crocodile as a fish, amphibian, reptile, bird, or mammal.

Birds

- Birds are warm-blooded.
- Birds have feathers and wings.
- Most birds can fly.
- Birds breathe with lungs.
- Birds hatch from eggs. Most birds build nests in which to lay their eggs.
- Robins, cardinals, chickens, and eagles are birds.

Most birds feed their young until they are big enough to leave the nest and survive on their own.

Mammals

Dogs are mammals. Mother dogs produce milk for their babies.

- Mammals are warm-blooded.
- Mammals have hair on their bodies.
- Mammals breathe with lungs.
- Baby mammals need care and feeding.
- Female mammals produce milk for their young.
- Horses, cats, dogs, monkeys, and humans are mammals.
- Most mammals live on land, although some mammals live in water. Whales and dolphins live in the water, but they are not fish. They breathe with lungs, not gills, and they need to come to the surface to breathe air. They are mammals.

Some mammals, like this bottlenose dolphin, swim underwater. Dolphins breathe with lungs, so they swim up to the surface for air.

The Human Body

The Skeletal and Muscular Systems

Muscle and Bone

Imagine that you're eating a drumstick of fried chicken. (Or, if you're a vegetarian, imagine someone else eating that drumstick!) The drumstick has skin, muscle, and bone. When you eat the meat, do you know what you're eating? You are eating muscle.

Do you know what part of a chicken the drumstick is? It's the lower leg. Now touch your own lower leg, which is also called your calf, between your knee and your ankle. Your calf has skin, muscle, and bone, too. You can see and touch the skin. You can feel your muscles when you flex your foot. You can feel the hard bone of your shin.

There are two big bones in your lower leg, called the tibia and the fibula. The bone you feel along your shin is the tibia, the larger of the two lower leg bones. The fibula is deeper inside your muscle.

See all the muscles in this picture? Can you feel any of them in your own body?

Bones and Connections

Most of your body is soft and squishy, but not your bones, which are very hard. Your bones give your body its shape, the way a stiff clothes hanger gives shape to a floppy shirt. Your bones also protect the soft organs inside your body.

Is Your Skeleton Inside or Out?

Insects have an **exoskeleton**, which means their bodies are made of a tough outer layer surrounding softer insides. Human beings have an **endoskeleton**, which means their soft skin and muscles surround the hard bones inside their bodies.

All Together

Play Simon Says with your child, but instead of body parts, use the names of these bones on your body: cranium, scapula, sternum, humerus, rib cage, pelvis, femur, and tibia.

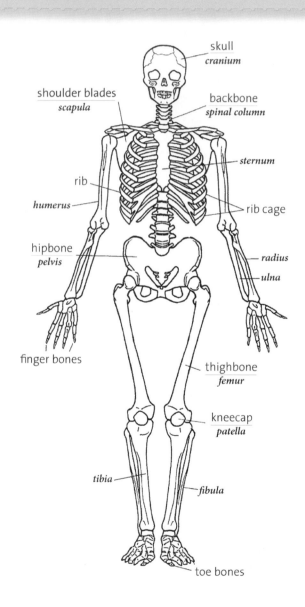

skull
cranium

shoulder blades
scapula

backbone
spinal column

sternum

rib

humerus

rib cage

hipbone
pelvis

radius

ulna

finger bones

thighbone
femur

kneecap
patella

tibia

fibula

toe bones

All your bones put together make up your skeleton. From head to toe, the skeleton of an adult human contains 206 bones. (A baby has more bones, but some of them **fuse** together as the baby grows.)

Bones come in many shapes and sizes. The biggest bone in your body is your thighbone, also called your femur [FEE-mur]. The smallest bone in your body is a tiny little bone inside your ear, called the stirrup. It's about the size of a grain of rice!

Lift your arm and bend it. Your arm bends at your elbow. Your elbow is a joint. A joint is a place where your bones come together. At each joint, the bones are connected by strong, stretchy tissue, like big rubber bands, called ligaments. Joints make it possible for you to bend, twist, run, chew, kick a ball, touch your toes, and hold a pencil. Can you point to some other joints in your body?

Touch the tip of your nose. That tough stuff you feel is called cartilage. In some places in your body, such as in your knee, cartilage keeps bones from rubbing together. When you were born, some of your skeleton was made of cartilage. But as you grew up, hard bone replaced the soft cartilage.

Let's learn about your most important bones.

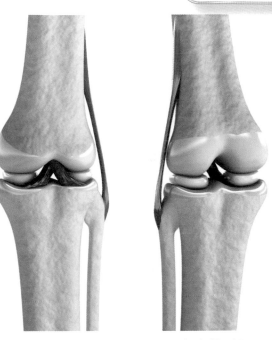

From the front and back, your knee joint looks like this. Ligaments and cartilage have been shaded different colors.

The Skull

The bones in your head are called your skull. Your skull surrounds and protects one of the most important organs in your body, your brain. The top part of your skull is called the cranium. It is made up of eight bones that fit tightly together to act like a helmet around your brain.

The Spinal Column

Remember when you felt the vertebrae that make up your backbone? A human has 24 vertebrae, stacked on top of one another. Stretchy ligaments join the vertebrae into a long, flexible chain of bones called the spinal column, the spine, or the backbone. A thick pad of cartilage provides a cushion between each vertebra.

When someone tells you to stand tall and strong, you straighten your spinal column. Your spinal column helps hold up your head and upper body. Your spine can bend forward, back, and sideways. It can swivel in both directions. All of these movements are possible because of the way the bones, ligaments, and cartilage join.

The Ribs

Start just under your armpits and run your fingers along your sides. Do you feel ribs? Your ribs connect with cartilage to a hard bone in the center of your chest called the sternum, or breastbone. From your sternum, your ribs curve around and connect to your spinal column in the back. You have 12 ribs on each side of your body, and together they form your rib cage. Your rib cage is a strong yet flexible set of bones that protects your lungs, heart, and stomach.

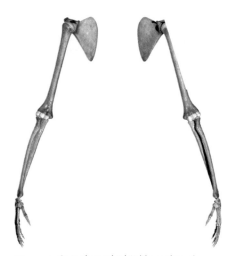

The scapula is shaped a bit like a shovel.

The Scapula

How many ways can you move your arms? You can point down to the ground. You can lift your arms above your head. You can swing your arms forward and back. Your arms can move in all these directions because of the way they are attached to your body at the shoulder bone, or scapula [SKAP-yuh-luh]. The word "scapula" comes from the Latin word for "shovel." Your scapula looks sort of like the blade of a shovel. It's a big, flat, triangle-shaped bone that joins the arm to the spine. People often call the scapula the shoulder blade.

The Pelvis

When you sit down, stand up, walk, or run, you are moving your pelvis. The pelvis is a set of bones at your hips. Your legs connect to your upper body at the pelvis. The word "pelvis" comes from the Latin word for "basin" or "sink." If you look at the pelvis on a skeleton, you can see why the name fits. The bones that make up the pelvis come together in a shape like a big bowl. The bowl shape of the pelvis protects your intestines and other digestive organs. When a baby is growing inside a mother's body, the mother's pelvis cradles the baby until birth.

Inside Your Bones

Bones are living, growing parts of the body. Bones feel hard, but they are not solid. While the outside of most bones is like a hard shell, inside the bone is light and spongy. This spongy part of your bones contains a substance called marrow. Red bone marrow produces new blood cells for your body.

This illustration shows the red marrow that makes up a bone's spongy inside.

Will You Sign My Cast?

Sometimes bones break, but they do grow back together. To examine a broken bone, a doctor looks at a special kind of picture taken with an X-ray machine. X-ray machines use a special kind of light, called X-rays, which can travel through muscle but not bone. This creates a picture that shows the bones inside your body.

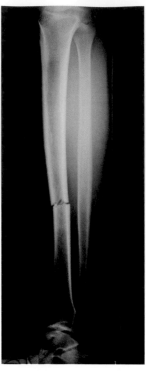

Here's an X-ray of Harry's leg after he broke it. To help it heal, Harry's doctor carefully lined up the broken pieces of bone. Then she put a cast around his calf. Harry had to wear the cast for six weeks to hold the bone in place and protect it while new bone cells were growing.

This X-ray shows a broken tibia, which is the larger of the two bones in the lower leg.

What About You?

Have you or your child ever broken a bone? If so, talk about how it happened and how long it took for the bone to heal. How do your experiences confirm what your child has just learned about bones being soft on the inside and alive?

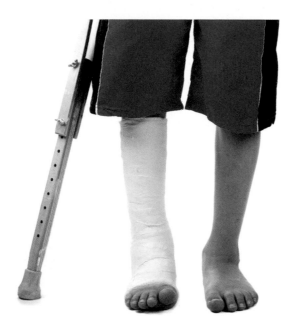

Many Muscles

Let's pretend that you're a powerful Olympic athlete. Now, show me your muscles—stand up, stretch out your arms, then bend them at the elbow as you curl your fists toward your head.

When you do that, you are tightening the muscles on the upper part of each arm, called the biceps [BIE-seps]. So you've shown me two of your muscles. But did you know that you have about 650 muscles in your body?

Some muscles, such as the ones in your ears, are as tiny as a thread. Other muscles, such as the hamstring muscles in the back of your leg, are thick and wide. Where do you think your biggest muscle is? It's called the gluteus maximus [GLOO-tee-us MAX-i-mus], and it's the muscle you sit down on (your rear end).

You use hundreds of different muscles when you play soccer or any other sport. Exercise helps keep your muscles strong.

You use your muscles when you walk, run, jump, swim, skate, play soccer, or ride a bicycle. Every time you move, you use your muscles.

Even when you're not exercising, you use muscles. When you read, your neck muscles hold your head up and your eye muscles move your gaze across the page.

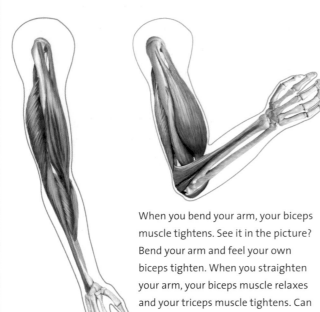

When you bend your arm, your biceps muscle tightens. See it in the picture? Bend your arm and feel your own biceps tighten. When you straighten your arm, your biceps muscle relaxes and your triceps muscle tightens. Can you point to the triceps in this picture? Can you feel it in your arm?

When you smile, you use about 15 different face muscles. When you frown, you use more than 40 different face muscles. So smile—it's easier than frowning!

When you move, your muscles work in pairs. When you bend your arm, you tighten your biceps, while another muscle on the lower part of your arm, called the triceps, relaxes. When you stretch your arm out straight again, the opposite occurs: the biceps relaxes and the triceps tightens.

That's how many muscles work in your body. When one pulls tight, a companion muscle relaxes.

Voluntary and Involuntary Muscles

When you tighten your biceps, you use voluntary muscles. Voluntary muscles are the ones you can control. You can choose whether to kick a ball or raise your hand or sit down. Whenever you do these things, you are using voluntary muscles.

But your body also depends on many muscles that move whether or not you want them to. These are called involuntary muscles. For example, your heart is an involuntary muscle. It keeps on pumping blood without your telling it when to do so. Involuntary muscles in your intestines work automatically to help you digest the food you eat. Involuntary muscles work all the time, whether you're awake or asleep, and whether or not you think about them.

Connecting Muscles and Bones

Muscles make you move by pulling on the bones of your skeleton. To do this, the muscles must be attached to the bones. Throughout your body, strong fibers called tendons connect muscles to bones.

Your largest and strongest tendon is called the Achilles [ah-KIL-eez] tendon. It connects your calf muscle to your heel bone. It's easy to find your Achilles tendon. Gently pinch the back of your foot, just above your heel. Do you feel something like a strong, tough rope? Wag your foot up and down and feel how the Achilles tendon stretches and relaxes.

Why is it called the Achilles tendon? A myth from ancient Greece tells of a boy named Achilles who would become a great warrior. When he was a baby, his mother dipped him in the river Styx. She believed its water would protect him from all harm. But to dip Achilles in the river, she had to hold him by his heel, and as a result, his heel did not touch the protective water.

Achilles grew up to become a great hero in the Trojan War. It seemed that no sword, spear, or arrow could harm him. But when a poisoned arrow pierced his heel, he died. Today people still use the phrase "Achilles' heel" to refer to a person's special weakness.

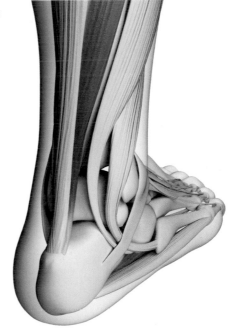

The Achilles tendon stretches from the calf to the heel.

The Human Body: The Brain and Nervous System

Your Powerful Brain

Inside your body there's an organ that you use to think, talk, listen, look, hear, smell, taste, dream, feel, decide, and remember. Sounds like a computer, a telephone, a camera, a television, and a scrapbook all wrapped up in one, doesn't it? It's your brain, which connects with your nerves to do all these things.

Your brain is in charge of everything you do. It's sort of like the president of your body. It keeps your heart beating. It makes sense of the information coming to it from your sensory organs—your eyes, ears, nose, tongue, and skin. It sends orders all over your body. It stores information in memory, such as the aroma of an orange peel, your best friend's favorite color, or the way to solve the math problems you learned last week.

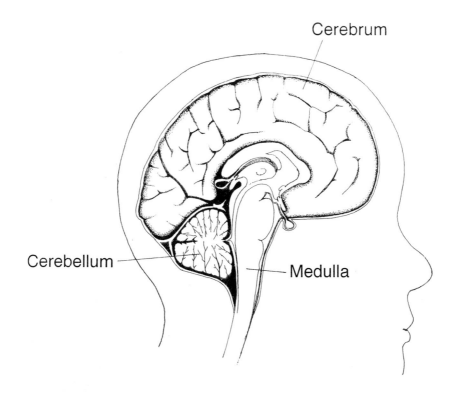

Cerebrum

Cerebellum

Medulla

The human brain is a pinkish-gray, wrinkled, spongy organ. An adult's brain weighs about three pounds. That's about the same weight as a half gallon of milk. The brain is divided into three main parts, which you can see in the picture. The cerebrum [suh-REE-brum] is by far the biggest section, about nine-tenths of your brain. Most brain activity takes place in the outer layer of the cerebrum, called the cerebral cortex. It's full of deep, wiggly grooves. Different parts of the cerebrum do different things. Some parts make sense of speech, other parts store memories, others control appetite or eye movements, and so on.

Deep in the back of your brain is the cerebellum [ser-uh-BELL-um]. It coordinates your balance and movements. When you first ride a bicycle, for example, you have to concentrate really hard. Soon you learn to balance and move your body easily, without even thinking about what you're doing. When that happens, your cerebellum is in control.

The medulla [me-DOO-la], or brain stem, lies even deeper than the cerebellum. It controls involuntary body functions. These are the functions that go on without your choosing to do them, such as your heartbeat, breathing, and digestion.

You've Got Nerves

You've probably seen telephone wires running from pole to pole, carrying messages back and forth from homes and businesses all over. If you imagine your brain as your central communications headquarters, then you can think of your nerves as the wires running throughout your body.

The medulla connects your brain to a thick bundle of nerve fibers called your spinal cord. The spinal cord runs through your backbone, through a hole in each vertebra. The spinal cord connects to many nerves that stretch throughout your body, branching out to your legs, arms, toes, and fingers.

Your nerves carry messages back and forth, to and from your brain. How does this work? Let's see what happens in the nervous system when you lean down toward a rose. First, your eyes send signals along special nerves to the brain. Your brain recognizes the image of a flower, compares the image with others in your memory, and then recalls that this kind of flower often has a pleasant smell. Your brain sends signals through your spinal cord and nerves to many muscles, giving the orders to make you bend toward the flower. Your brain then sends a message to breathe in deeply. The scent of the rose comes into your nose, and then signals of that scent travel through nerves to your brain. Ah, the sweet smell of a beautiful rose!

What About You?

Talk with your child about the relationship between memory and smells. Do either of you have any memories connected to smells that always come back when you smell that scent again? Why do you think the brain might connect memories and smells in this way?

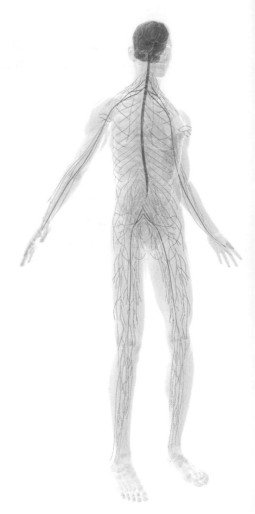

The spinal cord connects nerves in the brain to nerves in the rest of the body.

What signals might be traveling through this girl's nervous system?

Reflex Responses

Imagine you've just sniffed that lovely rose. You reach to bring the flower close to you when suddenly a sharp thorn pricks your thumb. Without thinking, you jerk your hand away.

When this happens, it is called a reflex action. Reflex actions happen almost instantly, without the brain's sending a message to perform the action.

When you touched the sharp thorn, a signal of pain raced from your finger to your spinal cord, which then sent back an immediate command to your muscles, saying, "Pull back!" Your body didn't wait for your brain to receive the pain message and respond to it. Instead, your reflexes

A doctor may use a soft rubber hammer near your knee to test your reflexes.

took over and saved you from feeling even more pain. Your reflexes will work the same way if, for example, you accidentally touch something hot, such as a pan that's just been taken out of the oven.

Has a doctor ever tested your reflexes? Try this. Sit in a chair and cross one leg loosely over the other. Ask someone to give you a *gentle* "karate chop" just below the kneecap. If the chop comes gently in just the right place, your leg will kick out automatically. You didn't have to think about it—it's a reflex. Kicking your leg out is not the only reflex action your body makes. Blinking and sneezing are other common reflex actions.

Light and Vision

Fast and Straight

You walk into a dark room, flip on the light switch, and presto—the room instantly fills with light. It seems to happen all at once. That's because light travels amazingly fast! The speed of light is 186,000 miles per second. Light travels so fast that in the time it takes you to blink your eyes three times light could travel to the moon and back.

Rays of light travel in straight lines, spreading in all directions from a source. Light cannot bend or curve around objects without help. You can see this by making shadows. In a darkened room, shine a desk lamp or flashlight at a wall. Now hold this book in front of the light. What happens? The light doesn't bend or curve around the book. Instead, the book blocks the rays of light, which are traveling in straight lines. That's why you see the shadow of your book on the wall.

Do you like to make shadow figures? How does it happen? The light rays don't bend. Your hand blocks the rays of light coming from the lamp and casts a shadow.

Your book does not let light pass through it because it is opaque [oh-PAKE]. Opaque materials block light. A wooden door is opaque. So is a metal can. Can you name some other things that are opaque?

Some materials are the opposite of opaque—they are transparent. Transparent materials are clear. You can see through them. They let light pass through almost unchanged. Glass and water are transparent.

Mirrors Flat and Curved

When you need to look your best, you wash your face, comb your hair, and then look at your reflection in a mirror.

A mirror reflects light, which means that it bounces back the light rays that hit it. How does this happen? First the light rays pass through the transparent glass part of a mirror. The back of the glass is coated with a special silver paint. When the light rays hit the silver surface, they bounce back through the glass. Shine a flashlight at a mirror, and you can see how almost all the light is reflected.

The mirrors that hang on the walls at your home or school are flat mirrors. A flat mirror is also called a plane mirror. When you look in a flat mirror, you see a reflection that appears almost exactly like yourself. But even though you see a clear image of your smiling face, the image is reversed. If you hold this book up to a mirror, the writing will appear backward. But if you hold backward writing up to a mirror, you can read it. Use a mirror to read this secret message:

ƨint əʞil əmɒn ɿuoy ətiɿw uoy nɒƆ

Some mirrors are made with curved glass. Mirrors that curve inward are called concave. (To help remember this name, think of a cave as something you go into.) The inner surface of a shiny spoon can work as a concave mirror, because the surface curves inward. Concave mirrors make objects appear larger than they are—as happens in the rearview mirrors of some automobiles.

Curved mirrors change the look of things because of the ways they bounce light rays back. What kind of mirror produced this image of a school bus?

Do It Yourself

Give your child a concave or convex mirror. A metal spoon will work for both: the side that holds food is concave, and the reverse side is convex. Instruct your child to look at himself in the mirror and draw what he sees. Encourage your child to view himself from different distances and note how his image changes. When does it increase or decrease in size? When does it appear upside down?

Have you ever seen yourself in a fun-house mirror? It can make your body look like it has a very strange shape. How do these mirrors work? The reflection you see is made of light rays bouncing back to your eyes. Fun-house mirrors are curved, and curved mirrors bounce light rays back in odd directions.

Mirrors that curve outward are called convex. Have you ever seen your face reflected in a shiny ball, like a Christmas tree ornament? The surface of the ornament curves outward, so it works as a convex mirror. It collects light rays from a wider area and reflects them to your eyes as a smaller image. Objects reflected in a convex mirror appear smaller than they really are.

Lenses

Put a straw in a glass of water. What do you see? The straw appears to be crooked. Why?

Whenever you see something, you are seeing the light rays reflected from the object. In the case of the straw, the light reflected from it travels through the water and the glass,

A straw sitting in a clear glass of water looks crooked. That's because the light rays change their path just a bit as they move from the water to the glass and from the glass to the air.

then through the air, before it reaches your eyes. The light rays change path just a little when they move from water to glass, and then from glass to air. Those slight changes in the path of the light rays between the straw and your eyes make the straw appear crooked underwater.

Sometimes we want to change the path of light rays coming from the things we are viewing to see them better. For that, we use things called lenses. If you have looked through a magnifying glass or binoculars, or if you wear glasses, then you have looked through lenses.

A lens is a curved piece of transparent material, usually glass or plastic. We say that a lens "bends the light," but actually, the curve of the lens makes the light rays change their path. That's how a magnifying glass works. When you hold a magnifying glass at the correct distance from a book, the words come into focus and appear bigger. The light rays coming from the page of the book have traveled through the lens glass and changed their path slightly to appear larger to your eyes.

Lenses can make things appear bigger or smaller. Have you ever looked through a pair of binoculars? Binoculars use lenses to make faraway things appear bigger. But what happens when you look through binoculars backward? Because you are looking the opposite way through the lenses, they make things appear smaller.

Because of lenses, we can see the world better than we ever could with only our eyes. Lenses in telescopes help us see as far away as the moon, planets, and stars. Lenses in microscopes help us see tiny things close-up, including things we cannot see with our eyes alone, such as the cells in our bodies or the little creatures that live in a drop of pond water.

Lenses, lenses everywhere! How many different lenses do you see in this picture?

What Color Is Light?

What color is sunlight? You might think it has no color at all. But scientists call the light that comes from the sun white light. What's amazing is that the white light of sunshine is actually made up of all the colors in the rainbow!

You can prove this if you have a wedge-shaped piece of clear glass called a prism. If you hold the prism near a sunny window, the light will shine through and make a rainbow-like band of colors. This shows that even though light may appear to be white or colorless, light is really made up of all colors.

When light rays move through a prism, the glass slows down the rays and changes their paths. As you can see in the diagram, rays that produce different colors are affected differently. The process is called refraction. A prism refracts light. A lens also refracts light. Remember the glass of water with the straw in it? Both the water and the glass are refracting light.

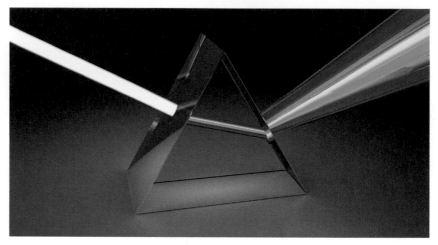

A prism separates white light into the spectrum of colors. The prism bends the rays of light, but rays of each color bend differently. Red bends the least. Violet bends the most. The colors from top to bottom are red, orange, yellow, green, blue, indigo, and violet.

Raindrops in the sky refract the light, which is what causes a rainbow. When light is refracted, it often separates into a combination of colors called the spectrum. The colors of the spectrum always appear in the same order: red, orange, yellow, green, blue, indigo, and violet. You can use a funny name to help you remember that order: "Roy G. Biv."

Somewhere Over the Rainbow

Is there a pot of gold at the end of a rainbow? Rainbows are so unusual and beautiful that you almost want to believe the magical stories about them.

When you see a rainbow in the sky, you see sunlight reflected off water droplets in the sky. The droplets work like prisms to refract the sunlight and separate it into colors. If you've been lucky enough to see a rainbow more than once, you might have noticed that rainbow colors always come in the same order as the colors of the spectrum, from red to violet. On a sunny day, you can make a little rainbow by turning on a hose and putting your thumb over the end to make the water come out as a mist. When the light bounces off the droplets of mist, you should see your own little rainbow.

How Your Eyes See

Close your eyes and what do you see? Nothing, of course! But why? You might say, "Because my eyes are closed, silly!" Or you could answer, "Because no light is coming into my eyes."

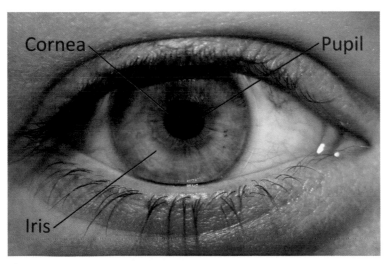

The parts of an eye.

You see things because light bounces off the objects in your line of sight, and then this light enters your eyes. Another way of saying this is that things reflect light, and we see the reflected light. But that's just the beginning. Let's find out what happens when you see.

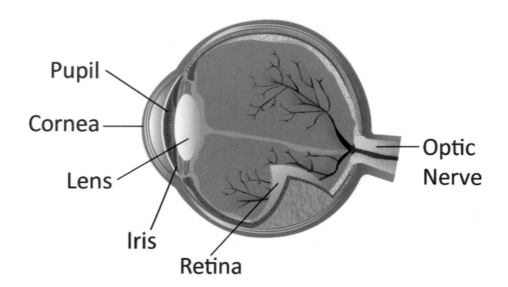

Look at the picture of the eyeball and its parts. First, rays of light pass through your cornea [KOR-nee-uh], a transparent covering on the outside of your eye. (Remember, "transparent" means "clear" or "see-through," like glass.) Next, the light goes through the pupil, which is a hole in the middle of the iris. The iris, the colored part of your eye, helps the pupil open and close. On a bright sunny day, the iris makes the pupil grow smaller to let in less light. In a dark room, such as a theater, the iris makes the pupil grow wider to let in more light. (By the way, the iris is an involuntary muscle—it works without your thinking about it.)

After light rays pass through the iris, they go through the lens. Muscles attached to the lens change the shape of the lens just a little bit, to help the lens focus. The lens focuses the light rays onto the surface at the back of the eyeball, called the retina [RET-in-ah].

Inside the retina, light rays change into electrical signals. These signals travel along the optic nerve to your brain. The brain makes sense of the signals and recognizes the image as, for example, a tree, a cat, a car, or the letters on this page. It all happens so fast, you don't even notice. All you do is open your eyes and see.

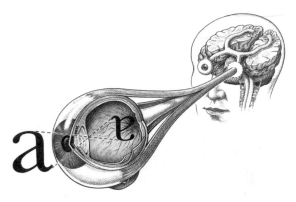

Light passes through the lens in the eye and makes an upside-down image on the retina. The brain turns the image right-side up!

Getting in Focus

In some people's eyes, the lenses don't change and focus as well as they should. Those are the people who need glasses. A person who can see things close-up but who needs glasses to focus on things far away is called nearsighted. A person who can see things far away but who needs glasses to focus on things close-up—to read, for example—is called farsighted. Glasses made of differently shaped lenses correct each of these seeing problems.

There are even glasses designed to help people see both far away and close-up. They are called bifocals. Can you guess why? Here's a hint: The prefix "bi-" means "two." Bifocal glasses are made from two differently shaped lenses. They help a person's eyes focus in two different ways, to see close-up and to see far away.

What About You?

If possible, allow your child to briefly try on someone else's glasses. (Don't allow her to wear the glasses for very long, or she may strain her eyes and get a headache.) How does her vision change as a result of wearing these glasses? What does this suggest about how the glasses affect the light rays entering her eyes?

Look Deep into My Iris

The iris, the colorful part of your eye, gets its name from Iris, the goddess of the rainbow in ancient Greek mythology. Look at your eyes in a mirror. What color are they? Brown, blue, green? The parts of your eye that you can see make up only a small portion of the entire eyeball. Much of the eye is inside the skull, protected behind hard bone.

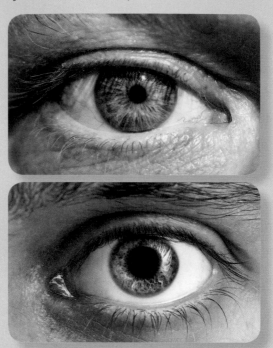

The pupil opens or closes to let more or less light into the eye, responding to the amount of light coming into it. Which picture shows the eye on a bright, sunny day? Which shows the eye in a dark room?

Want to see your iris at work? Go into the bathroom and turn the light on. Look at your eyes in the mirror and see how small the pupil is (the black circle in the center of your eye). Now turn the light off and count slowly to 20. Flip the light back on and—quick!—look at your pupils. They grew larger in the dark, because of the work of the iris muscle.

Sound and Hearing

Good Vibrations

An alarm clock rings, a dog barks, a voice calls, "Time to get up!" Every day is full of familiar sounds. But what exactly is sound?

Sound is caused by a back-and-forth movement called vibration. Try this: Close your lips and hum. While you're humming, feel your throat under your chin. Do you feel a tingling? It is caused by something moving back and forth very fast. When you hum, the vocal cords in your throat are vibrating back and forth, which makes the air around them vibrate. These vibrations of air strike your eardrums and make them vibrate, creating the sound you hear.

Here's a way you can see how sound makes the air vibrate. Stretch a piece of plastic wrap over the surface of a bowl and fasten it tightly with a rubber band. Sprinkle a few grains of dry sand or rice on the plastic. Now take a big pan, hold it near the bowl, and strike the pan with a spoon a few times. Do you see the grains jump when you hit the pan? That is because the pan is vibrating, which causes the air and then the plastic to vibrate. We call the vibrating air sound waves. When you hit the pan, sound waves travel through the air and cause the plastic to vibrate, which in turn makes the grains jump. If you lightly touch your fingertips to the side of a radio, television, or stereo speaker when the sound is coming out, you should be able to feel the vibrations from the sound these devices make.

Sound waves move out from a vibrating object in all directions. They compress and decompress the air, making it move back and forth in a way we can't see. Those back-and-forth vibrations spread out from the source that made them, getting weaker as they get farther away. That's why you hear your friend standing right next to you more clearly than you hear someone calling from across the street.

Do It Yourself

Our word "telephone" comes from two old Greek words: "tele" means "at a distance," and "phone" means "sound." Your child can make his own telephone using two paper or plastic cups, two paper clips, and about 20 feet of string. Help your child poke a small hole in the bottom of each cup. Stick one end of the string into each hole and knot it tightly around a paper clip. Give one cup to your child, and you take the other. Walk apart from each other until the string is straight and tight. When you talk into your "telephone," your child should be able to hear you. Ask your child to explain how this works.

Make a Connection

Have your child read about the inventor of the telephone, Alexander Graham Bell, on page 420. Encourage her to connect what she is learning about sound waves to Bell's experiments and inventions.

What Does Sound Travel Through?

Sound can travel through all kinds of matter: gases, liquids, and solids. Every time you speak, you prove that sound travels through gases. The air through which the sound of your voice travels is made of gases like oxygen.

Can you think of an example that proves sound travels through liquid? Have you ever heard someone's voice underwater in a swimming pool? It sounded funny, but you could hear it. That sound was traveling through a liquid. Some animals, like whales and dolphins, depend upon sound that travels through the water. Whales sing underwater and can hear each other from more than a mile away.

At first, you might not think that sound travels through solids, because we build walls to keep out sounds. But in your room, sometimes you hear laughter or talking from the room next door, don't you?

In general, vibrations from sound waves move more easily through solids. This is because in most solids, matter is packed more densely than in liquids or gases. Try this. Drum your fingers on a table. Now rest your ear right on the table's surface and drum your fingers on it again. Doesn't it sound louder? That's because the sound is traveling through the solid table.

When the Native Americans of the Great Plains hunted for buffalo, they would sometimes put their ear to the ground. Why do you think they did this? Think about how sounds travel through solids.

The hunters might not hear the sound of faraway hoofbeats in the air, but they could hear the sound as it traveled through the solid earth.

The Speed of Sound

Remember how fast light travels? Faster than anything else—an amazing 186,000 miles per second. Sound travels much more slowly than light. In air, sound travels at about 1,086 feet per second, or about 740 miles per hour. Of course, that's still very fast compared to a car going 55 miles per hour on the highway! But there are jets that can fly as fast as the speed of sound. When these jets go even faster than the speed of sound, we say that they have "broken the sound barrier."

Here's an example that shows how light travels faster than sound. During a thunderstorm, a crash of thunder and a bolt of lightning happen at the same time. When you're far away, you see the lightning before you hear the thunder. Why? Because the light traveled faster to your eyes than the sound did to your ears.

Loud and Quiet

If you're listening to the radio and a favorite song comes on, you might say, "Turn it up!" and reach for the knob marked VOLUME.

When you turn up the volume, you are making the sound louder. A scientist might say that you are increasing the sound's intensity. How far away you can hear a sound depends on its intensity. A quiet sound, like a whisper, doesn't travel very far. But a really loud sound can travel for hundreds of miles. More than 100 years ago, when a volcano exploded on the Indonesian island of Krakatoa, the sound could be heard in Australia, more than 2,000 miles away!

How would you arrange these sounds in order of intensity, from quietest to loudest?

A doorbell
A lawn mower
A whisper
A rocket blasting off
A dog barking

How high is the highest pitch you can sing?

High and Low

Pretend that you're a pop star. Sing the highest note you can sing. Now sing the lowest. When we describe how high or low a sound is, we are talking about the sound's pitch. A bird singing makes a high-pitched sound. A dog growling makes a low-pitched sound. Think of a flute and a tuba. Which instrument makes high-pitched sounds? Which makes low-pitched sounds?

When you sing a high note, your vocal cords vibrate very fast. When you sing a low note, your vocal cords vibrate more slowly. Faster vibrations make a sound with a higher pitch. Slower vibrations make a sound with a lower pitch.

Try this. Take a large rubber band and loop it around a drawer knob. Pull it tight and pluck it. Now loosen it and pluck again. Can you hear the difference? When it's pulled tight, the rubber band makes a higher-pitched sound. Is the rubber band vibrating faster when it's loose or when it's pulled tight?

Your Own Personal Noisemaker

You carry a noisemaker around with you wherever you go. It's called your larynx [LAIR-inks], or voice box, and it's in your throat. When you felt your throat and hummed, you were feeling the vibration of your larynx.

How does your body make a sound? Air travels from your lungs and past your vocal cords, which stretch open and shut like two thick rubber bands inside your larynx. You use muscles to relax or tighten your vocal cords, which changes the pitch of your voice from low to high. You use your tongue, teeth, and lips to form words.

How the Ear Works

Let's find out what happens when sound waves enter your ears.

If you look at someone's head, you see the outer ear. The outer ear is made of cartilage. Nature has cleverly designed the outer ear to catch and direct sound waves through an opening into the ear canal.

The vibrations travel through the air inside the ear canal to the eardrum. Like a drum, the eardrum is made of thin tissue stretched tightly across an opening. Each of your eardrums is only about as big as the fingernail on your little finger. Sound waves enter the ear and make the eardrum vibrate.

Next, those vibrations travel through three bones deep inside the ear. They're called the hammer, anvil, and stirrup. These are the tiniest bones in your body. They get their names from their shapes. The hammer looks like a tiny hammer. The anvil looks like an anvil, the heavy iron surface that a blacksmith uses. And the stirrup is shaped like a stirrup, the metal ring for a horseback rider's foot.

Vibrations pass from the hammer to the anvil to the stirrup, and then on to the cochlea [COH-clee-uh]. The cochlea is spiral-shaped. Can you find it in the picture? Does its shape remind you of a certain animal? ("Cochlea" comes from the Latin word for "snail.")

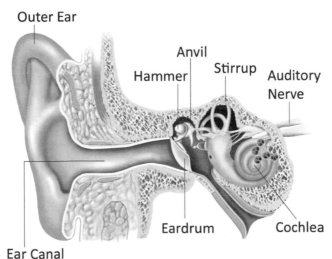

A cross section of the ear.

New Word

Does your child know what the word **auditory** means? Explain that "auditory" refers to anything to do with hearing or the ears.

The cochlea is filled with liquid, which vibrates as sound enters. When the liquid vibrates, it shakes tiny hairs inside the cochlea. The hairs are connected to nerves that send signals to a big nerve called the **auditory** nerve. The auditory nerve carries the signals to the brain and, ta-dah!, you hear the sound.

Eardrum: Handle with Care

The eardrum is a delicate, airtight seal. Never poke anything long or sharp into your ear, because it could damage your eardrum. Extremely loud sounds can damage the eardrum, too. Try not to stand close to loudspeakers, and if you listen to music through headphones, don't turn up the volume too loud. Damaged eardrums are hard to heal. Without healthy eardrums, you won't hear well.

Alexander Graham Bell

Even as a boy, Alexander Graham Bell was fascinated by sound. "How do the vocal cords make noise?" he asked. "How does the ear hear?" He and his brother dissected the larynx of a sheep and then built a machine of tin and rubber, designing it to work like the sheep's vocal cords. When they blew through the machine, it made a noise.

Bell was born in 1847. His father and his grandfather were teachers who taught students who could not speak or hear. Many of their students had been deaf all their lives. Bell's father and grandfather invented "visible speech," which showed deaf people how to move their mouths to pronounce different letters.

The young Bell learned that when air vibrations come into the ear, we hear sounds. A friend of his father's had demonstrated that principle to him by scattering sand on top of a drum, then playing the violin nearby—just like the demonstration mentioned on page 415. Vibrations from the violin made the drumhead vibrate. The sand, in turn, vibrated and shifted around.

In those days, around 1860, people had two ways to communicate over long distances. They could write letters or use the telegraph, which had been invented by Samuel Morse in 1840. The telegraph worked by sending electrical pulses through long wires. By following a code, now called Morse code, the pulses spelled out words.

Aleck Bell, as he was known to close family and friends, wondered whether wires could carry more complicated signals. Could they carry the sounds of the human voice? In an electrical shop in Boston, Massachusetts, Bell and another inventor named Thomas Watson began building machines to test the idea.

Bell designed a machine with two parts that worked like the voice box and the ear, connected by electrical wire. One part of the machine, the transmitter, turned sounds into electricity and sent them through the wire. The other part, the receiver, turned the electrical signals back into sound.

In March 1876, the invention finally worked. Alexander Graham Bell spoke into the transmitter: "Mr. Watson! Come here—I want to see you!" Thomas Watson, 60 feet away in the next room, heard the words quite clearly.

In June 1876, Bell showed his invention at America's Centennial Exhibition in Philadelphia. The emperor of Brazil was there. The emperor held the receiver to his ear, and from the far end of the hall, Bell spoke into the transmitter, reciting words from Shakespeare's play *Hamlet*: "To be, or not to be: That is the question."

For his new invention, Bell received the

Alexander Graham Bell (1847–1922).

Centennial Prize. Later that year, Bell and Watson attached their instruments to telegraph wires and spoke to each other between Boston and Cambridge, Massachusetts, two miles apart. It didn't take very long before people wanted telephones. Within a year, hundreds of households in Boston were connected by telephone wires.

Throughout the rest of his life, Alexander Graham Bell continued experimenting. He worked on early versions of phonograph records, air conditioners, and X-ray machines. He even designed a circular kite. But he will always be remembered for his most important invention: the telephone.

Astronomy

On a clear night, go outside and look up at the sky. What do you see? Is the moon shining? Are the stars twinkling?

There you are, a single person on this planet called Earth, looking up into the vastness of space. It seems to go on forever. But for every star you see, there are billions more you can't see. On and on the universe goes, stretching out in all directions, farther and bigger than anyone can imagine.

The stars in the universe are grouped into huge galaxies. Some galaxies, like ours, are spiral-shaped, like pinwheels. Others look like big oozing blobs of light.

Our sun is only a single star among the billions of stars that make up the galaxy we live in, which is called the Milky Way. Why is our galaxy called the Milky Way? On a dark night, you can sometimes see a fuzzy, milky-looking white stripe running across the sky. That white stripe is made up of billions of stars in the Milky Way.

> **New Word**
> The science of outer space, planets, and stars is called **astronomy**. That word comes from the Greek word "astron," which means "star."

From those who study **astronomy**, we know that beyond the Milky Way there are billions more stars in the galaxies that are our closest neighbors. One of our close neighbors is the Andromeda Galaxy, but don't expect to travel there soon. Even though Andromeda is closer to us than most other galaxies, it is almost 2 million light-years away. That means that light traveling from Andromeda to Earth takes nearly 2 million years to arrive!

Beyond Andromeda, there are still billions more galaxies. Astronomers— the scientists who study outer space—have made an amazing discovery. All

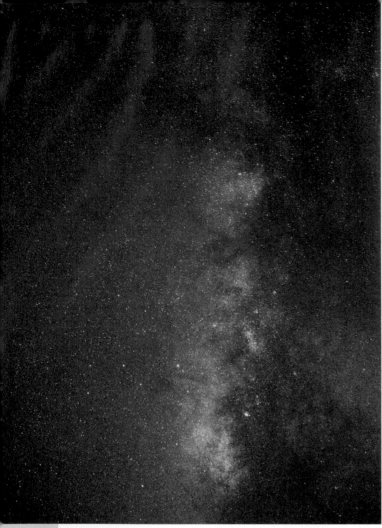

The Milky Way galaxy, as seen from Earth.

these billions of galaxies seem to be flying out and away from each other. In other words, the universe is *growing bigger*!

When astronomers observed how galaxies seem to be flying away from each other, they came up with a theory for how the universe began. (A theory is an idea or explanation based on the best available evidence.) Their idea, which most scientists accept, is called the big bang theory. Many scientists think that about 15 billion years ago, all the matter in the universe was packed into a super-dense ball. No one knows exactly what happened or why, but something caused this ball to explode. The explosion sent chunks of matter flying out into space. Eventually this matter became the stars, planets, and everything else in our universe.

Just think—if the big bang theory is correct, then all matter came from that super-dense ball that exploded billions of years ago. And because you are made of matter, that means you are made of the stuff of stars!

How Do We Learn About Outer Space?

Astronomers learn about distant planets, stars, and galaxies by looking through powerful telescopes. An optical telescope uses lenses and mirrors to focus rays of visible light, allowing the human eye to see objects far, far away. As soon as the first telescopes were invented, in the 1600s, people began to observe the stars and planets. What they learned also taught them a lot about this planet of ours called Earth.

The biggest telescopes need to be in special buildings in faraway places, where city lights don't make it hard to see out into the night sky. This building on the top of a mountain in Hawaii is part of the Mauna Kea Observatory. The mountain is so tall that it rises above the clouds.

Today's astronomers also use another kind of telescope, called a radio telescope. Stars and galaxies give off other kinds of energy in addition to visible light. Radio telescopes use radio waves, which are much longer than visible light rays, to learn about the universe. These telescopes gather information that cannot be seen through optical telescope lenses.

In 1990, the space shuttle put the Hubble Space Telescope into orbit about 370 miles above Earth. The Hubble is about as big as a school bus. It weighs 12 tons. It uses a concave mirror eight feet across to collect light from faraway stars and then radios information about that light back to Earth.

Astronomers also learn a great deal from unmanned space probes. These spacecraft carry cameras, computers, and scientific instruments far into space. They send radio signals back to Earth. Sometimes astronomers turn those signals into pictures, like postcards sent from outer space!

Take a Look
Since its launch, the Hubble Space Telescope has made more than a million observations of space. You and your child can view many of the images created from these observations at www.hubblesite.org.

The Hubble Space Telescope.

Our Solar System

When we say "solar system," what do we mean? We mean all the planets, moons, and other heavenly bodies that move around the sun. "Solar" comes from the Latin word "sol," which means "sun." "System" refers to the group of things that move in great, round paths around our sun.

Hundreds of years ago, people believed that the sun, the stars, and the other planets moved around Earth. Some Greek astronomers guessed that Earth moved around the sun, but their ideas didn't take hold. Then in the 1500s, a Polish astronomer named Nicolaus Copernicus argued that the sun, not Earth, was at the center of our solar system. Not many people believed Copernicus during

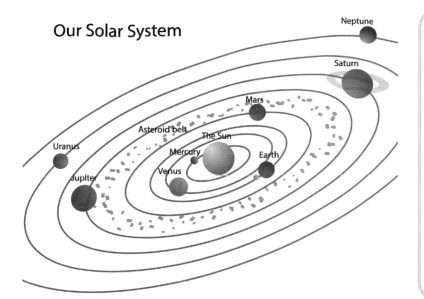

Our Solar System

Neptune

Saturn

Mars

Asteroid belt

The Sun

Uranus

Mercury

Earth

Venus

Jupiter

Do It Yourself

Using craft materials, help your child to make a model of our solar system, based on this diagram. An orange or yellow tennis ball might represent the sun. What might you use to represent the planets and asteroids and their orbital paths? Try to maintain an appropriate scale in terms of the size of each object and its distance from the sun.

The objects in our solar system move in elliptical, or oval-shaped, paths around the sun.

his lifetime, but today no one would argue with him. (You can read more about Copernicus and his ideas on page 450 in this book.)

The sun is a star like other stars you see at night. The sun looks bigger and brighter than other stars because it is closer to us. Even though it's the closest star, the sun is still 93 million miles from Earth.

You know that light travels fast. When you turn on a lamp, think how quickly its light reaches your eyes. For the sun's light to travel 93 million miles to reach us here on Earth, it takes about eight minutes.

How big is Earth compared to the sun? The sun is so large, you could fit about 1,300,000 planet Earths inside of it.

Like other stars, the sun is a giant ball of churning, glowing, exploding gas. On a very hot day on Earth, the temperature might reach 100 degrees Fahrenheit. The surface of the sun can reach 10,000 degrees Fahrenheit, and astronomers think that the deep core inside the sun might be as hot as *27 million degrees*!

The natural world depends upon the energy that comes from the sun. Without the light and heat we get from the sun, life simply wouldn't exist. But don't worry. The sun isn't going anywhere. It's been around for billions of years, and it will still be around billions of years from now.

Planets in Motion: Orbit and Rotation

Around the sun travel the eight planets: Mercury, Venus, Earth, Mars, Jupiter, Saturn, Uranus, and Neptune. The word "planet" comes from an old Greek word that means "wanderer." But the planets do not wander around the solar system. They travel around the sun in fixed paths called orbits.

Ex-Planet Pluto

Until recently, you would have learned about *nine* planets: the eight listed above, and Pluto. Pluto is so small and located so far from the sun, only the most powerful telescopes on Earth can see it. Astronomers did not discover it until 1930.

In 2006, astronomers voted that Pluto is too small to be a planet. Today Pluto is considered a dwarf planet. It is part of a ring of icy, rocky bodies called the Kuiper [KAHY-per] belt. The Kuiper belt contains several other dwarf planets, as well as millions of smaller objects.

As the planets orbit (go around) the sun, they also rotate. That means they spin around like a top. Like the other planets, Earth both orbits the sun and rotates. We say that Earth rotates on an axis, which is an imaginary pole running through the planet from the North Pole to the South Pole.

If you were to spend a day keeping track of the position of the sun in the sky, it might appear as though the sun is moving. Get up early some morning and notice where you see the sun. A few hours later, Earth has rotated, so it looks as though the sun has moved to a different place in the sky. But really, the sun isn't moving. It only appears to move because Earth is rotating. When evening comes, notice where the sun sets. It always sets in the west and rises in the east. We talk about the sun "rising" and "setting" because that's what the sun appears to do. But remember: it only looks that way. Earth is moving, not the sun.

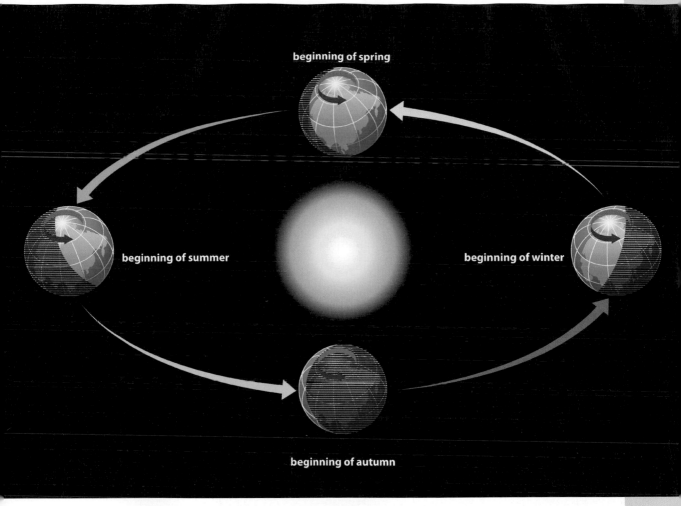

beginning of spring

beginning of summer

beginning of winter

beginning of autumn

Earth revolves around the sun in one year. Earth rotates on its axis in one day.

It takes a day for Earth to make one complete spin on its axis. When the place where you live is turned toward the sun, it is day for you, while it is night for people on the opposite side of Earth. As Earth continues to rotate, the place where you live turns away from the sun, and it becomes night for you.

Do you know how long it takes for Earth to make one complete orbit around the sun? In other words, do you know how long it takes Earth to go around the sun and come back to where it started? It takes one year (365 days) for Earth to orbit the sun.

Earth doesn't stand straight up and down on its axis as it spins. It tilts slightly, and this tilt causes the different seasons. When we have summer, our part of Earth is tilting toward the sun. When we have winter, our part of Earth is tilting away from the sun. This position makes the sunlight shine less directly on us. The areas tilted away from the sun receive less sunlight. Winter is cold because we get less heat from the sun.

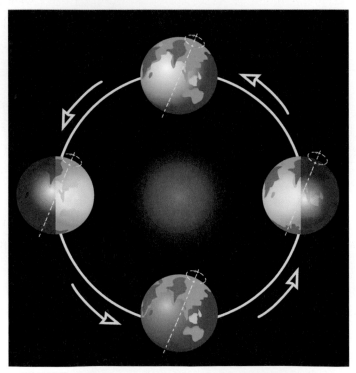

People living in different parts of the globe experience winter and summer in different months of the year. Can you see why?

Depending on the location and time of year, the sun never sets for 24 hours in some places and never rises in others. Let's find out about a girl who lives in a place where the sun never sets during the summer and never rises during the winter. How would you like to live in such a place?

Midnight Sun

"Just think, Erik, the very sun we're looking at right now will still be in the sky at midnight!" Astrid exclaimed as she and her friend Erik ate lunch together in the school cafeteria.

"I won't believe it until I see it!" Erik replied. "The idea of the sun in the sky when I'm supposed to be in bed sleeping is just crazy!"

Astrid chuckled. The idea of the midnight sun is usually unbelievable to people who come to Tromsø, Astrid's hometown. Tromsø is a city in Norway, located more than 200 miles north of the Arctic Circle, near the North Pole. Not long ago, during Tromsø's winter, the sun was never out. Starting today, the sun would be out for 24 hours straight.

"It's not crazy to me! I'm used to seeing the sun never setting," Astrid told Erik.

"Well, I'm used to the sun rising in the morning and setting at night. How am I supposed to sleep with the sun shining brightly in the sky?" Erik asked.

"Oh, there are lots of things you can do! We have blackout curtains. Really good blackout curtains will keep the sunlight out of your room. It's almost as good as the sun setting," Astrid explained.

"I'll have to tell my mom about those. We never needed blackout curtains in Oslo." Erik sighed. Erik had moved from Oslo, the capital of Norway, located more than 700 miles to the south of Tromsø. In Oslo, the sun sets close to midnight in the summer, leaving the city in an extended twilight.

As lunch ended, Astrid and Erik left the cafeteria and headed to their separate classes. Before parting, Astrid waved good-bye to Erik and said, "I'll see you later. I can't wait to see the midnight sun with you and your family." Erik smiled and waved back.

All afternoon Astrid struggled to pay attention to her teachers. All she could think about was the midnight sun. Luckily, her science teacher's lesson was all about the midnight sun.

"Does anyone know why today is such a special day in Tromsø?" Mrs. Franzen asked.

"It's the first day of the midnight sun," a classmate named Sven answered.

"Excellent," said Mrs. Franzen. "Does anyone know why we have the midnight sun here in Tromsø?"

Astrid's hand shot in the air, and Mrs. Franzen called on her to answer.

"Tromsø is very close to the North Pole. Earth's axis is on a tilt. The tilt makes the North Pole face toward the sun in our summer and away from it in winter. This explains why the sun is out all the time during summer and why it seems to disappear during Tromsø's winter."

"Exactly right, Astrid! The midnight sun is one of the things that make Tromsø so special!" Mrs. Franzen told the class.

Is Tromsø really special? Astrid thought. To Astrid, it was just home. She was used to the summers of long sunlight and the winters of darkness. During the winter, the days were lit by a special kind of light called blue twilight. A faint glow that bathed the city in midnight blue was the only hint of sunlight. Astrid found it comforting. She liked that the pretty lights in the city stayed on all day in the winter.

Astrid could not wait for school to end so that she and her parents could continue a family tradition. Every year on the first day of the midnight sun, Astrid would go up Mount Storsteinen with her parents in the city's cable car. The cable car went high up in the air. From a peak on Mount Storsteinen, Astrid and her family would count down to midnight and find the sun still high in the sky. When school ended, Astrid raced home. She raced through her homework and dinner almost as fast as she raced home from school.

After what seemed like forever, her parents were ready to leave. They drove to the cable car that would take them up Mount Storsteinen and boarded a car together. During the ride, Astrid enjoyed looking down on the city and the thou-

Do It Yourself

With your child, create a simple model of the seasons. As your child holds a globe at the poles, shine a desk lamp or flashlight at the equator. Then instruct your child to tilt the top (north) of the globe slightly toward the lamp. When Earth tilts like this on its axis, where is it summer and where is it winter? Next, instruct your child to tilt the top of the globe away from the lamp. Now where is it summer and winter?

sands of people below. From the height of the cable car, Astrid could barely make out the fjord where she and her friends would hike and kayak along during the long summer days and nights. It was hard for Astrid to believe that an icy glacier had once stood in the valley with steep cliffs where the winding and deep waters of the fjord flowed. Thousands of years ago, in the last ice age, the great glacier had cut through the rock. The cut remained after the glacier retreated and seawater flooded in, creating the fjord. Astrid enjoyed the beautiful view as the car chugged up the mountainside.

Finally the cable car came to a stop. Astrid and her parents stepped out onto the mountain, where they found a small crowd had gathered. It was getting late, but the warmth of the sun gave Astrid a boost of energy. She looked around the crowd until she spotted Erik and his parents.

"Mom and Dad, this is my friend Erik," Astrid said, introducing her parents to Erik.

"It's great to meet you, Erik. Astrid tells us that you've never seen the midnight sun before," said Astrid's mother. "Do you know what causes the midnight sun?"

"Let me explain," Astrid interrupted. "I learned about it in school today. Earth's axis is tilted, which causes some places to get more sunlight than other places. In the summer in Tromsø, the sun keeps shining on the North Pole. In the winter, it shines on the South Pole. We live in Tromsø, which is near the North Pole. That's why the sun stays in the sky all day in our summer!"

"That's right!" Astrid's dad said proudly.

"It's midnight!" Erik exclaimed. Astrid looked to the sun. It was like seeing sunset and sunrise at the same time. In the orange glow, Astrid could see the freckles on Erik's cheeks. She looked down on the city and could make out cars moving on the streets. She knew that for the next two months the sun would dip to the horizon of the pink and orange sky and then rise up again.

With the sun still in the sky, Astrid's father placed his hand on her shoulder. "Come on, Astrid, we're going home. It's way past your bedtime!" It was hard for Astrid to think about falling asleep when the sun was about to rise higher in the sky. Luckily, the windows in her room were fitted with blackout curtains that kept it dark. At least while she was falling asleep, she could feel like it was really night-time. For more than two months, the sun would not set on Tromsø.

Earth's Satellite: The Moon

Earth orbits the sun. And what orbits Earth? The moon. Another way of saying this is that the moon is a satellite of Earth. You may think of a satellite as a device that gets blasted into space by a rocket and then orbits Earth, sending down radio signals and scientific measurements. That's one kind of satellite. In astronomy, the word "satellite" can refer to any heavenly body that orbits another. The word "satellite" comes from the Latin for "attendant," meaning someone who waits on an important person.

On some nights, you might look up at the sky and say, "Look, the moon is shining so brightly!" The moon may look bright, but it does not make its own light, as the sun does. The moon reflects the light cast on it by the sun.

There are nights when no moon appears in the sky at all, even if the sky is clear. That's the time we call the new moon. Of course, the moon is out there, but you can't see it. In fact, when there's a new moon, the moon is overhead during the day, but the bright sunlight makes it impossible to see from Earth.

The moon appears to change shape, but the moon doesn't actually change. What does happen? The moon reflects the light of the sun. Depending on the positions of the moon and sun in relation to our eyes, we on Earth see all, part, or none of the moon.

Over the course of a month, the moon may look as if it is changing shape and size, but what changes is the way the moon reflects sunlight to our eyes on Earth. It takes about 30 days for the moon to go through all its phases, from new moon to full moon and back to new moon again. When more of the moon is becoming visible each night, we say the moon is waxing. When less of the moon is becoming visible each night, we say it is waning. It's fun to pay attention to the moon every night for a few weeks to notice how it waxes and wanes.

What is the moon made of? Not green cheese! The moon is mostly a big ball of rock. There is no atmosphere on the moon—no air, no water, no clouds, no rain. Nothing grows on the moon. All you can see on the **lunar** landscape are rocks and moon dust.

When you were little, did you ever look up at night and see the face of "the man in the moon"? It is fun to imagine a face there, even though what you are seeing are huge mountains and craters on the surface of the moon.

> ### New Word
> Lunar is a word for anything that has to do with the moon. It comes from "luna," the Latin word for the moon.

Apollo 11 astronauts Neil Armstrong and Buzz Aldrin left footprints and a flag on the moon.

What About You?

Ask your child to imagine that she is the first person to set foot on the moon. What would she say? What would she want to see and do first?

Human beings have visited the moon and walked on its surface. In July 1969, three American astronauts—Michael Collins, Buzz Aldrin, and Neil Armstrong—blasted off from Cape Kennedy on the *Apollo 11* space mission to the moon. On July 20, 1969, Neil Armstrong became the first person to set foot on the moon. As he stepped from his spacecraft onto the moon's surface, he said, "That's one small step for a man, one giant leap for mankind."

The Force of Gravity

What keeps the moon orbiting Earth instead of floating off into space? *Gravity.* Gravity is a force between bits of matter. Through the force of gravity, each bit of matter attracts and is attracted to every other bit.

You may not feel it, but gravity affects you all the time. Gravity is the force that keeps your feet on the ground. When you jump up into the air, what happens? No matter how high you jump, you always come back down. The gravitational force between Earth and your body pulls you down to the ground. If it were not for the pull of gravity, you would just keep going up. In fact, without gravity, if you jumped away from Earth, you would keep moving out into space!

Earth's gravity pulls on the moon, and the moon's gravity pulls on Earth. Those forces keep the moon in orbit around Earth. In the same way, the sun's gravity pulls on Earth and the other planets and keeps them in their orbits around the sun.

The strength of the pull of gravity between objects depends on two things: the distance between the objects and the mass of each object—that is, how much matter each object contains. Objects that are close together and objects that have lots of mass attract each other strongly. Things that are far apart and things that have little mass attract only weakly.

Let's think about what these rules mean. If you were on the moon, you could jump much higher than you can when you are on Earth. You could jump high and slam-dunk a basketball as easily as a seven-foot-tall basketball star can. Why?

Because the moon is much smaller than Earth and contains much less matter than Earth, its gravitational pull is weaker than Earth's. With gravity pulling more weakly on you, you could jump higher.

You would even weigh less on the moon, though your mass would not change. This is because weight is a measure of the force of gravity on an object. The moon has about one-sixth of Earth's gravity. Therefore, on the moon you would weigh about one-sixth of what you weigh on Earth. Can you figure out how much you would weigh on the moon?

Although the moon has less gravity than Earth, its gravity still affects us. The gravity of the moon (with just a little help from the gravity of the sun) pulls on the waters of the oceans here on Earth. That gravitational pull causes the tides, which are the regular patterns by which the ocean's water level rises and falls.

If you've spent a day at the beach, you've probably noticed the difference between low tide and high tide. At low tide, you can play on a broad, sandy beach. But when high tide comes, the ocean's water level rises and covers part of the beach, leaving less room for you to play. So if your sand castle gets washed out by the tide, blame the man in the moon!

The Powerful Force of Gravity

Astronomers think there are some places in the universe where the force of gravity is so strong that it captures everything that comes near it. These super-dense places pull in everything—nothing can escape their pulling power, not even light. This is why astronomers call these places black holes.

When Day Becomes Night: A Solar Eclipse

As the moon orbits Earth, it sometimes moves right between Earth and the sun. Then the moon blocks our view of the sun and casts a shadow on Earth. And when that happens, we on Earth see a solar eclipse.

As a solar eclipse begins, it looks as if a dark disk is creeping slowly across the face of the sun. The disk—which is the moon—seems just as big as the sun, but that's because the moon is so much closer to Earth than the sun is. As more and more of the moon blocks the light of the sun, day seems to turn to night, no matter what time it is. The sky darkens. Stars become visible. Some animals curl up and go to sleep.

During a solar eclipse, the moon passes between Earth and the sun.

A solar eclipse lasts only a few minutes. The moon moves out of its position between Earth and the sun. The sky brightens. Roosters crow as if it were dawn! Hundreds of years ago, before people understood about the solar system, they were terrified by solar eclipses. They didn't understand why the sun seemed to be getting darker in the middle of the day.

Avert Your Eyes

Even when you're studying the sun, *never* look directly at it, either with your eyes alone or through binoculars or a telescope. You could damage your eyes or even blind yourself. If you happen to be somewhere where you can see a solar eclipse, here's a simple way to view it safely. Poke a little hole in an index card. Hold it about three feet above a piece of white paper, and look at the paper. A little image of the sun will be projected by the hole onto the paper.

When Earth moves between the moon and the sun, what do you think will happen? Remember that the moon does not make its own light. It just reflects the light of the sun. If Earth blocks sunlight from reaching the moon, Earth will cast a shadow on the moon. When that happens, it's called a lunar eclipse.

During a lunar eclipse, Earth passes between the sun and the moon.

The Inner Planets

Let's take a quick tour of the solar system. We'll visit all eight planets, but let's start with the four planets closest to the sun—Mercury, Venus, Earth, and Mars. These four are often called the inner planets.

Mercury

The closest planet to the sun, Mercury, was named after the Roman god Mercury, the swift and speedy messenger of the gods. The name fits because compared to Earth, Mercury orbits the sun quickly. A year on Mercury—one complete orbit around the sun—takes only 88 of our Earth days.

In 1974, the spacecraft *Mariner 10* flew by Mercury and sent back pictures of its surface. We learned that Mercury gets very hot and very cold—almost 800 degrees Fahrenheit when facing the sun and down to almost 300 degrees below zero when facing away from the sun.

Venus

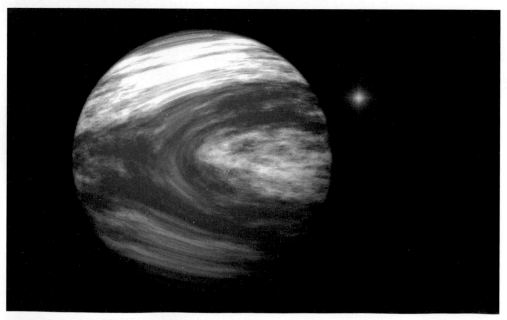

Venus's thick atmosphere traps large amounts of heat. The planet's average surface temperature is over 850 degrees Fahrenheit.

The second planet from the sun, Venus, gets its name from the ancient Roman goddess of love and beauty, perhaps because the planet appears to shine so brightly and beautifully in the sky. In the morning or the evening, you can often see Venus. It has been nicknamed the "morning star" and "evening star" because you can see it, brighter than any star, just above the horizon at dawn or dusk. But Venus isn't a star. It's a planet. Thick clouds always cover Venus. Those clouds reflect sunlight, making the planet look bright.

Earth

The *Apollo 17* spacecraft took this photograph of Earth from space. Look closely and see if you recognize the continent of Africa through the clouds. Can you see Antarctica, too?

As you sit at your desk or lie in your bed, it's hard to think of Earth as a huge round planet spinning on its axis and orbiting the sun. But like the other seven planets in our solar system, Earth is always moving in relation to the sun. It moves in a nearly round path, speeding around the sun at more than 60,000 miles per hour!

If you were an astronaut looking back at Earth from your spacecraft, you would see a blue-and-white ball. What do you think the white is? Clouds, lots of clouds. And the blue is water, lots of water. Nearly three-fourths of Earth is covered with water. All that water is one of the main reasons there is life on Earth.

As far as we know now, Earth is the only planet with life on it. But with all those billions of other galaxies out there, you can't help but wonder.

Mars

The fourth planet from the sun is Mars, named after the Roman god of war. Sometimes you can see Mars in the night sky, even without a telescope. Mars is nicknamed the "red planet" because of its orange-red color. That color comes from the large amount of rusty iron on the planet's rocky surface.

Mars has two moons. Astronomers think these moons may once have been asteroids that were captured by the planet's gravity.

For many years, people thought that, among all the other planets in the solar system besides Earth, Mars was the one most likely to have life. In 1976, two space probes from the Viking Mission, launched by the United States, landed on the surface of Mars and found no life. The Viking probes sent back pictures of a bare, rocky, dusty planet. More recently, NASA launched two robot rovers to explore the geology of Mars. They searched for rocks and soils that will tell us more about signs of water on Mars.

The Mars rovers search for rocks and soils that will tell us more about signs of water on Mars.

War of the Worlds

In 1898, an English writer named H. G. Wells wrote a book called *The War of the Worlds* that told a story about Martians invading Earth. Forty years later, on Halloween night, 1938, an American radio station broadcast a play based on Wells's story. Thousands of people tuned in to the broadcast without knowing it was a play. They were terrified— they believed Martians were really attacking!

The Asteroid Belt

Between Mars and Jupiter, the fifth planet from the sun, is the asteroid belt, which is made up of thousands of chunks of rock and metal that are orbiting the sun. Some asteroids are as small as a basketball. Others are as big as a mountain. The biggest is one-fourth the size of our moon!

Where did the asteroids come from? Some scientists think they are bits and pieces left over from the time of the big bang, when the solar system was first formed.

Sometimes asteroids escape from the asteroid belt and wander toward the inner planets. Some scientists think that a huge asteroid might have hit Earth about 65 million years ago, creating tidal waves, fires, and a thick cloud of dust that blocked out the sunlight for years. These scientists think that this terrible disaster wiped out much of the life on our planet, including the dinosaurs.

This picture helps to show the size of each planet in our solar system. The sun is at the far left, followed by Mercury, Venus, Earth, Mars, Jupiter, Saturn, Uranus, and Neptune. Which planet is largest? Which is smallest? Where is the asteroid belt located?

The Outer Planets

Now you have learned about the four inner planets in the solar system. Can you name them? They are Mercury, Venus, Earth, and Mars. The inner planets are all solid and rocky. But when we move to the four outer planets, we find that they are made mostly of liquid and gas. These four, called the gas giants, are Jupiter, Saturn, Uranus, and Neptune.

Jupiter

Jupiter, the largest planet in our solar system, was named for the Roman king of the gods. Jupiter is so big that more than a thousand Earths could fit inside it. Jupiter is mostly made of hydrogen, in liquid form inside the planet and as gas on the surface. Strong winds swirl that gas into colorful clouds of red, orange, yellow, and brown.

Imagine looking up and seeing *many* moons in the sky. Galileo, the great Italian astronomer who lived around 1600, looked through a telescope and discovered four moons around Jupiter. Since then, astronomers have found 12 more moons. In the 1990s, a space probe traveled toward Jupiter. It was called the *Galileo*—can you guess why? In 1995, *Galileo* reached Jupiter. In 1999, it flew past one of Jupiter's moons, called Io, and sent back amazing pictures.

Ask your child why she thinks so many spacecraft are named for famous explorers. Work with your child to learn about examples in addition to those listed above.

Make a Connection

Instruct your child to read the names of the eight planets in our solar system and then to review the names of the Roman deities on page 128. Ask your child why he thinks certain planets were named for certain gods and goddesses.

Talk and Think

Point out that many spacecraft and probes are named for famous astronomers, such as Galileo and Cassini, a 17th-century astronomer who observed Saturn's rings. Others are named for explorers.

- In 1999, the United States sent two probes, *Amundsen* and *Scott*, to search for water at the South Pole of Mars. The probes were named for the first explorers to reach Earth's South Pole.

- Between 1990 and 1994, the *Magellan* spacecraft orbited Venus and sent back pictures by radio. The *Magellan* was named for a Portuguese explorer who sailed around South America to the Pacific Ocean.

- The *Viking 1* and *Viking 2* probes that landed on Mars in 1976 were named for the Scandinavian peoples who colonized much of Europe and sailed to North America in the 10th and 11th centuries.

Saturn

Saturn, the second-largest planet in our solar system, was named for the Roman god of the harvest. This planet looks different from all the rest because of its spectacular rings. Astronomers know that the rings are made of ice, dust, and rock, but they aren't sure where all that stuff came from. Some think the rings may be the remains of a moon that shattered long ago. At least 18 moons still orbit Saturn.

With its distinctive rings, Saturn may be the most recognizable planet in our solar system.

Uranus

The farther we get into outer space, the less we know about the planets. Uranus, the seventh planet from the Sun, was named for the ancestor of all the Greek gods. Uranus has rings as well, but they are much fainter than Saturn's. Until 1986, only five moons were known to circle Uranus. Then the *Voyager 2* spacecraft flew by and sent back information showing 10 more moons around the planet.

Neptune

The last of the four gas giants, Neptune is the eighth planet from the Sun. It was named for the Roman god of the sea. This planet is so far away that it takes about 165 Earth years to complete one orbit around the sun. We learned a lot about Neptune when the *Voyager 2* space probe flew by the planet in 1989. It revealed Neptune to be a frozen and stormy world, bluish in color, with the strongest winds in the solar system—up to 1,200 miles per hour!

Dirty Snowballs and Shooting Stars

Chunks of matter called comets and meteoroids are zipping through space. As-tronomers think that, like asteroids, these heavenly bodies may be left over from the beginnings of the solar system.

Comets are sometimes called dirty snowballs because they're made of ice, rock, and dust. When a comet passes near the sun, the sun's rays melt some of the ice, which causes a huge tail of gas and dust to form. The tail of a comet can stretch out for hundreds of thousands of miles!

Millions of comets orbit the sun. Sometimes a comet that passed close enough to Earth for people to see will come back hundreds of years later and be visible again. The English astronomer Edmund Halley predicted that a big comet, seen in 1531 and 1607, would return in the 1750s. He was right, and scientists named the comet after him. Halley's Comet last came into view in 1986. It takes about 76 years for it to return to Earth's view. You can look forward to seeing it in the year 2061.

Comets don't appear very often, but on many nights you might be able to see something bright streak across the night sky. These shooting stars, as they're often called, are not really stars at all. They are caused by meteoroids, bits of matter that soar through space and sometimes cross the path of Earth. When a meteoroid falls through Earth's atmosphere at a super-fast speed, it gets so hot that it burns up and makes the fiery streak you might see in the sky. We call this streak a meteor.

Scientists estimate that several hundred million meteoroids

> **What About You?**
> Have you or your child ever seen a comet or meteor? Meteor showers happen throughout the year. With your child, research the date of the next meteor shower that might be visible from your home.

enter Earth's atmosphere every day! Most burn up and never reach the ground. A meteoroid that makes it through to the ground is called a meteorite.

Most meteorites are made of iron and rock. Scientists are very eager to collect and study all the meteorites they can find. What do you think these scientists are hoping to find?

Constellations: Shapes in the Stars

Long ago, when the earliest humans looked up into the night sky, what thoughts do you imagine passed through their minds? As they stared at the stars, they began to see shapes and patterns—bears and lions, maidens and hunters. These "connect-the-dot" pictures that people have imagined in the stars are called constellations. They have names like Leo (the Lion), Taurus (the Bull), and Orion (a mighty hunter).

One star pattern you might easily be able to see is the Big Dipper, which looks like a cup with a long handle. The Big Dipper is part of the constellation called Ursa Major, or the Great Bear.

Make a Connection

Read a Native American tale about the Big Dipper, "The Hunting of the Great Bear," on page 38.

If you live in a region where you can view the Big Dipper, you can use its stars to figure out which way is north. Find the two stars that form the front of the Big Dipper's cup. Let your eyes follow an imaginary line starting at the bottom star, going through the top one, then moving out into space. The first bright star you see, brighter than any others around, is Polaris, or the North Star. Polaris is part of another constellation. It's the first star in the handle of the constellation called the Little Dipper.

Follow the line formed by the outer two stars in the Big Dipper to the North Star, a bright star in the handle of the Little Dipper.

In the days before radio and satellites, stars and constellations were important to sailors, who used them to determine compass directions. You can do that, too. When you look at the North Star, you are facing north. Once you know where north is, you can find your way south, east, or west.

The Space Shuttle

It wasn't so very long ago that people first blasted off into space. In the spring of 1961, the Union of Soviet Socialist Republics (which has since become Russia and other countries) sent the first man into space. About a month after that voyage, an American astronaut, Alan Shepard, climbed into a space capsule named *Freedom 7*, which was attached to a powerful rocket. The rocket blasted off and sent the capsule 116 miles into space, making Shepard the first American in space. He stayed in space for 15 minutes, and then his capsule fell back through Earth's atmosphere and into the ocean, where he was picked up by a U.S. Navy ship.

In 1962, John Glenn became the first American astronaut to orbit Earth. Many more flights led to that exciting moment in 1969 when Neil Armstrong took the first steps on the moon.

Until recently, American astronauts flew in the space shuttle. Today American astronauts fly on Russian Soyuz spacecraft to the International Space Station. However, the U.S. space program plans to send its own shuttles again before 2020. Unlike the old space capsules, which could fly only once, the space shuttle can fly many times. So far, five different shuttles have flown in space: *Atlantis, Columbia, Discovery, Endeavour,* and *Challenger.*

As many as seven people traveled together on the space shuttle, and their missions could last for many days. During one shuttle mission, the astronauts fixed the Hubble Space Telescope. Several times, an American shuttle and a Russian spacecraft named *Mir* met in space so that astronauts from the two ships could work together.

In 1998, the space shuttles began carrying astronauts to work on the International Space Station, a place where astronauts from many countries can live and work in space for months at a time. The United States ended its space shuttle program in 2011. However, the International Space Station remains in use. It currently houses a six-person crew.

The International Space Station has been in orbit around Earth for more than 15 years. Its many solar panels turn energy from sunlight into electricity.

Nicolaus Copernicus

Today we know the real reason the sun seems to go around Earth every day. It's because Earth spins on its axis, and the view of the sun from any one point of Earth changes as our planet spins. It's Earth that moves.

But 500 years ago, people believed Earth was still and the sun moved around it. This belief supported the church's teachings that Earth was the center of the universe—the most important part of creation. Nicolaus Copernicus [nic-o-LAY-us co-PER-ni-cus] was brave enough to question that belief.

Copernicus was born in Poland in 1473. He studied astronomy at a Polish university. Then, wanting to learn more, he traveled to Italy. If you can find Poland and Italy on a map, you will see that he had to cross the Alps to make that journey. Some say he and his brother walked the whole way across the Alps, just to get to Italy to study. In the Italian city of Bologna [ba-LO-nya], he studied not only astronomy but also medicine and law.

Copernicus was 19 years old in 1492—a big year for people who were interested in science. What happened in 1492? Christopher Columbus sailed across the Atlantic Ocean to North America. Why would that matter to an astronomer like Copernicus? Because Columbus's experience helped more people understand that Earth is a sphere-shaped planet that orbits the sun.

Nikolaus Kopernikus.

Nicolaus Copernicus (1473–1543).

Columbus's voyage must have set Copernicus thinking. By then, he had traveled home to Poland, where his work kept him from studying astronomy all the time. He was a canon (or priest) in the church, and he also helped run the government in the part of the country where he lived. No matter what work he did, though, he kept thinking about and studying the planets.

Copernicus wrote down his proofs for why Earth must revolve around the sun and sent them to the pope, the head of the Roman Catholic Church. Other people heard about his ideas as well. Friends told Copernicus he should publish his ideas in a book so that more people could read them. But Copernicus was not ready. He knew that rumors about his ideas were upsetting some people, who didn't want to change their minds about the importance of Earth in the universe.

Finally a younger man named Rheticus came to work with Copernicus on a book. The book was called *De revolutionibus orbium coelestium*, which is Latin for "about the revolutions of the planets in the sky." Copernicus waited so long to write and publish his book that not long after he got a printed copy in his hands, he died, at the age of 70. Now we consider that book to be an important step toward our modern understanding of how Earth and the other planets in our solar system revolve around the sun.

Women on the Final Frontier

In the 1500s and 1600s, the New World of the Americas was the great frontier. Today outer space is our New World, with many places yet to be discovered. There's one big difference between then and now. Five hundred years ago, few women took part in exploration. Today women work together with and even lead men, making discoveries in space.

Almost as soon as flight began, women flew airplanes. Bessica Raiche was America's first woman aviator, flying in 1910, only seven years after the Wright brothers' first flight. One year later, Harriet Quimby was the first American woman to earn a pilot's license. Amelia Earhart became the first woman to fly alone across the Atlantic, in 1932, and the first person, man or woman, to fly alone from Hawaii to California, in 1935.

The first woman to go into

Amelia Earhart in an airplane.

space was from Russia. Her name was Valentina Tereshkova, and she flew as a cosmonaut in 1964. In 1978, six of the people chosen to be American space shuttle astronauts were women. They all studied hard, becoming experts in science and engineering. They were physically fit and eager to put their learning to the test by flying in the space shuttle.

Five years later the first of those female astronauts was assigned to be part of the space shuttle crew. On June 18, 1983, the seventh shuttle mission took off from the Kennedy Space Center in Florida with a crew of five, including Sally Ride. Sally Ride grew up in California and studied physics. She was the first woman assigned to a space shuttle mission. She flew on one other space shuttle mission, and then she decided that she wanted to go back to work as a scientist. She taught physics at a university in California until she died in 2012.

Kathryn Sullivan was the first woman to walk in space, in 1984. She and fellow astronaut David Leestma spent three and a half hours outside the shuttle, testing whether they could refuel a satellite in space.

A tragic accident happened in 1986. The space shuttle *Challenger* was set to take off, carrying a crew of seven. Among those seven was Christa McAuliffe, an elementary school teacher from New Hampshire. She was the first person chosen for a shuttle mission who had not spent years training as an astronaut. The plan was for her to send messages from the space shuttle to all the schoolchildren in America.

Only 73 seconds after takeoff, the *Challenger* exploded. All the astronauts, including Christa McAuliffe, died. It was a horrible time for all the schoolchildren who had been hoping to hear from McAuliffe in outer space, and for all the people around the world who were excited about space travel. Engineers spent months determining what went wrong in the machinery of the shuttle. After three years and 300 changes in shuttle design, the remaining shuttles were ready to fly again.

During the 1990s, one out of every four American astronauts was a woman. Many shuttle crews have included at least one woman. In 1992, Mae Jemison flew her first shuttle mission on the *Endeavour*, making her the first African American female astronaut. A physician and a scientist, she helped conduct experiments in space.

How did Mae Jemison grow up to become such a special person? Science—especially astronomy—fascinated her all her life. She attended Stanford University in California and studied chemical engineering and African American history. Then she decided to become a doctor. While still a medical student, she traveled far, helping in places where there aren't enough doctors, like Cuba, Kenya, and Thailand. She worked as a doctor in the Peace Corps in West Africa. The first time she applied to be an astronaut, she was not chosen. She worked hard and tried again, and in 1987 she became an astronaut. It took five more years of hard work and study before she was ready for her first space flight.

Make a Connection

Look back at the geography and history chapter and recall the fate of Henry Hudson's quest to find a Northwest Passage. Why do you think people would want to name a ship after the *Discovery*?

In 1993, Ellen Ochoa became the first Hispanic woman among the American astronauts. She and her crewmates flew on the *Discovery*, named after the last ship that Henry Hudson sailed from England to the New World in search of a Northwest Passage.

In 1995, Eileen M. Collins took the helm of the space shuttle, becoming the first woman pilot in the U.S. space program. Collins had been a pilot for the Air Force. She knew how to fly 30 different kinds of jets and planes. Before becoming an astronaut, she taught mathematics and piloting to Air Force cadets. She flew the space shuttle during two flights in which it met and hooked up with the Russian space station *Mir*.

Women took on many important jobs in the space shuttle missions. In 1993, Kathryn Thornton stepped out of the space shuttle and worked in outer space twice during one shuttle mission, repairing the Hubble Space Telescope. In 1996, Shannon Lucid launched with crew members on the shuttle *Atlantis*. They docked with *Mir*, and Lucid moved onto the *Mir*, where she stayed for six months. At the end of that space flight, Shannon Lucid had traveled 75 million miles over 188 days—the longest any American astronaut, male or female, has ever stayed in space.

Ecology

Close your eyes and imagine it's a cool summer day, and you're sitting on a dock that juts out into a little pond. Look around in your imagination. How many different living things are in this pond environment?

You might see frogs and toads, turtles and salamanders. You might see dragonflies skimming the surface of your imaginary pond. Hear that buzz? Is it a fly or a mosquito? Both of these insects can be found near a pond. If the water is clear and still, you might be able to see the fish that live underwater.

And don't forget all the plants. Plants are living things, too. Think how many plants live near, and even in, a pond. Little plants grow right up to the pond's edge, and some plants may even grow underwater.

There arc also beings, so tiny you can't see them, living in the mud and in the water. All these living things depend on each other and on the kind of world a pond setting provides. In other words, these plants and animals share the pond as their habitat.

If you were walking along the edge of this pond, what living things would you hear and see? They all share the pond environment.

Living Things Depend on One Another

Let's see how some of the creatures living in and near the pond depend on one another. Green ferns grow at the edge of the pond. The ferns absorb light from the sunshine. Their roots take in water and nutrients from the muck underwater. The ferns use sunlight, water, and nutrients to grow big and healthy.

A tadpole swims up and nibbles on one of the roots. But watch out, little tadpole! What's that coming up behind you? It's a hungry bass. Chomp! The bass eats the tadpole in one gulp.

A few months later the bass grows old and dies. Its body sinks to the bottom of the pond. Down under the water, tiny worms and bacteria—creatures so tiny you can't see them—break down the dead bass's body as they use it for food. Nutrients from the decaying flesh and bones of the bass settle into the soil at the bottom of the pond. Those nutrients are absorbed by the roots of the ferns growing at the water's edge. And so we're back where we started.

Look at how many ways the living things of this pond depend on one another—and we haven't talked about how big fish eat little fish, or how raccoons and bears catch fish to eat them, or how deer graze on the plants at the pond's edge! All these creatures, living together, are part of a cycle of nature.

How Natural Cycles Work

The pond's cycle of nature depends on three groups of living things:

Producers

Consumers

Decomposers

Producers make their own food. Can you name a kind of living thing that makes its own food? Not your parents in the kitchen, but something in nature that uses sunshine and water and nutrients from the soil? A plant uses solar energy—energy from sunlight—to produce its own food. Plants are producers. In our pond, the plants at the pond's edge are producers.

All living things need energy to live, and all living things need food for energy. In our pond, the tadpole eats the plants. Then the fish eats the tadpole. The tadpole and the fish are consumers, because both of them consume (or eat) other living things. The tadpole is a primary, or first-level, consumer because it eats plants. The fish is a secondary consumer because it eats other animals.

Are you a consumer? Yes, indeed. You eat plants and you may eat other animals. If you eat a bacon, lettuce, and tomato sandwich, you are eating plants (the lettuce, tomato, and the wheat in the bread) and animals (the bacon). You and all the other animals in the world are consumers, because you consume food to get the energy you need.

When plants and animals die, they provide food for the decomposers. To "decompose" means to "break something down into smaller pieces." In the pond, the little worms and bacteria are decomposers because as they seek food to eat, they decompose the body of the dead fish and break it into smaller pieces. They eat some, but they drop some, too. Those pieces become part of the soil at the bottom of the pond. Worms and bacteria are also decomposers on land, as are mushrooms.

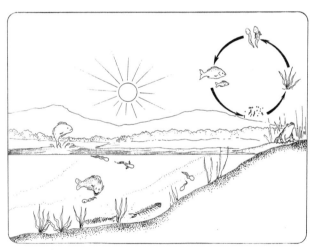

Can you trace the cycle of producers, consumers, and decomposers in and around this pond?

You can see how producers, consumers, and decomposers connect in a kind of natural cycle. Plants produce food. Animals eat plants or other animals that have eaten plants. When plants and animals die, decomposers break down their remains, leaving nutrients in the soil. Plants use those nutrients to produce their own food. And so, like a circle, this cycle of nature goes on and on.

Depending on One Another

In northern Arizona, when farmers killed wolves to protect their cows and sheep, they changed the balance of nature.

If one part of the cycle of nature changes, other parts may feel the change. This happened not long ago in the southwestern United States, in Arizona. For centuries, wolves and deer had lived side by side in the forests in northern Arizona. The wolves, which are carnivores (meat eaters), killed and ate the deer. The deer, which are herbivores (plant eaters), ate moss, leaves, fruits, and twigs. Then people moved in and began farming in that part of Arizona. The wolves started eating the cows and sheep on the farms. To protect their animals, the farmers killed the wolves. They kept on hunting the wolves until there were no wolves left.

What do you think happened? Without wolves to eat some of the deer, more deer lived. More and more deer went looking for food, and they ate all the green plants they could find. They even ate the very young trees. As the years passed, no trees grew big enough to make seeds from which new trees could grow. Finally, there were no plants left for the deer to eat. The forest was destroyed, and the deer began to starve.

People did not realize that the wolves were an important part of the natural cycle in their habitat. When this link disappeared, the balance of nature changed. Since then, people have brought wolves back to northern Arizona and set them free. The number of deer is decreasing, and the trees are beginning to grow again.

A Web of Living Things

You have been learning about cycles of nature. You've read about producers, consumers, and decomposers and how they all depend on one another. You read about the farmers, wolves, and deer in Arizona, and you saw what happens when part of a natural cycle changes.

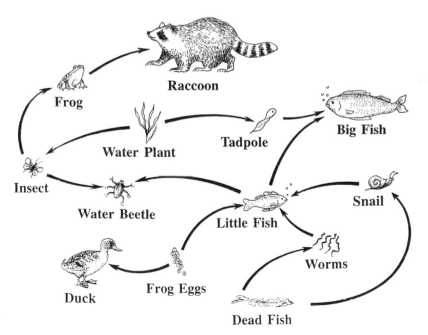

Frog

Raccoon

Water Plant

Tadpole

Big Fish

Insect

Water Beetle

Little Fish

Snail

Duck

Frog Eggs

Worms

Dead Fish

These animals all share an ecosystem. Who eats what? See how many ways one kind of animal depends on another.

Take a Look
With your child, talk through the food web diagram. Have your child guess what would happen if each animal were removed from the food web.

In learning about these things, you have been studying ecology. Ecology is the study of the relations between living things and their environment—the world around them. (The word "environment" comes from a French word for "all around.")

In nature, living things depend on one another in an ecosystem, which is another word for "environment." The pond you have been thinking about is an ecosystem. It includes the pond itself, the stream that flows into it, and the surrounding forest, as well as the community of creatures living in and near the pond, all affecting one another and depending on one another.

You can imagine an ecosystem as being something like a delicate, invisible web that holds life together for a group of living things. It changes whenever anything new comes into the web or anything old leaves it. If one or two strands of the web get damaged, the web might still hold together. But if too many strands are broken, that web changes its shape altogether. That is what happened in the Arizona ecosystem when the farmers got rid of the wolves.

As you can see from the example of the wolves in Arizona, human beings are part of ecosystems, too. People are part of the world of nature, and what we do affects it. Let's look at some of the things people do to the environment.

Pollution

Hold Your Breath!

Have you ever smelled the exhaust coming out of a truck or school bus? Have you ever seen thick smoke pouring from a factory's smokestack?

Exhaust and smoke often contain unhealthful chemicals that pollute the air. "Pollute" means "to make something dirty or impure or unsafe."

Cars, trucks, and buses are one cause of air pollution. Their engines burn fuel, usually gasoline. From their exhaust pipes these vehicles put out unhealthful emissions. (Emissions are what cars and other vehicles put in the air as a result of burning fuel in their engines.) Now imagine a city full of cars, trucks, and buses, every one of them burning fuel and releasing emissions. That's one big reason

Smoke from this factory pollutes the air.

why the air in many big cities is polluted. When city air gets so dirty that the sky starts looking brown, it is called smog, a word made up from the two words "smoke" and "fog." If people breathe in too much smog, it can hurt their lungs.

Should You Drink the Water?

Go to a sink, turn on the faucet, and out comes a nice, clear stream of water. Do you know where that water comes from?

People get most of their water from lakes, rivers, and water under the ground. If you live in the country, your water may come from an underground well. This water is often very pure because it has passed through layers of sand and soil and rock that filter out particles and leave the water clean and clear.

Cities often get their water from rivers and lakes. The city engineers use human-made filters to clean this water. Then they add small amounts of chemicals, such as chlorine, to kill germs. (You may have smelled chlorine in the water of a swimming pool.)

Talk and Think

Ask your child if he has any ideas for reducing pollution in his home or community. As a family, try to implement at least one of these ideas in your daily life.

Litter pollutes the environment, too.

Of course, we want to drink only water that is clean and pure. But water can get polluted. Sometimes factories pollute water by dumping chemicals and waste products into lakes and rivers. Sometimes farmers put chemicals, such as fertilizers and insect killers, into the soil, and then the rain washes these chemicals into nearby rivers, lakes, and underground water supplies. These chemicals and other particles pollute the water, which can make it unhealthful for people and other animals to drink.

Conservation and Recycling

Do you help recycle in your neighborhood?

You can help fight pollution. Do you have any ideas how?

One way is by conserving, which means using something carefully and not wasting it. When you don't leave the bathroom faucet dripping, you are conserving. Lights and the television use electricity, and electricity is often made by factories that burn fuel and send emissions into the air. When you turn off the lights and the TV when you're not using them, you are conserving and helping to fight pollution.

Are you practicing conservation at home or school? For example, do you recycle? When you recycle something, it will be used again.

Recycling can help reduce water and air pollution. If you recycle glass and aluminum containers, for example, factories won't have to

Do It Yourself
Look around the room where you and your child are reading. Together, count how many things in the room are recyclable.

burn as much fuel to make new containers. If a factory burns less fuel, it puts fewer unhealthful chemicals into the air and water.

Lots of stuff can be recycled: aluminum cans, tin cans, glass bottles, plastic bottles, cardboard, newspapers, even junk mail. Recycling helps make sure we don't use up what nature has to offer.

Maybe you have seen this symbol on a bottle, a cardboard box, or a trash can. It means "Recycle!" It reminds us that instead of throwing things away, we can use them, or the materials they are made from, again.

John Muir

John Muir [MYOOR] loved wild places. He spent years of his life in the American wilderness, recording what he found. He is remembered as one of the foremost defenders of our natural heritage.

Muir and his family came to the United States from Scotland in 1849, settling on a farm in Wisconsin. He was interested in machines and enrolled in engineering classes at the University of Wisconsin. Soon, though, he decided that instead of human inventions, he wanted to "study the inventions of God," by which he meant the world of nature. He set out on foot—carrying only a compass, a small bag of clothes, and a wood press—to collect flower specimens. For his first adventure, he walked from the Midwest to the Gulf of Mexico. Here's how John Muir described the way he studied nature.

> *I drifted about from rock to rock, from stream to stream, from grove to grove.*
> *Where night found me, there I camped. When I discovered a new plant,*
> *I sat down beside it for a minute or a day, to make its acquaintance and hear*
> *what it had to tell.*

He arrived in California's Yosemite [yo-SEM-i-tee] Valley in 1868. He spent six years there, studying, writing, and making sketches of the valley. Legend has it that he once climbed a 100-foot pine tree in a windstorm and clung there, swaying in the gale, to get a better sense of the forest in a storm.

John Muir understood how important it was to observe details. He measured California's giant sequoia trees, one of which he estimated was 4,000 years old. Noticing deep scratches on some rock walls, he developed a hypothesis that the mountains and valleys of the Sierra Nevada had been formed by glaciers—slow-moving rivers of ice. Muir went on to explore other regions of western North America, including Nevada, Utah, and Alaska. He wrote his observations in personal journals, and using those journals, he wrote articles and books.

John Muir believed that people needed the solitude and pleasure they could find in nature. He began to think that the United States should set aside large, beautiful natural areas for all Americans to enjoy. Although most of us agree with this idea today, in Muir's time few people did. Most of them viewed nature as a wild thing that needed to be tamed.

When he was 42, Muir stopped traveling and started working as a fruit farmer. But every year he took four months for a retreat in the wilderness. He was more and more disturbed by how logging, farming, and other human projects were destroying the natural woodlands and river valleys. He wrote and spoke publicly about preserving the wilderness. Thanks to his ideas and work, the

> **What About You?**
> With your child, discuss whether you like to spend time outdoors. Why or why not? If so, where does each of you like to go?

United States now protects millions of acres as national parks and forests, such as Yellowstone, Yosemite, and Sequoia National Parks. If you ever visit one of these places, remember to think about John Muir.

John Muir (1838–1914).

Suggested Resources

Classifying Animals

About Amphibians: A Guide for Children, by Cathryn Sill (Peachtree Publishers, 2001)

About Birds: A Guide for Children, by Cathryn Sill (Peachtree Publishers, 1997)

About Fish: A Guide for Children, by Cathryn Sill (Peachtree Publishers, 2002)

About Mammals: A Guide for Children, by Cathryn Sill (Peachtree Publishers, 1999)

About Reptiles: A Guide for Children, by Cathryn Sill (Peachtree Publishers, 1999)

Amphibians: Water-to-Land Animals, by Laura Purdie Salas (Picture Window Books, 2009)

Animals Called Fish, by Kristina Lundblad and Bobbie Kalman (Crabtree Publishing, 2005)

Animals with Backbones, by Keith Pigdon (National Geographic Society, 2003)

Birds: Winged and Feathered Animals, by Suzanne Slade (Picture Window Books, 2009)

Mammals: Hairy, Milk-Making Animals, by Laura Purdie Salas (Picture Window Books, 2009)

Reptiles: Scaly-Skinned Animals, by Laura Purdie Salas (Picture Window Books, 2009)

The Human Body: The Skeletal and Muscular Systems

Bones and Muscles (Your Body Inside and Out), by Angela Royston (Sea-to-Sea Publications, 2012)

Bones: Our Skeletal System, by Seymour Simon (HarperTrophy, 1998)

Muscles: Our Muscular System, by Seymour Simon (HarperTrophy, 2000)

The Muscular System, by Kay Manolis (Children's Press, 2009)

The Muscular System (Early Bird Body Systems), by Rebecca L. Johnson (Lerner Publications, 2006)

The Skeletal System, by Kay Manolis (Children's Press, 2009)

The Skeletal System (Early Bird Body Systems), by Caroline Arnold (Lerner Publications, 2006)

Your Body Battles a Broken Bone, by Vicki Cobb, Dennis Kunkel, and Andrew N. Harris (Lerner Publishing Group, 2009)

The Human Body: The Brain and Nervous System

The Astounding Nervous System, by John Burstein (Crabtree Publishing, 2009)

The Brain, by Seymour Simon (Collins, 2006)

The Nervous System, by Kay Manolis (Children's Press, 2009)

The Nervous System, by Christine Taylor-Butler (Children's Press, 2008)

The Nervous System (Early Bird Body Systems), by Joelle Riley (Lerner Publications, 2006)

Touch (A True Book), by Patricia J. Murphy (Children's Press, 2003)

Your Brain, by Terri DeGezelle (Capstone Press, 2002)

Light and Vision

Eyes and Ears, by Seymour Simon (HarperCollins, 1998)

How Sight Works, by Sally Morgan (Rosen Publishing Group, 2010)

Light and Color (Making Sense of Science), by Peter Riley (SmartApple Media, 2005)

Light and Color (Straightforward Science), by Peter Riley (Franklin Watts, 1998)

Light and Dark (Science Alive), by Terry Jenkins (Smart Apple Media, 2009)

Light (Science Alive), by Darlene Lauw and Lim Cheng Puay (Crabtree Publishing, 2002)

The Sense of Sight, by Ellen Weiss (Children's Press, 2009)

The Sense of Sight (The Senses), by Mari Schuh (Bellwether Media, 2008)

Sight (A True Book), by Patricia J. Murphy (Children's Press, 2003)

What Is Sight?, by Jennifer Boothroyd (Lerner Publishing Group, 2010)

Sound and Hearing

Hearing (A True Book), by Patricia J. Murphy (Children's Press, 2003)

Now Hear This!, by Melissa Stewart (Marshall Cavendish, 2010)

The Sense of Hearing, by Elaine Landau (Children's Press, 2009)

Sound and Hearing, by Julie Murray (Abdo Consulting Group, 2007)

Sounds and Vibrations (Making Sense of Science), by Peter Riley (Smart Apple Media, 2005)

Sound, Heat and Light: Energy at Work, by Melvin Berger (Scholastic, 2002)

What Is Hearing?, by Jennifer Boothroyd (Lerner Publishing Group, 2010)

Astronomy

Astronomy (Amazing Science Discoveries), by Dr. Bryson Gore (Stargazer Books, 2009)

The Big Dipper, by Franklyn M. Branley (HarperCollins, 1991)

Comets, Meteors, and Asteroids, by Seymour Simon (Mulberry Books, 1998)

Constellations (True Books), by F. S. Kim (Children's Press, 2010)

Destination: Space, by Seymour Simon (HarperCollins, 2006)

Forces Make Things Move, by Kimberly Brubaker Bradley (HarperCollins, 2005)

Galaxies (True Books), by Howard K. Trammel (Children's Press, 2010)

Galileo's Leaning Tower Experiment, by Wendy Macdonald (Charlesbridge, 2009)

The Hubble Space Telescope: Understanding and Representing Numbers in the Billions, by Greg Roza (Rosen Publishing Group, 2005)

The Moon, by Seymour Simon (Simon and Schuster Books for Young Readers, 2003)

Pluto: A Dwarf Planet, by Ralph Winrich (Capstone Press, 2010)

Sun Up, Sun Down: The Story of Day and Night, by Jacqui Bailey (Picture Window Books, 2006)

When Is a Planet Not a Planet?: The Story of Pluto, by Elaine Scott (Clarion Books, 2007)

Ecology

Food Chain Frenzy (The Magic School Bus Chapter Book), by Anne Capeci (Scholastic, 2003)

Food Chains, by Peter Riley (Franklin Watts, 1998)

The Green Alphabet: A First Look at Ecology, by Donna L. Hurst and Allison Wagner Taylor (Eloquent Books, 2010)

Recycling (A True Book), by Rhonda Lucas Donald (Children's Press, 2001)

Wetland Food Chains, by Bobbie Kalman and Kylie Burns (Crabtree Publishing, 2007)

What Are Food Chains and Webs?, by Bobbie Kalman and Jacqueline Langille (Crabtree Publishing, 2005)

Who Eats What?: Food Chains and Food Webs, by Patricia Lauber (HarperCollins, 1995)

Why Should I Recycle?, by Jen Green (Barron's, 2005)

Why Should I Save Energy?, by Jen Green (Barron's, 2005)

Why Should I Save Water?, by Jen Green (Barron's, 2005)

The Lives of Famous Scientists

Alexander Graham Bell, by Victoria Sherrow (Millbrook Press, 2001)

Alexander Graham Bell: An Inventive Life, by Elizabeth MacLeod (Scholastic, 1999)

Alexander Graham Bell: Inventor of the Telephone, by the editors of Time for Kids, with John Micklos, Jr. (HarperCollins, 2006)

Alexander Graham Bell: Setting the Tone for Communication, by Mike Venezia (Children's Press, 2009)

John Muir: America's Naturalist, by Thomas Locker (Fulcrum Publishing, 2003)

Listen Up!: Alexander Graham Bell's Talking Machine, by Monica Kulling (Random House Children's Books, 2007)

Mae Jemison: Out of This World, by Corinne J. Naden and Rose Blue (Millbrook Press, 2003)

Illustration and Photo Credits

Poems

• •

"By Myself," by Eloise Greenfield. Copyright © 1978 by Eloise Greenfield. Used by permission of HarperCollins Publishers.

"Catch a Little Rhyme," from *Catch a Little Rhyme* by Eve Merriam. Copyright © 1966 Eve Merriam, renewed 1994. Used by permission of Marian Reiner.

"Dream Variation" from *The Collected Poems of Langston Hughes* by Langston Hughes, edited by Arnold Rampersad with David Roessel, Associate Editor, copyright © 1994 by the Estate of Langston Hughes. Used by permission of Alfred A. Knopf, an imprint of the Knopf Doubleday Publishing Group, a division of Random House LLC. All rights reserved. Any third-party use of this material, outside of this publication, is strictly prohibited. Interested parties must apply directly to Random House LLC for permission. Reprinted by permission of Harold Ober Associates Incorporated.

"Jimmy Jet and His TV Set," from *Where the Sidewalk Ends* by Shel Silverstein. © 1974, renewed 2002 Evil Eye, LLC. By permission of Edite Kroll Literary Agency Inc. Reprinted with permission from the Estate of Shel Silverstein and HarperCollins Children's Books.

"Knoxville, Tennessee," From *Black Feeling, Black Talk, Black Judgment* by Nikki Giovanni. Copyright © 1968, 1970 by Nikki Giovanni. Reprinted with permission of HarperCollins Publishers, Inc.

Stories

• •

"Gone Is Gone," copyright 1935 by Wanda Gág; copyright renewed 1963 by Robert Janssen. First University of Minnesota Press Edition, 2003.

"The Hunting of Great Bear," by Joseph Bruchac.

"The River Bank," from Kenneth Grahame's *The Wind in the Willows*, adapted by Rosie McCormick, Core Knowledge Foundation, 2014.

Index

igloos, 171
imperative sentences, 96–97
indexes, 91
indigo, 225
Indus River, 118
inequality signs, 321, 363
insects, 387
instrument families, 271–77, 281
The Interior of the Pantheon (Panini), 243
International Space Station, 449–50
Internet suggested resources (coreknowledge.org), xxxiii
interrogative sentences, 96–97
"In the Good Old Summertime," 291
Inuit people, 169, 170–71
inverse operations, 305, 311–12, 368
invertebrates, 387–88
involuntary muscles, 400
Iroquois people, 38–41, 169, 177
Isabella (of Spain), 183
Istanbul, 157–58

J

James I (of England), 197, 199, 203, 205, 216
Jamestown colony, 197–204
"Jason and the Golden Fleece," 69–71
jazz, 274
Jemison, Mae, 385, 453–54
Jesus, 154–55, 160
"Jimmy Jet and His TV Set" (Silverstein), 14–15
Julius Caesar, 137–41, 160
Juno, 128

Jupiter (planet), 445
Jupiter (Roman god), 128–29, 153
Justinian Code, 160–61

K

kachina dolls, 175, 411–14
kettle drum, 271
knowledge-rich curricula, xxviii–xxxv
commonly shared knowledge, xxviii–xxxii
Core Knowledge Sequence, xxxiii–xxxv
fairness, xxxi–xxxii
foundation knowledge, xxx–xxxi
reasons for, xxix–xxxii
vs. skills, xxviii–xxx, xxxii
"Knoxville, Tennessee" (Giovanni), 10
Kuiper Belt, 428

L

lacrosse, 180–81
land bridges, 169–70
language skills, xxx, 90–106
abbreviations, 106
double negatives, 103
homophones, 105–6
paragraphs, 3, 93
parts of speech, 3, 98–101
prefixes and suffixes, 3, 103–4, 132
punctuation, 3, 101–3
sentence parts, 95–96
sentence types, 3, 96–97
syllables, 3
writing a letter, 94–95
writing a report, 90–93
See also literature; writing skills

larynx, 418
Latin, 132
Lays of Ancient Rome (Macaulay), 80
leap year, 430
Leif "the Lucky" Ericson, 167–68
length measurement, 350–51, 353–55
lenses, 408–9
letter-writing, 94–95
light, 406–14, 468
color, 410–11
lenses, 408–9
mirrors, 407–8
opaque and transparent materials, 407
shadow, 236–37, 406–7
speed of light, 406
vision, 411–14
in visual art, 234–36, 245–46
"Li'l Liza Jane," 285
linear measurements, 354–55
line graphs, 341
line of symmetry, 345–46
lines and movement (in visual art), 246–48
line segments, 342–43, 353–54
literature, 6, 106–7
biography and autobiography, 82–83
chapter books, 3
familiar sayings, 83–89
fiction and nonfiction, 83
myths, 6, 64–81, 107
poetry, 7–19, 106
stories, 6, 20–63, 106
Little Dipper, 448
"The Little Matchgirl" (Andersen), 46–47

About the Editors

E. D. HIRSCH, Jr., is the founder and chairman of the Core Knowledge Foundation and professor emeritus of education and humanities at the University of Virginia. He is the author of several acclaimed books on education issues including the bestseller *Cultural Literacy*. With his subsequent books *The Schools We Need and Why We Don't Have Them*, *The Knowledge Deficit*, and *The Making of Americans*, Dr. Hirsch solidified his reputation as one of the most influential education reformers of our time. He and his wife, Polly, live in Charlottesville, Virginia, where they raised their three children.

JOHN HOLDREN is senior vice president of content and curriculum at K12 Inc., America's largest provider of online education for grades K–12. He lives with his wife and two daughters in Greenwood, Virginia.